# Metrics and Models in Software Quality Engineering

# Metrics and Models in Software Quality Engineering

Stephen H. Kan, Ph.D.

**ADDISON–WESLEY**

Boston • San Francisco • New York • Toronto • Montreal
London • Munich • Paris • Madrid
Capetown • Sydney • Tokyo • Singapore • Mexico City

Many of the designations used by manufacturers and sellers to distinguish their products are claimed as trademarks. Where those designations appear in this book, and we were aware of a trademark claim, the designations have been printed in initial capital letters or in all capitals.

The author and publisher have taken care in the preparation of this book, but make no expressed or implied warranty of any kind and assume no responsibility for errors or omissions. No liability is assumed for incidental or consequential damages in connection with or arising out of the use of the information or programs contained herein.

The publisher offers discounts on this book when ordered in quantity for special sales. For more information, please contact:

Pearson Education Corporate Sales Division
One Lake Street
Upper Saddle River, NJ  07458
(800) 382-3419
corpsales@pearsontechgroup.com

Visit AW on the Web: www.awl.com/cseng/

*Library of Congress Cataloging-in-Publication Data*

Kan, Stephen H.
    Metrics and models in software quality engineering / Stephen H. Kan.
       p.  cm.
    Includes bibliographical references and index
    ISBN 0-201-63339-6
    1. Computer software-Quality control.   I. Title.
 QA76.76.Q35K35   1995
 005.1'068'5–dc20                           94-26972
                                                     CIP

ISBN 0-201-63339-6
Text printed on recycled paper
8 9 10 11 12—MA—03 02 01
8th printing, April 2001

*In memory of my brother Yiu Kun
and my sister Kuan.*

# Contents

**Chapter 3: Fundamentals in Measurement Theory      53**

**Chapter 4: Software Quality Metrics      83**

# Foreword

Quality management and engineering have enjoyed a diversity of applications over the past few years. For example:

- [ ] A system of teaching hospitals conservatively estimates $17.8 million saved on an investment of $2.5 million in quality management over a five-year time period.

- [ ] The US Air Force Military Airlift Command improved capacity so much through quality improvement problem solving during the Gulf War that they avoided having to deploy civilian aircraft (thus avoiding the suspension of next-day mail delivery, among other conveniences).

- [ ] The US Bureau of Labor Statistics reduced the time needed to produce the monthly Consumer Price Index (CPI), compiled by 650 people in five departments by 33%, with no loss in accuracy.

- [ ] The University of Pennsylvania saved over $60,000 a year from one project focused on reducing mailing costs.

The examples go on and on, from industries such as telecommunications, health care, law, hospitals, government, pharmaceuticals, railways, and schools. The variety of terrains where the seeds of TQM successfully take hold is almost baffling.

As the rest of the world moves headlong into quality improvement at revolutionary rates, the software developers and engineers—consumed in debates over metrics and process models, over methodologies and CASE tools—often lag far behind. Some of the reasons include unique challenges in defining user requirements, the "guru" mentality prevalent in many software organizations, and the relative immaturity of the application of software engineering. Whereas the first two are fascinating topics in their own right, it is the third challenge at which Stephen Kan's book is squarely aimed.

Imagine designing an airplane using a small fraction of the aeronautical engineering knowledge available. Imagine designing an automobile while ignoring mechanical engineering. Imagine running a refinery with no knowledge of chemical process engineering. It is not surprising that the first recommendations from consultants offering credible software quality solutions would be to apply proven software engineering methods first. Just as these methods only slowly find acceptance in software development communities, so also have the methods of quality engineering.

One reason for this slow adoption lies with the relative lack of literature that gives clear descriptions of the fundamentals in these fields while illustrating actual use within leading-edge software development organizations. Stephen Kan's book, *Metrics and Models in Software Quality Engineering*, represents a laudable move to fill this need.

Dr. Kan provides a uniquely comprehensive reference to the field of software quality engineering. He has managed a delightful balance between the technical details needed and practical applications of the models and techniques. This book is peppered with industry examples, not only from Kan's own employer, the Malcolm Baldrige National Quality Award-winning IBM Rochester, but from NEC's Switching Systems Division, Hewlett-Packard, Motorola, NASA Software Engineering Laboratory, and IBM Federal Systems Division. Concepts and theory are illustrated by software industry examples, which make the reading that much richer.

Whereas the reader will likely return to this book many times during his or her career, I would like to draw particular attention to Chapter 12, which describes the AS/400 system. This real-life case study pulls together the elements introduced elsewhere in the book and provides them the important context of a success story. The last chapter provides an exciting peek forward into the emerging field of data quality.

Dr. Joseph Juran, one of the key founders of modern quality management and engineering, describes "life behind the quality dikes." As society becomes more reliant on technology, failures of that technology have increasing adverse impacts. Quality helps to insulate society from these dangers. This role of quality in software development certainly rivals that of business competitiveness, and gives another compelling reason to read, understand, and apply the ideas within this book.

Brian Thomas Eck, Ph.D.
Vice President
Juran Institute, Inc.
Wilton, Connecticut

# Preface

Looking at software engineering from a historical perspective, the 1960s and earlier could be viewed as the functional era, the 1970s the schedule era, and the 1980s the cost era. In the 1960s we learned how to exploit information technology to meet institutional needs and began to link software with the daily operations of institutions. In the 1970s, as the industry was characterized by massive schedule delays and cost overruns, the focus was on planning and control of software projects. Phase-based life-cycle models were introduced and analysis, like the mythical man-month, emerged. In the 1980s hardware costs continued to decline. Information technology permeated every facet of our institutions and also became available to individuals. As competition in the industry became keen and low-cost applications became widely implemented, the importance of productivity in software development increased significantly. Various cost models in software engineering were developed and used. In the late 1980s, the importance of quality was also recognized.

The 1990s and beyond is certainly the quality era. With state-of-the-art technology now able to provide abundant functionality, customers demand high quality. Demand for quality is further intensified by the ever-increasing dependence of our society on software. Billing errors, large-scale disrupted telephone services, and even a missile failure during the recent Gulf War can all be traced to the issue of software quality. In this era, quality has been brought to the center of the software development process. From the standpoint of software vendors, quality is no longer an advantage factor in the marketplace; it has become a necessary condition if a company is to compete sucessfully.

Measurement plays a critical role in effective software development. It provides a scientific basis for software engineering to be a true engineering discipline. This book describes the metrics and models in software quality engineering: quality planning, process improvement and quality control, in-process quality management, product engineering (design and code complexity), reliability estimation and projection, and analysis of customer satisfaction data. Most measurement books take an encyclopedic approach in which every possible software measurement is included. This book confines its scope to the metrics and models on software quality. Areas such as cost estimation, productivity, staffing, and performance measurement, for which numerous publications exist, are not covered.

This book is intended for use by software product managers, software development managers, software engineers, software product assurance personnel, and students in software engineering, management information systems, systems engineering, and in quality management. For students, it is intended to provide a basis for a course at the undergraduate upper division or the graduate level. It provides practical guidelines and examples in the practice of quality engineering in software development. Although equations and formulas are involved, the focus is on the understanding and applications of the metrics and models (rather than mathematical derivations). Throughout the book, numerous real-life examples are used from the development of the IBM Application System/400 (AS/400) at IBM Rochester, Minnesota, and from other companies in the software industry. (IBM Rochester won the Malcolm Baldrige National Quality Award in 1990 and became ISO 9000 registered in 1992.) Chapter 12 details a case study of the AS/400 software quality management system and provides links with the AS/400 examples in previous chapters.

Chapter 1 discusses the definition of software quality and the total quality management framework. Chapter 2 reviews various development process models that are used in the software industry and discusses the process maturity framework and several quality standards. Chapter 3 examines the fundamentals in measurement theory, which are very important for the practice of software measurement. Chapter 4 presents the major software quality metrics associated with the software life-cycle phases, describes the metrics programs of several large software companies, and discusses software engineering data collection. Chapter 5 describes the application of the basic statistical tools for quality control, known as Ishikawa's seven basic tools, in software development. Chapter 6 examines the central concept of defect removal effectiveness, its measurements, and its role in quality planning.

Chapters 7 through 10 cover the three categories of software quality engineering models, each of which is intended for a separate purpose: (1) the reliability models for quality assessment and projection (Chapter 7 on the Rayleigh model and Chapter 8 on the exponential distribution and the reliability growth models), (2) the quality management models for managing quality during the development process (Chapter 9), and (3) the complexity metrics and models that can be used by software engineers for quality improvement in their design and implementation (Chapter 10).

Chapter 11 discusses the measurement and analysis of customer satisfaction data. Chapter 12 describes the software quality management system that was used for the development of the AS/400 computer system. This chapter explicitly or implicitly refers to the approaches, methods, metrics and models, and AS/400 examples discussed in previous chapters. Finally, Chapter 13 provides several observations with regard to software measurement in general and software quality metrics and models in particular, and offers a perspective on the future of measurement in software engineering.

I would like to thank Richard Hedger, David Amundson, and Kathy Dunham for their continuing support and encouragement during the preparation of this book. Thanks are also due to my former and present colleagues, especially Lionel Craddock and members of the department of development quality and process technology at IBM Rochester, for the many informal discussions and insights on the subject of software metrics. I also thank the Technical Vitality program at IBM Rochester for providing editing assistance.

I am thankful to the reviewers, particularly Dr. Brian Eck of the Juran Institute, Richard Hedger of Quality Software Technologies, Inc., Dr. Alan Yaung of IBM Westlake, Texas, Lionel Craddock of IBM Rochester, Dr. Wei-Tsek Tsai of the University of Minnesota, and James Abraham of Skill Dynamics, Inc. They contributed many constructive suggestions. Thanks are also due to the authors, journals, and publishers who granted permission to reproduce some of the figures and examples used in the book; acknowledgments are specified individually in the book.

Stephen H. Kan, Ph.D.
Rochester, Minnesota
August 1994

# 1

---

# What Is Software Quality?

Quality must be defined and measured if improvement is to be achieved. Yet, a major problem in quality engineering and management is that the term *quality* is ambiguously defined, such that it is commonly misunderstood. The confusion may be attributed to several reasons. First, quality is not a single idea, but rather a multidimensional concept. The dimensions of quality include the entity of interest, the viewpoint on that entity, and the quality attributes of that entity. Second, for any concept there are different levels of abstraction; when people talk about quality, one party could be referring to it in its broadest sense, whereas another might be referring to its specific meaning. Third, the term *quality* is a part of our daily language and the popular views of the term may be very different from its use in professions in which it is approached from the engineering or management perspective.

In this chapter we discuss the popular views of quality, formal definitions from quality experts and their implications, the meaning and specific uses of quality in software, and the approach and key elements of total quality management.

## 1.1  Quality: Popular Views

A popular view of quality is that it is an intangible trait—it can be discussed, felt, and judged, but cannot be weighed or measured. To many people, quality is similar to what a federal judge once commented about obscenity: "I know it when I see it." Terms such as *good quality, bad quality,* and *quality of life* exemplify how people talk about something vague, which they don't intend to define. This view reflects the fact that people perceive quality and interpret it in different ways. The implication of this view is that quality cannot be controlled and managed, nor can it be quantified. This view is in vivid contrast to the professional view held in the discipline of quality engineering that quality can, and should, be operationally defined, measured, monitored, managed, and improved.

Another popular view is that quality is luxury, class, and taste. Expensive, elaborate, and more complex products are regarded as offering a higher level of quality than their humbler counterparts. Therefore, a Cadillac is a quality car, but a Chevrolet is not, regardless of their actual reliability and repair records; or, a surround-sound hi-fi system is a quality system, but a single-speaker radio is not. According to this view, quality is restricted to a limited class of expensive products with sophisticated functionality and items that have a touch of class. Products that are simple in functionality and inexpensive can hardly be classified as quality products.

## 1.2  Quality: Professional Views

The misconceptions and vagueness of the popular views do not help the quality improvement effort in the industries. To that end, quality must be described in a workable definition. Crosby (1979) defines quality as "conformance to requirements" and Juran defines it as "fitness for use" (Juran and Gryna, 1970). These two definitions are interrelated and consistent with each other, as we will see later. These definitions of quality have been adopted and used among quality professionals.

"Conformance to requirements" implies that requirements must be clearly stated such that they cannot be misunderstood. Then, in the development and production process, measurements are taken continually to determine conformance to those requirements. The nonconformances are then regarded as defects—the absence of quality. For example, one of the requirements (specifications) for a certain radio may be that it must be able to receive certain frequencies more than 30 miles away from the source of broadcast. If the radio fails to do so, then it does not meet the quality requirements and should be rejected. By the same token, if a Cadillac conforms to all the requirements of a Cadillac, then it is a quality car. If a Chevrolet conforms to all the requirements of a Chevrolet, then it is also a quality car. The two cars may be very different in style, performance, and economy. But if both measure up to the standards set for them, then both are quality cars.

The "fitness for use" definition takes customers' requirements and expectations into account. Customers' requirements and expectations involve whether the products or services fit their uses. Since different customers may use the products in different ways, it means that products must possess multiple elements of fitness for use. According to Juran, each of these elements is a quality characteristic and they can be classified into categories known as parameters for fitness for use. The two most important parameters are *quality of design* and *quality of conformance.*

Quality of design in popular terminology is known as grades or models, which are related to the spectrum of purchasing power. The differences between grades are the result of intended or designed differences. Using the example of cars again, all automobiles provide to the user the service of transportation. However, models differ in size, comfort, performance, style, economy, and status conferred. In contrast, quality of conformance is the extent to which the product conforms to the intent of the design. In other words, quality of design can be regarded as the determination of requirements and specifications and quality of conformance is conformance to requirements.

The two definitions of quality (conformance to requirements and fitness for use), therefore, are essentially similar. The difference is that the fitness for use concept implies a more significant role for customers' requirements and expectations.

### 1.2.1 The Role of the Customer

The role of the customer, as it relates to quality, can never be overstated. From a customer's standpoint, quality is the customer's perceived value of the product he or she purchased, based on a variety of variables such as price, performance, reliability, and satisfaction. In Guaspari's book *I Know It When I See It* (1985), he discussed quality in the customers' context as follows:

> Your customers are in a perfect position to tell you about quality, because that's all they're really buying. They're not buying a product. They're buying your assurances that their expectations for that product will be met.
> And you haven't really got anything else to sell them but those assurances. You haven't really got anything else to sell but quality.

From a high-level definition of a concept to a product being operationally defined, many steps are involved, each of which may be exposed to possible shortcomings. For example, to achieve the state of conformance to requirements, the customers' requirements must be first gathered and analyzed, specifications from those requirements must be produced, and the product must be developed and manufactured accordingly. In each phase of the process, errors can occur that will affect the quality of the finished product. The requirements may be erroneous (this is especially the case for software development), the development and manufacturing process may be subject to variables that induce defects, and so forth. From the customer's perspective, satisfaction after the purchase of the product is the ultimate validation that the product conforms to requirements and is fit to use. From the producer's perspective, once requirements are specified, developing and producing the product in accordance with the specifications is the basic step to achieving quality. Usually, for product quality, the lack of defects and good reliability are the most basic measures.

Because of the two perspectives on quality (customer satisfaction as the ultimate validation of quality and producer's adherence to requirements to achieve quality), the *de facto* definition of quality consists of two levels. The first is the intrinsic product quality, often operationally limited to product defect rate and reliability. This narrow definition is referred to as the "small q" (q for quality). The broader level of the definition of quality includes product quality, process quality, and customer satisfaction, and it is referred to as the "big Q." One can observe that this two-level approach to the definition of quality is being used in many industries, including the automobile industry, the computer industry (both software and hardware) and the consumer electronics industry.

The two-level concept of quality is supposed to form a closed-loop cycle: customer's wants and needs → requirements and specifications → products designed, developed, and manufactured in accordance with the requirements, and with continuous focus on process improvement → excellent product quality, plus good distribution and service processes → achieve total customer satisfaction. However, this was not always the case in many industries, especially before the late 1980s, when the modern quality era began. Product requirements were often generated without customer input, and customer satisfaction was not always a factor in business decision making. Although the final products conformed to requirements, they may not have been what the customers wanted. Therefore, the role of customers should be explicitly spelled out in the definition of quality: conformance to customers' requirements.

## 1.3  Software Quality

In software, the narrowest sense of product quality is commonly recognized as lack of "bugs" in the product. It is also the most basic meaning of conformance to requirements, because if the software contains too many functional defects, the basic requirement of providing the desired function is not met. This definition is usually expressed in two ways: defect rate (e.g., number of defects per million lines of source code, per function point, or other units), and reliability (e.g., number of failures per $n$ hours of operation, mean time to failure, or the probability of failure-free operation in a specified time).

Customer satisfaction is usually measured by percent satisfied or nonsatisfied (neutral and dissatisfied) from customer satisfaction surveys. To reduce bias, techniques such as blind surveys (the interviewer not knowing who the customer is, and the customer not knowing what company the interviewer represents) are usually used. In addition to overall customer satisfaction with the software product, satisfaction toward specific attributes is also gauged. For instance, IBM monitors the CUPRIMDSO satisfaction levels of its software products [capability (functionality), usability, performance, reliability, installability, maintainability, documentation/information, service, and overall]. Hewlett-Packard focuses on FURPS (Functionality, usability, reliability, performance, and serviceability). Similar dimensions of software customer satisfaction are used by other companies. Quality attributes such as these are what Juran called *quality parameters* or parameters for fitness for use.

To increase overall customer satisfaction as well as satisfaction toward various quality attributes, the quality attributes must be taken into account in the planning and design of the software. However, these quality attributes are not always congruous with each other. For example, the higher the functional complexity of the software, the harder it becomes to achieve maintainability. Depending on the type of software and customers, different weighting factors are needed for different quality attributes. For large customers with sophisticated networks and real-time processing, performance and reliability may be the most important attributes. For customers with stand-alone systems and simple operations, on the other hand, ease of use, installability, and documentation may be more important. Figure 1.1 shows the possible relationships among some quality attributes. Some relationships are mutually supportive, some are negative, and yet others are not clear, depending on the types of customers and applications. For software with a diverse customer set, therefore, the tasks to set goals for various quality attributes and to meet customers requirements are not easy ones.

In view of these discussions, the updated definition of quality (i.e., conformance to customers' requirements), is especially relevant to the software industry. It is not surprising that requirements errors constitute one of the major problem categories in software development. According to Jones (1992), 15% or more of all software defects are requirements errors. A development process that does not address requirements quality is bound to produce poor-quality software.

Yet another view of software quality is that of process quality versus end-product quality. From customer requirements to the delivery of software products, the development process is complex and often involves a series of stages, each with feedback paths. In each stage, an intermediate deliverable is produced for an intermediate user—the next stage. Each stage also receives an intermediate deliverable from the preceding stage. Each intermediate deliverable has certain quality attributes that affect the quality of the end product. For instance, Figure 1.2 shows a simplified representation of the most common software development process, the waterfall process.

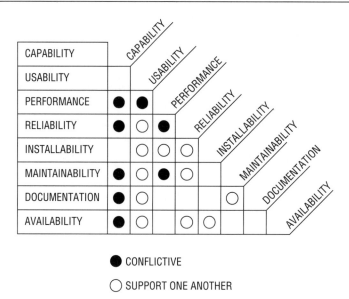

CONFLICTIVE

SUPPORT ONE ANOTHER

BLANK NONE

FIGURE 1.1
Interrelationships Among Software Attributes — A CUPRIMDA Example

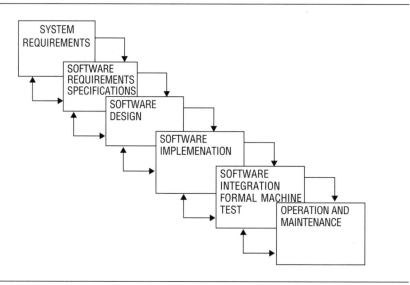

FIGURE 1.2
Simplified Representation of the Waterfall Development Process

Intriguingly, if we extend the concept of customer in the definition of quality to include both external and internal customers, the definition also applies to process quality. If each stage of the development process meets the requirements of its intermediate user (the next stage), the end product thus developed and produced will meet the specified requirements. This statement, of course, is an oversimplification of reality, because in each stage numerous factors exist that will affect that stage's ability to fulfill its requirements completely. To improve quality during development, we need models of the development process, and within the process we need to select and deploy specific methods and approaches, and employ proper tools and technologies. We need measures of the characteristics and quality parameters of the development process and its stages, as well as metrics and models to help ensure that the development process is under control to meet the product's quality objectives. Quality metrics and models are the very focus of this book.

## 1.4 Total Quality Management

*Total quality management* (TQM) is a term that was originally coined in 1985 by the Naval Air Systems Command to describe its Japanese-style management approach to quality improvement. It has taken on a number of meanings, depending on who is interpreting it and how they are applying it. In general, however, it represents a style of management aimed at achieving long-term success by linking quality with customer satisfaction. Basic to the approach is the creation of a culture in which all members of the organization participate in the improvement of processes, products, and services. Various specific methods for implementing the TQM philosophy are found in the works of Philip Crosby (1979), W. Edwards Deming (1986), Armand V. Feigenbaum (1961, 1991), Koru Ishikawa (1985), and J. M. Juran (1970).

Since the 1980s, many companies in the U.S. have begun adopting the TQM approach to quality. The Malcolm Baldrige National Quality Award (MBNQA), established by the U.S. government in 1988, highlighted the embracing of such a philosophy and management style. The adoption of ISO 9000 as the quality management standard by the European Community and the acceptance of such standards by the U.S. private sector in the past several years further illustrates the importance of the quality philosophy in today's business environments. In the computer and electronic industry, examples of successful TQM implementation include Hewlett-Packard's Total Quality Control (TQC), Motorola's Six Sigma Strategy, and IBM's Market Driven Quality. In fact, Motorola won the first MBNQA award (in 1988) and IBM's AS/400 Division in Rochester, Minnesota, won in 1990.

Hewlett-Packard's TQC focuses on key areas such as management commitment, leadership, customer focus, total participation, and systematic analysis. There are strategies and plans in each area to drive the improvement of quality, efficiency, and responsiveness, with the final objective being to achieve success through customer satisfaction (Shores, 1989). In software development, the Software Quality and Productivity Analysis (SQPA) program (Zimmer, 1989) is one of the approaches taken to improve quality.

Motorola's Six Sigma strategy focuses on achieving stringent quality levels in order to obtain total customer satisfaction. Cycle time reduction and participative management are among the key initiatives of the strategy (Smith, 1989). Six Sigma is not just a measure of the quality level; inherent in the concept are product design improvements and reductions in process variations (Harry and Lawson, 1992). Six Sigma is applied to product quality as well as everything that can be supported by data and measurement.

"Customer is the final arbiter" is the key theme of IBM's Market Driven Quality strategy. The strategy is comprised of four initiatives: defect elimination, cycle time reduction, customer and business partner satisfaction, and adherence to the Baldrige assessment discipline.

Despite variations in its implementation, the key elements of a TQM system can be summarized as follows:

- □ *Customer focus:* The objective is to achieve total customer satisfaction. Customer focus includes studying customers' wants and needs, gathering customer requirements, and measuring and managing customer satisfaction.

- □ *Process:* The objective is to reduce process variations and to achieve continuous process improvement. Process includes both the business process and the product development process. Through process improvement, product quality will be enhanced.

- □ *Human side of quality:* The objective is to create a company-wide quality culture. Focus areas include leadership, management commitment, total participation, employee empowerment, and other social, psychological, and human factors.

- □ *Measurement and analysis:* The objective is to drive continuous improvement in all quality parameters by the goal-oriented measurement system.

Furthermore, an organization that practices TQM must have executive leadership, must focus on infrastructure, training, and education, and must do strategic quality planning.

Figure 1.3 shows the schematic representation of the key elements of TQM. Clearly, measurement and analysis are the most fundamental elements for gauging continuous improvement.

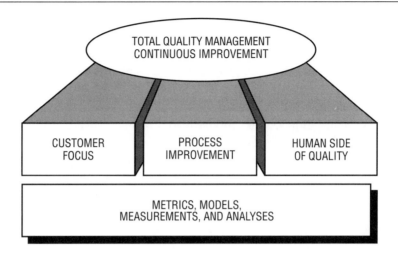

FIGURE 1.3
Key Elements of Total Quality Management

Various organizational frameworks have been proposed to improve quality that can be used to substantiate the TQM philosophy. Specific examples include Plan-Do-Check-Act (Shewhart, 1931, Deming, 1986), Quality Improvement Paradigm/ Experience Factory Organization (Basili, 1985, 1989; Basili and Rombach, 1987, 1988; Basili *et al.*, 1992), Software Engineering Institute (SEI) Capability Maturity Model (Radice *et al.*, 1985; Humphrey, 1989), and Lean Enterprise Management (Womack *et al.*, 1990).

Plan-Do-Check-Act is a quality improvement process based on a feedback cycle for optimizing a single process or production line. It uses techniques, such as feedback loops and statistical quality control, to experiment with methods for improvement and build predictive models of the product. Basic to the assumption is that a process is repeated multiple times, so that data models can be built that allow one to predict results of the process.

The Quality Improvement Paradigm (QIP)/Experience Factory Organization aims at building a continually improving organization, based on its evolving goals and an assessment of its status relative to those goals. The approach uses internal assessments against the organization's own goals and status (rather than process areas) and such techniques as Goal/Question/Metric (GQM), model building, and qualitative/quantitative analysis to improve the product through the process. The six fundamental steps of the QIP are (1) characterize the project and its environment,

(2) set the goals, (3) choose the appropriate processes, (4) execute the processes, (5) analyze the data, and (6) package the experience for reuse. The Experience Factory organization separates the product development from the experience packaging activities. Basic to this approach is the need to learn across multiple project developments.

The SEI Capability Maturity Model is a staged process improvement, based on assessment with regard to a set of key process areas, until you reach a level 5, which represents a continuous process improvement. The approach is based on organizational and quality management maturity models developed by Likert (1967) and Crosby (1979), respectively. The goal of the approach is to achieve continuous process improvement via defect prevention, technology innovation, and process change management.

As part of the approach, a five-level process maturity model is defined based on repeated assessments of an organization's capability in key process areas. Improvement is achieved by action plans for poor areas. Basic to this approach is the idea that there are key process areas that will improve your software development.

Lean Enterprise Management is based on the principle of concentration of production on "value-added" activities and the elimination or reduction of "not-value-added" activities. The approach has been used to improve factory output. The goal is to build software with the minimum necessary set of activities and then to tailor the process to the product needs. The approach uses such concepts as technology management, human-centered management, decentralized organization, quality management, supplier and customer integration, and internationalization/regionalization. Basic to this approach is the assumption that the process can be tailored to classes of problems.

---

## 1.5  Summary

This chapter discussed the definition of quality from both the popular views and the professional views, and described total quality management (TQM) as it relates to software quality. From the popular views, quality cannot be quantified and is some type of thing: *I know it when I see it*. Quality and grade (or class) are often confused. From the professional views, quality must be defined and measured for improvement and is best defined as "conformance to customers' requirements." In software as well as other industries, the *de facto* operational definition of quality consists of two levels: the intrinsic product quality (small q) and customer satisfaction (big Q).

The TQM philosophy aims at long-term success by linking quality with customer satisfaction. Despite variations in its implementation, there are four key common elements of a TQM system: (1) customer focus, (2) process improvement, (3) human side of quality, and (4) measurement and analysis.

It is not surprising that the definition of quality fits perfectly in the TQM context. That definition correlates closely with the first two of the TQM elements (customer focus and process improvement). To achieve good quality, all TQM elements must definitely be addressed, with the aid of some organizational frameworks. In this book, our key focus is on metrics, measurements, and quality models as they relate to software engineering. In the next chapter we discuss various software development models and the process maturity framework.

## References

1. Basili, V. R., "Quantitative Evaluation of Software Engineering Methodology," *Proceedings First Pan Pacific Computer Conference,* Melbourne, Australia, September 1985 (also available as Technical Report, TR-1519, Department of Computer Science, University of Maryland, College Park, July 1985).

2. Basili, V. R., "Software Development: A Paradigm for the Future," *Proceedings 13th International Computer Software and Applications Conference (COMPSAC),* Keynote Address, Orlando, Fl., September 1989.

3. Basili, V. R., and H. D. Rombach, "Tailoring the Software Process to Project Goals and Environments," *Proceedings Ninth International Conference on Software Engineering,* Monterey, Calif.: IEEE Computer Society, March 30–April 2, 1987, pp. 345–357.

4. Basili, V. R., and H. D. Rombach, "The TAME Project: Towards Improvement-Oriented Software Environments," *IEEE Transactions on Software Engineering,* Vol. SE-14, No. 6, June 1988, pp. 758–773.

5. Basili, V. R., G. Caldiera, F. McGarry, R. Pajersky, G. Page, and S. Waligora, "The Software Engineering Laboratory: An Operational Software Experience Factory," *International Conference on Software Engineering,* IEEE Computer Society, May 1992, pp. 370–381.

6. Basili, V. R., and J. D. Musa, "The Future Engineering of Software: A Management Perspective," *IEEE Computer,* 1991, pp. 90–96.

7. Bowen, T. P., "Specification of Software Quality Attributes," RADC-TR-85-37 (3 volumes), *Rome Air Development Center,* February 1985.

8. Crosby, P. B., *Quality Is Free: The Art of Making Quality Certain,* New York: McGraw-Hill, 1979.

9. Deming, W. E., *Out of the Crisis,* Cambridge, Mass.: Massachusetts Institute of Technology, 1986.

10. Feigenbaum, A. V., *Total Quality Control: Engineering and Management,* New York: McGraw-Hill, 1961.

11. Feigenbaum, A. V., *Total Quality Control,* New York: McGraw-Hill, 1991.

12. Guaspari, J., *I Know It When I See It: A Modern Fable About Quality,* New York: American Management Association, 1985.

13. Guaspari, J., *Theory Why: In Which the Boss Solves the Riddle of Quality,* New York: American Management Association, 1986.

14. Guaspari, J., *The Customer Connection: Quality for the Rest of Us,* New York: American Management Association, 1988.

15. Harry, M. J., and J. R. Lawson, *Six Sigma Producibility Analysis and Process Characterization,* Reading, Mass.: Addison-Wesley, 1992.

**16.** Humphrey, W.S., *Managing the Software Process,* Reading, Mass: Addison-Wesley, 1989.

**17.** Ishikawa, K., *What Is Total Quality Control? The Japanese Way,* Englewood Cliffs, N.J.: Prentice-Hall, 1985.

**18.** Jones, C., *Programming Productivity,* New York: McGraw-Hill, 1986.

**19.** Jones, C., *Applied Software Measurement: Assuring Productivity and Quality,* New York: McGraw-Hill, 1991.

**20.** Jones, C., "Critical Problems in Software Measurement," Version 1.0, Burlington, Mass.: Software Productivity Research (SPR), August 1992.

**21.** Juran, J. M., and F. M. Gryna, Jr., *Quality Planning and Analysis: From Product Development Through Use,* New York: McGraw-Hill, 1970.

**22.** Likert, R., *The Human Organization: Its Management and Value,* New York: McGraw-Hill, 1967.

**23.** Radice, R. A., J. T. Harding, P. E. Munnis, and R.W. Phillips, "A Programming Process Study," *IBM Systems Journal,* Vol. 24, No. 2, 1985, pp. 91–101.

**24.** Shewhart, W. A., *Economic Control of Quality of Manufactured Product,* New York: D. Van Nostrand Company, 1931.

**25.** Shores, D., "TQC: Science, Not Witchcraft," *Quality Progress,* April 1989, pp. 42–45.

**26.** Smith, W. B., "Six Sigma: TQC, American Style," presented at the National Technological University television series on October 31, 1989.

**27.** Womack, J. P., D. T. Jones, and D. Ross, *The Machine that Changed the World: Based on the Massachusetts Institute of Technology 5-Million-Dollar, 5-Year Study of the Future of the Automobile,* New York: Rawson Associates, 1990.

**28.** Zimmer, B., "Software Quality and Productivity at Hewlett-Packard," *Proceedings of the IEEE Computer Software and Applications Conference,* 1989, pp. 628–632.

# 2

# Software Development Process Models

Software metrics and models cannot be discussed in a vacuum; they must be referenced to the software development process. In this chapter we summarize the major process models available that are being used in the software development community. We start with the waterfall process life-cycle model and then cover the others including the prototyping approach, the spiral model, and the iterative development process. We also discuss a proposed development process for the object-oriented approach, for which numerous methodologies have emerged but little has been established in terms of development process. Processes pertinent to the improvement of the development process, such as the Cleanroom methodology (formalized approach) and the defect prevention process, are also described.

In the last part of the chapter we shift our discussion from specific development processes to the evaluation of development processes and quality management standards. Presented and discussed are the process maturity framework, including the Software Engineering Institute's (SEI) Capability Maturity Model (CMM) and the Software Productivity Research's (SPR) assessment approach, and two bodies of quality standards—the Malcolm Baldrige assessment discipline and ISO 9000—as they relate to software process and quality.

## 2.1 The Waterfall Development Model

In the 1960s and 1970s software development projects were characterized by massive cost overruns and schedule delays; the focus was on planning and control (Basili and Musa, 1991). The emergence of the waterfall process to help tackle the growing complexity of development projects was a logical event (Boehm, 1976). As shown in Figure 1.2 in Chapter 1, the waterfall process model encourages the development team to specify first what the software is supposed to do (gather and define system requirements) before developing the system. It then breaks the complex mission of development into several logical steps (design, code, test, and so forth) and intermediate deliverables that lead to the final completion of the product. To ensure that each step is executed properly with good-quality deliverables, validation, entry, and exit criteria exist for each step. This Entry-Task-Validation-Exit (ETVX) paradigm is a key characteristic of the waterfall process and the IBM programming process architecture (Radice *et al.,* 1985).

The divide and conquer approach of the waterfall process has several advantages. It enables tracking of project progress more accurately and uncovering of possible slippages early. It forces the organization that develops the software system to be more structured and manageable. This structural approach is very important for large organizations with large, complex development projects. It demands that the process generate a series of documents that can later be used to test and maintain the system (Davis *et al.,* 1988). The bottom line of this approach is to make large software projects more manageable and delivered on time without cost overrun.

Experiences from the past couple of decades showed that the waterfall process is very valuable. Many major developers, especially those who were established early and those who are involved with systems development, have adopted this process. This includes commercial corporations, government contractors, and governmental entities. Although a variety of names have been given to each of the stages in the model, the basic methodologies remain more or less the same. Thus, the system-requirements stages are sometimes called system analysis, customer-requirements gathering and analysis, or user needs analysis; the design stage may be further broken down into high-level design and detail-level design; the implementation stage may be called code and debug; and the testing stage may include component-level test, product-level test, and system-level test.

Figure 2.1 shows an actual implementation of the waterfall process model for a large project. Note that the requirements stage is followed by a stage for system architectural design. When the system architecture and design are in place, design and development work for each function begins. This consists of high-level design (HLD), low-level design (LLD), code development, and unit test (UT). Despite the waterfall concept, parallelism exists because various functions can proceed simultaneously. As shown in the figure, the code development and unit test stages are also implemented iteratively. As UT is an integral part of the implementation stage, it makes little sense to separate it into another formal stage. Before the completion of the HLD, LLD, and code, formal reviews and inspections occur as part of the validation and exit criteria. These inspections are called I0, I1, and I2 inspections, respectively. The subsequent stages after the code is completed and unit tested are integration, component test, system test, and early customer programs. The final stage is to release the software system to customers.

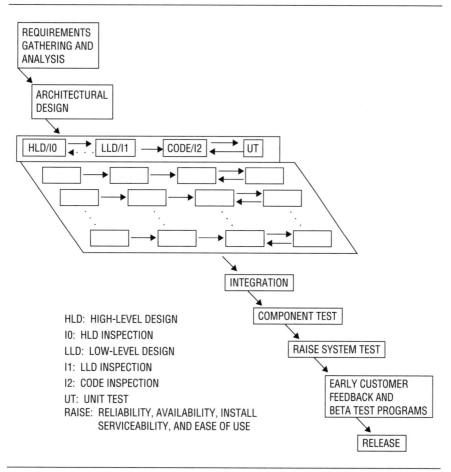

FIGURE 2.1
An Example of the Waterfall Process Model

In the following subsections, the objectives of the various stages from high-level design to early customer programs are described.

**High-Level Design**

High-level design is the process of defining the externals and internals from the perspective of a component. Its objectives are as follows:

- ☐ Develop the external functions and interfaces, including:
  external user interfaces
  application programming interfaces
  system programming interfaces: intercomponent interfaces and data structures.
- ☐ Design the internal component structure.
  intracomponent interfaces and data structures.
- ☐ Ensure all functional requirements are satisfied.
- ☐ Ensure the component fits into the system/product structure.
- ☐ Ensure the component design is complete.
- ☐ Ensure the external functions can be accomplished—"doability" of requirements.

**Low-Level Design**

Low-level design is the process of transforming the HLD into a more detailed level from the perspective of a part (modules, macros, includes, and so forth). Its objectives are as follows:

- ☐ Finalize the design of components and parts (modules, macros, includes) within a system or product.
- ☐ Complete the component test plans.
- ☐ Feedback to HLD, verify changes in HLD.

**Code Stage**

The coding portion of the process results in the transformation of the LLD for a function to completely coded parts. The objectives of this stage are as follows:

- ☐ Code parts (modules, macros, includes, messages, and so forth).
- ☐ Code component test cases.
- ☐ Verify changes in HLD and LLD.

**Unit Test**

This is the first test performed on an executable module. Its objectives are as follows:

- ☐ Verify the code against the component's
  high-level design
  low-level design.
- ☐ Execute all new and changed code to ensure:
  all branches are executed in all directions
  correctness of logic, and data paths are verified.
- ☐ Exercise all error messages, return codes, and response options.
- ☐ Feedback to code, LLD, and HLD.

The level of unit test is for verification of limits, internal interfaces, and logic and data paths in a module, macro, or executable include. Unit test is performed on non-integrated code and may require scaffold code to construct the proper environment.

**Component Test**

Component test is the testing of the combined software parts that make up a component after the software parts have been integrated into the system library. The objectives of this test are as follows:

- ☐ Test external user interfaces to the component's design documentation—user requirements.
- ☐ Test intercomponent interfaces to the component's design documentation.
- ☐ Test application program interfaces to the component's design documentation.
- ☐ Test function to the component's design documentation.
- ☐ Test intracomponent interfaces (module level) to the component's design documentation.
- ☐ Test error recovery and messages to the component's design documentation.
- ☐ Verify that component drivers are functionally complete and at the acceptable quality level.
- ☐ Test the shared paths (multitasking) and shared resources (files, locks, queues, and so forth) to the component's design documentation.
- ☐ Test ported and unchanged functions to the component's design documentation.

**System-Level Test**

The system-level test phase is comprised of the following tests:

- ☐   System test
- ☐   System regression test
- ☐   System performance measurement test
- ☐   Usability tests.

The system test follows the component tests and precedes system regression tests. The system performance measurement test usually begins shortly after system test starts and proceeds throughout the system-level test phase. Usability tests occur throughout the development process (prototyping during design stages, formal usability testing during system test period).

- ☐   *System test objectives:*
      Ensure software products function correctly when executed concurrently and in stressful system environments.
      Verify overall system stability when development activity has been completed for all products.

- ☐   *System regression test objective:*
      To verify that the final programming package is ready to be shipped to external customers. During this phase the focus is to make sure original functions work correctly as before after new functions were added to the system.

- ☐   *System performance measurement test objectives:*
      Validate the performance of the system.
      Verify performance specifications.
      Provide performance information to marketing.
      Establish base performance measurements for future releases.

- ☐   *Usability tests objective:*
      To verify that the system contains the usability characteristics required for the intended user audience, user tasks, and user environment.

**Early Customer Programs (ECP)**

The ECP include testing of the following support structures to verify their readiness:

- ☐   Service structures
- ☐   Development fix support

    □    Electronic customer support

    □    Market support

    □    Ordering, manufacturing, and distribution.

In addition to these objectives, a side benefit from having production systems installed in a customer's environment for the ECP is the opportunity to gather customer feedback so development can evaluate features and improve for future releases. Collections of such data or user opinion include:

    □    Product feedback: function offered, ease of use, and quality of on-line documentation

    □    Installability of hardware and software

    □    Reliability

    □    Performance (measure throughput under the customer's typical load)

    □    System connectivity

    □    Customer acceptance.

As the preceeding lists illustrate, the waterfall process model is a disciplined approach to software development. It is most appropriate for systems development that is characterized by a high degree of complexity and interdependency. Although expressed as a cascading waterfall, parallelism and some amount of iteration among process phases often exist in actual implementation. When using this process, the focus should be on the intermediate deliverables (for example, design document, interface rules, test plans and test cases, etc.), rather than on the sequence of activities for each development phase. In other words, it should be entity-based instead of step-by-step based. Otherwise the process could become too rigid to be efficient and effective.

## 2.2 The Prototyping Approach

The very first step in the waterfall model is the gathering and analysis of customers' requirements. When the requirements are defined, design and development work begins. The model assumes that requirements are known, and that once requirements are defined, they will not change or any change will be insignificant. This may well be the case for system development where the purpose of the system and its architecture are thoroughly investigated. However, in the case where requirements change significantly between the time when the specifications of the system are finalized and when the development of the product is complete, the waterfall model may not be well equipped to deal with the problems thus induced. Sometimes the requirements were not even known. In the past decades, various software process models have been proposed that attempt to deal with customer feedback on the product to assure that it satisfies the requirements. Each of these models provides some form of prototyping, either of a part or all of the system. Some of them build prototypes to be thrown away; others evolve the prototype over time, based on customer needs.

A prototype is a partial implementation of the product expressed either logically or physically with all external interfaces presented. The potential customers use the prototype and provide feedback to the development team before full scale development begins. *Seeing is believing*, and that is really what prototyping intends to achieve. By using this approach, both the customers and the development team can clarify both requirements and their interpretation.

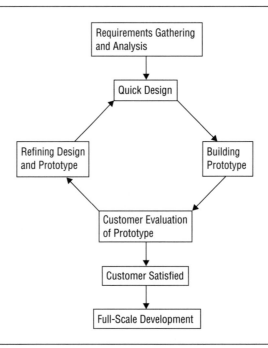

FIGURE 2.2
The Prototyping Approach

As shown in Figure 2.2, the prototyping approach usually involves the following steps:

1. Requirements gathering and analysis
2. Quick design
3. Building prototype
4. Customer evaluation of prototype
5. Refining design and prototype
6. If customers are not satisfied with the prototype, loop back to step 2
7. If customers are satisfied, begin full-scale product development.

The critical success factor of the prototyping approach is quick turnaround in designing and building the prototypes. There are several technologies that can be used to facilitate achieving such an objective. Reusable software parts could make the design and implementation of prototypes easier. Formal specification languages could be used to facilitate the generation of executable code, (for examples, the Z notation and the Input/Output Requirements Language (IORL) (Smith and Wood, 1989; Wing, 1990)). Fourth-generation languages and technologies could be extremely useful in the prototyping in the graphical user interface (GUI) domain. These technologies are, however, still emerging, and are used in varying degrees depending on the specific characteristics of the projects.

The prototyping approach is most applicable to small tasks or at the subsystem level. Prototyping a complete system is difficult. Another difficulty with this approach is knowing when to stop iterating. In practice, the method of *time boxing* is being used. This method involves setting arbitrary time limits (for example, three weeks) for each activity in the iteration cycle and for the entire iteration and then assessing progress at these checkpoints.

## Rapid Throwaway Prototyping

The rapid throwaway prototyping approach of software development was made popular by Gomaa and Scott (1981) and is now being used widely in the industry, especially in application development. It is usually used with the high-risk items or with the parts of the system where the development team does not have a deep understanding of the problem. In this approach, "quick and dirty" prototypes are built, verified with customers, and thrown away until a satisfactory prototype is reached, at which time full-scale development begins.

### Evolutionary Prototyping

In the evolutionary prototyping approach, a prototype is built based on some known requirements and understanding. The prototype is then refined and evolved instead of thrown away. Whereas throwaway prototypes are usually used with the aspects of the system that are poorly understood, evolutionary prototypes are more likely to be used with those aspects of the system that are best understood and thus build on the development team's strengths. These prototypes are also based on prioritized requirements, sometimes referred to as "chunking" in application development (Hough, 1993). For complex applications, it is not reasonable nor economical to expect the prototypes to be developed and thrown away rapidly.

## 2.3 The Spiral Model

The spiral model of software development and enhancement, developed by Boehm (1988), was based on experience with various refinements of the waterfall model as applied to large government software projects. Relying heavily on prototyping and risk management, it is much more flexible than the waterfall model. On the other hand, it is still in the maturing stage. The most complete application to date is the development of the TRW Software Productivity System (TRW-SPS) as described by Boehm.

Figure 2.3 shows the spiral model as presented by Boehm. The underlying concept of the model is that for each portion of the product and for each of its levels of elaboration, the same sequence of steps (cycle) is involved. For instance, the concept of operation, to software requirements, to product design, to detailed design and implementation each involves a spiral cycle. The radial dimension in Figure 2.3 represents the cumulative cost incurred to date in accomplishing the steps. The angular dimension represents the progress made in completing each cycle of the spiral. As indicated by the quadrants in the figure, the first step of each cycle of the spiral is to identify the objectives of the portion of the product being elaborated, the alternative means of implementation of this portion of the product, and the constraints imposed on the application of the alternatives. The next step is to evaluate the alternatives relative to the objectives and constraints, and to identify the associated risks and resolve them. Risk analysis and the risk-driven approach, therefore, are key characteristics of the spiral model, versus the document-driven approach of the waterfall model.

In this risk-driven approach, prototyping is an important tool. Usually prototyping is applied to the elements of the system or the alternatives that have highest risk. Unsatisfactory prototypes can be thrown away and when an operational prototype is in place, implementation can begin. In addition to prototyping, the spiral model also uses simulations, models, and benchmarks in order to reach the best alternative. Finally, as indicated in the illustration, an important feature of the spiral model, as with other models, is that each cycle is completed by a review involving the key members or organizations concerned with the product.

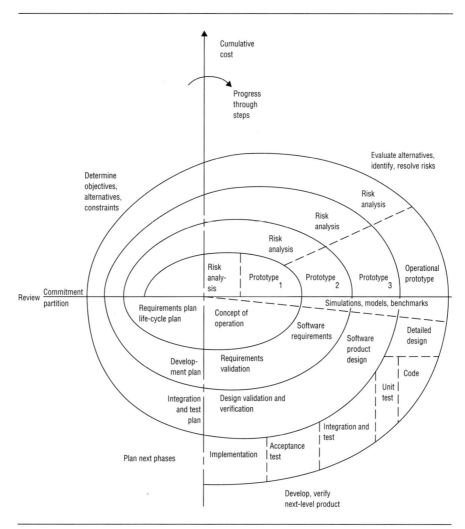

FIGURE 2.3
## Spiral Model of the Software Process (Copyright© 1988 IEEE)

(*Source:* B. W. Boehm, "A Spiral Model of Software Development and Enhancement," *IEEE Computer,* May 1988, pp. 61–72. Permission to reprint obtained from IEEE.)

For software projects with incremental development or with components to be developed by individual organizations or individuals, a series of spiral cycles can be used, one for each increment or component. In Figure 2.3, a third dimension can be added to better represent the model.

Boehm also provides a candid discussion on the advantages and disadvantages of the spiral model. Its advantages are as follows:

☐ Its range of options accommodates the good features of existing software process models, whereas its risk-driven approach avoids many of their difficulties. This is the primary advantage. Boehm also discussed the primary conditions under which this model becomes equivalent to other process models such as the waterfall model and the evolutionary prototype model.

☐ It focuses early attention on options involving the reuse of existing software. These options are encouraged because early identification and evaluation of alternatives is one of the key steps in each spiral cycle.

☐ It accommodates preparation for life-cycle evolution, growth, and changes of the software product.

☐ It provides a mechanism for incorporating software quality objectives into software product development.

☐ It focuses on eliminating errors and unattractive alternatives early.

☐ It does not involve separate approaches for software development and software enhancement.

☐ It provides a viable framework for integrating hardware-software system development. The risk-driven approach can be applied to both hardware and software.

On the other hand, difficulties the spiral model encounters include the following:

☐ *Matching to contract software:* Contract software relies heavily on control, checkpoint, and intermediate deliverables for which the waterfall model is good. The spiral model has a great deal of flexibility and freedom and is, therefore, more suitable for internal software development. The challenge is how to achieve the flexibility and freedom prescribed by the spiral model without losing accountability and control for contract software.

☐ *Relying on risk management expertise:* The risk-driven approach is the backbone of the model. The risk-driven specification carries high-risk elements down to a great deal of detail and leaves low-risk elements to be elaborated in later stages. However, an inexperienced team may also produce a specification just the opposite: a great deal of detail for the well-understood, low-risk elements and little elaboration of the poorly understood, high-risk elements. In such case, the project may fail seriously and the failure may be discovered only after a great deal of resources have been invested. Another concern is that a risk-driven specification is also people dependent. In the case where a design produced by an expert is to be implemented by nonexperts, the expert must furnish additional documentation.

☐ *Need for further elaboration of spiral steps:* The spiral model describes a flexible and dynamic process model that can be utilized to its fullest advantage by experienced developers. However, for nonexperts and especially for large-scale projects, the steps in the spiral must be further elaborated and more specifically defined so that consistency, tracking, and control can be achieved. Such elaboration and control are especially important in the area of risk analysis and risk management.

## 2.4 The Iterative Development Process Model

The iterative enhancement (IE) approach (Basili and Turner, 1975), or the iterative development process (IDP), was defined to begin with a subset of the requirements and develop a subset of the product that satisfies the essential needs of the users, provides a vehicle for analysis and training for the customers, and provides a learning experience for the developer. Based on the analysis of each intermediate product, the design and the requirements are modified over a series of iterations to provide a system to the users that meets evolving customer needs with improved design based on feedback and learning.

The IDP model combines prototyping with the strength of the classical waterfall model. Other methods such as domain analysis and risk analysis can also be incorporated into the process model. The model shares much commonality with the spiral model discussed earlier, especially with regard to prototyping and risk management. Indeed, the spiral model can be regarded as a specific IDP model, while the term *IDP* is a general rubric under which varying forms of the model can exist. The model also provides a framework for many of the modern systems and software engineering methods and techniques such as reuse, object-oriented development, and rapid prototyping.

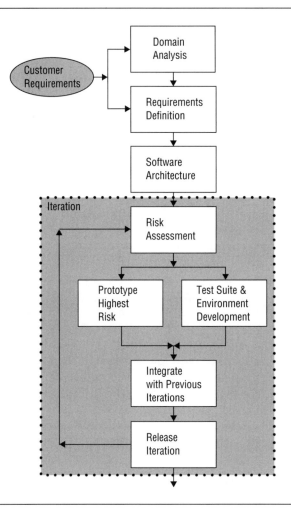

FIGURE 2.4
## An Example of the Iterative Development Process Model

(*Source:* P. H. Luckey, R. M. Pittman, and A. Q. LeVan, 1992, "Iterative Development Process with Proposed Applications," IBM Federal Sector Division, Route 17C, Owego, N.Y. 13827.)

Figure 2.4 shows an example of the iterative development process model as used by IBM Owego, New York. With the purpose of "building a system by evolving an architectural prototype through a series of executable versions, with each successive iteration incorporating experience and more system functionality," the example implementation contains eight major steps (Luckey *et al.,* 1992):

1.  Domain analysis
2.  Requirements definition
3.  Software architecture
4.  Risk analysis
5.  Prototype
6.  Test suite and environment development
7.  Integration with previous iterations
8.  Iteration release.

As illustrated in the figure, the iteration process involves the last five steps, while domain analysis, requirements definition, and software architecture are preiteration steps, which are similar to those in the waterfall model. During the five iteration steps, the following activities occur:

- ☐ Analyze or review the system requirements.
- ☐ Design or revise a solution that best satisfies the requirements.
- ☐ Identify the highest risk areas for the project and prioritize them. Mitigate the highest priority risk via prototyping, leaving lower priority risks for subsequent iterations.
- ☐ Define and schedule or revise the next few iterations.
- ☐ Develop the iteration test suite and supporting test environment.
- ☐ Implement the portion of the design that is minimally required to satisfy the current iteration.
- ☐ Integrate the software in test environments and perform regression testing.
- ☐ Update documents for release with the iteration.
- ☐ Release the iteration.

Note that test suite development along with design and development is extremely important for the verification of the function and quality of each iteration. Yet in practice this activity is not always emphasized appropriately.

The development of IBM's OS/2 2.0 operating system is a combination of the iterative development process and the small team approach. Different from the last example to some extent, the OS/2 2.0 iterative development process involved large-scale early customer feedback instead of just prototyping. The iterative part of the process involved the loop of subsystem design → subsystem code and test → system integration → customer feedback → subsystem design. Specifically, the previous waterfall process involved the steps of market requirements, design, code and test, and system certification. The iterative process went from initial market requirements to the iterative loop, then to system certification. Within the one-year development cycle, there were five iterations before the final completion of the system, each with increased functionality. For each iteration, the customer feedback involved a beta test of the functions available, a formal customer satisfaction survey, and feedback from various vehicles such as electronic messages on Prodigy, IBM internal electronic mail conference forums, customer visits, technical seminars, internal and public bulletin boards, and so forth. Feedback from various channels was also statistically verified and validated by the formal customer satisfaction surveys. More than 30,000 customers and 100,000 users were involved in the iteration feedback process. Supporting the iterative process was the small team approach in which each team assumed the full responsibility of a particular function of the system. Each team owned its project, functionality, quality, and customer satisfaction, and were held totally responsible. There were also cross-functional system teams providing support and services to make the subsystem teams successful and to help resolve cross-subsystem concerns (Jenkins, 1992).

The OS/2 2.0 development process and approach, although it may not be universally applicable to other products and systems, was apparently a true success as attested by customers' acceptance of the product and positive responses.

## 2.5 The Object-Oriented Development Process

The object-oriented approach to design and programming, which was introduced in the 1980s, represents a major paradigm shift in software development. This approach will continue to have a major effect in software for many years to come. Different from traditional programming, which separates data and control, in object-oriented programming an object is a set of defined data and a set of operations (methods) that can be performed on that data. Like the paradigm of structural design and functional decomposition, the object-oriented approach will become a major cornerstone in software engineering. Although there is a growing trend in object-oriented program-ming (OOP) in the industry, and a host of object-oriented analysis and design methods have been developed and documented, there is very little information avail-able about object-oriented development processes. Many of the discussions on methodology (for example, Booch's early work now available in Booch, 1991; McMenamin and Palmer, 1984; Meyer, 1988; Coad and Yourdon, 1990) can be implemented for small projects for which development processes are not always needed. However, for large development projects with many developers, informal channels of communication can no longer be relied on to design, implement, and test the software successfully; a development process is required. Branson and Herness (1992) proposed an OOP process for large-scale projects that centers on an eight-step methodology supported by a mechanism for tracking, a series of inspections, a set of technologies, and rules for prototyping and testing.

The eight-step process is divided into three logical phases:

☐   *The analysis phase* focuses on obtaining and representing customers' requirements in a concise manner; an essential system that represents the users' requirements regardless of which implementation platform (hard-ware or software environment) is developed.

☐   *The design phase* involves modifying the essential system so that it can be implemented on a given set of hardware and software. Essential classes and incarnation classes are combined and refined into the evolving class hierarchy. The objectives of class synthesis are to optimize reuse and to create reusable classes.

☐   *The implementation phase* takes the classes that are defined to completion.

The eight steps of the process are summarized as follows.

1.   *Model the essential system:* The essential system describes those aspects of the system required to make it achieve its purpose, regardless of the target hardware and software environment. It is composed of essential activities and essential data. This step has five substeps:

☐       Creating the user view.

☐       Modeling essential activities.

☐       Defining solution data.

☐       Refining the essential model.

☐       Constructing a detailed analysis.

This step focuses on the user requirements. Requirements are analyzed, dissected, refined, combined, and organized into an essential logical model of the system. This model is based on the perfect technology premise.

2. *Derive candidate essential classes:* This step uses a technique known as "carving" to identify candidate essential classes and methods from the essential model of the system. A complete set of data-flow diagrams, along with supporting process specifications and data dictionary entries, is the basis for class and method selection. Candidate classes and methods are found in external entities, data stores, input flows, and process specifications.

3. *Constrain the essential model:* The essential model is modified to work within the constraints of the target implementation environment. Essential activities and essential data are allocated to the various processors and containers (data repositories). Additional activities are added to the system as needed, based on the target implementation environment limitations. The essential model, when augmented with the additional activities needed to support the target environment, is referred to as the incarnation model.

4. *Derive additional classes:* Additional candidate classes and methods specific to the implementation environment are selected based on the additional activities added while constraining the essential model. These classes supply interfaces to the essential classes at a consistent level.

5. *Synthesize classes:* The candidate-essential classes and the candidate-additional classes are refined and organized into a class hierarchy. Common attributes and operations are extracted to produce superclasses and subclasses. Final classes are selected to maximize reuse through inheritance and importation.

6. *Define interfaces:* The interfaces, object-type declarations, or class definitions are written based on the documented synthesized classes.

7. *Complete design:* The design of the implementation module is completed. The implementation module comprises methods where each provides a single cohesive function. Logic, system interaction, and method invocations to other classes are used to accomplish the complete design for each method in a class. Referential integrity constraints that are specified in the essential model (using the data model diagrams and data dictionary) are now reflected in the class design.

8. *Implement solution:* The implementation of the classes is coded and unit tested.

The analysis phase of the process consists of steps 1 and 2, the design phase consists of steps 3 to 6, and the implementation phase consists of steps 7 and 8. Within the steps of analysis and design, it is expected that several iterations are involved. Prototyping may also be used to validate the essential model and to assist in selecting the appropriate incarnation. Furthermore, the process also calls for several reviews and checkpoints to enhance the control of the project. The reviews include the following:

- Requirements review after the second substep of step 1 (model essential system)
- External structure and design review after the fourth substep (refined model) of step 1
- Class analysis verification review after step 5
- Class externals review after step 6
- Code inspection after step 8 code is complete.

In addition to methodology, requirements, design, analysis, implementation, prototyping, and verification, Branson and Herness (1993) asserted that the object-oriented development process architecture must also addresses elements such as reuse, CASE tools, integration, build and test, and project management. The Branson and Herness process model, based on their object-oriented experience at IBM Rochester, represents one attempt to deploy the object-oriented technology in large organizations. It is certain that many more variations will emerge before a commonly recognized OOP model is reached.

Finally, the element of reuse merits more discussion from the process perspective, even in this brief section. Design and code reuse gives object-oriented development significant advantages in quality and productivity. However, reuse is not automatically achieved simply by using object-oriented development. Object-oriented development provides a large potential source of reusable components, which must be generalized to become usable in new development environments. In terms of development life cycle, generalization for reuse is typically considered as an "add-on" at the end of the project. However, the generalization activities take time and resources. Therefore, *developing with reuse* is what every object-oriented project is aiming for, but *developing for reuse* is difficult to accomplish. This reuse paradox explains the reality that today there are no significant amounts of business-level reusable code despite the promises object technology offers, although there are a large number of general-purpose reusable libraries (Henderson-Sellers and Pant, 1993). Therefore, development organizations that intend to leverage the reuse advantage of object-oriented development must deal with this issue in their development process.

Henderson-Sellers and Pant (1993) proposed a two-library model for the generalization activities for reusable parts. The model addresses the problem of costing and is quite promising. The first step is to put "on hold" project-specific classes from the current project by placing them in a library of potentially reusable components (LPRC). Thus the only cost to the current project is the identification of these classes. The second library, the library of generalized components (LGC), is the high-quality company resource. At the beginning of each new project, an early phase in the development process is an assessment of classes currently residing in both the LPRC and LGC libraries in terms of their reuse value for the project. If of value, additional spending on generalization is made and potential parts in LPRC then can undergo the generalization process and quality checks and be placed in LGC. Because the reusable parts are to benefit the new project, it is reasonable to allocate the cost of generalization to this new customer, for whom it will be a savings.

As the preceding example illustrates, it may take significant research, experience, and ingenuity to piece together the key elements of an object-oriented development process and for it to mature. There is no doubt, however, that once such a process is established, the ability of the software industry to produce large-scale object-oriented projects effectively will be greatly improved.

## 2.6  The Cleanroom Methodology

Cleanroom Software Engineering approaches software development as an engineering process with mathematical foundations rather than a trial-and-error programming process (Linger and Hausler, 1992). The Cleanroom process employs theory-based technologies such as box structure specification of user function and system object architecture, function-theoretic design and correctness verification, and statistical usage testing for quality certification. Cleanroom management is based on incremental development and certification of a pipeline of user-function increments that accumulate into the final product. Cleanroom operations are carried out by small, independent development and certification (test) teams, with teams of teams for large projects (Linger, 1993). Figure 2.5 shows the full implementation of the Cleanroom process (Linger, 1993).

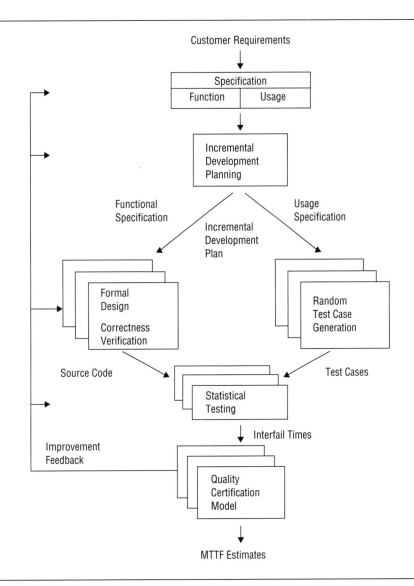

FIGURE 2.5
The Cleanroom Process (Copyright© 1993 IEEE)

(*Source:* R. C. Linger, "Cleanroom Software Engineering for Zero-Defect Software," *Proceedings 15th International Conference on Software Engineering,* May 17–21, 1993, IEEE Computer Society Press. With permission to reprint.)

The Cleanroom process emphasizes the importance of the development team having intellectual control over the project. The bases of the process are proof of correctness (of design and code) and formal quality certification via statistical testing. Perhaps the most controversial aspect of Cleanroom is that team verification of correctness takes the place of individual unit testing. Once the code is developed, it is subject to statistical testing for quality assessment. Proponents argue that the intellectual control of a project afforded by team verification of correctness is the basis for prohibition against unit testing. This elimination also motivates tremendous determination by developers that the code they deliver for independent testing be error-free on first execution (Hausler and Trammell, 1993).

The Cleanroom process proclaims that statistical testing can replace coverage and path testing. In Cleanroom, all testing is based on anticipated customer usage. Test cases are designed to rehearse the more frequently used functions. Therefore, errors that are likely to cause frequent failures to the users are likely to be found first. In terms of measurement, software quality is certified in terms of mean time to failure (MTTF).

The Cleanroom process represents one of the formal approaches in software development that have begun to see application in industry. Other examples of formal approaches include the Vienna Development Method (VDM) and the Z notation (Smith and Wood, 1989; Wing, 1990). It appears that Z and VDM have primarily been used by developers in the United Kingdom and Europe, whereas Cleanroom projects are mostly conducted in the United States.

Since the pilot projects in 1987 and 1988, more than a dozen projects have been completed using the Cleanroom process with more than half a million lines of code. The average defect rate found in first time execution was 2.9 defects per thousand lines of code (KLOC), which is significantly better than the industry average (Linger, 1993).

The adoption of Cleanroom thus far is mostly confined to small projects. Like other formal methods, the questions about its ability to be scaled up to large projects and the mathematical training required have been asked by many developers and project managers. Also, as discussed before, the prohibition of unit testing is perhaps the most controversial concern. Whether statistical testing could completely replace range/limit testing and path testing remains a key question in many developers' minds. This is especially true when the software system is complex or when the system is a common-purpose system where a typical customer usage profile is itself in question. Not surprisingly, some Cleanroom projects do not preclude the practice of the traditional methods (such as unit test and limit test) while adopting Cleanroom's formal approaches. Hausler and Trammell (1993) even proposed a phased implementation approach in order to facilitate the acceptance of Cleanroom. The phased implementation framework includes three stages:

- □ *Introductory implementation* involves the implementation of Cleanroom principles without the full formality of the methodology (for example, box structure, statistical testing, and certification of reliability).
- □ *Full implementation* involves the complete use of Cleanroom's formal methods (as illustrated in Figure 2.5).
- □ *Advanced implementation* optimizes the process for the local environment (for example, the use of an automated code generator, Markov modeling and analysis of system usage, certification using a locally validated reliability model, and so forth).

## 2.7 The Defect Prevention Process

The defect prevention process (DPP) is not itself a software development process. Rather, it is a process to continually improve the development process. It originated in the software development environment and thus far has been mostly implemented within software development organizations. We would be remiss if we did not discuss this process while discussing software development processes. For these reasons we include a brief discussion of DPP in this chapter.

The DPP was modeled on techniques used in Japan for decades and is in agreement with Deming's principles. It is based on three simple steps:

1. Analyze existing defects or errors to trace the root causes.
2. Suggest preventive actions to eliminate the defect root causes.
3. Implement the preventive actions.

The formal process, which was first used at the IBM Communications Programming Laboratory at Research Triangle Park, North Carolina (Jones, 1985; Mays *et al.,* 1990), consists of the following four key elements:

1. *Causal analysis meetings:* These are usually two-hour brainstorming sessions conducted by technical teams at the end of each stage of the development process. Developers analyze defects that occurred in the stage, trace the root causes of errors, and suggest possible actions to prevent similar errors from recurring. Methods for removing similar defects in a current product are

also discussed. Team members discuss any overall defect trends that may emerge from their analysis of this stage, particularly what went wrong and what went right, and examine suggestions for improvement. After the meeting, the causal analysis leader records the data (defects, causes, and suggested actions) in an action database for subsequent reporting and tracking. To allow participants at this meeting to more freely express their thoughts and feelings on why defects occurred without jeopardizing their career or next appraisal, management is not present during this meeting.

2. *Action team:* The action team is responsible for screening, prioritizing, and implementing suggested actions from causal analysis meetings. Each member has a percentage of his/her time allotted for this task. Each action team has a coordinator and a management representative (the action team manager). The team uses reports from the action database to guide their meetings. The action team is the engine of the process. Other than action implementation, the team is also involved in feedback to the organization, reports to management on the status of its activities, publishing success stories, and taking the lead in various aspects of the process. The action team relieves the programmers from having to implement their own suggestions, especially actions that have a broad scope of influence and require substantial resource. Of course, existence of the action team does not preclude action implemented by others. In fact, technical teams are encouraged to take improvement actions, especially those that pertain to their specific areas.

3. *Stage kickoff meetings:* The technical teams conduct these meetings at the beginning of each development stage. The emphasis is on the technical aspect of the development process and on quality: What is the right process? How do we do things more effectively? What are the tools and methods that can help? What are the common errors to avoid? What improvements and actions had been implemented? The meetings thus serve two main purposes: as a primary feedback mechanism of the defect prevention process and as a preventive measure.

4. *Action tracking and data collection:* To prevent suggestions from being lost over time, to aid action implementation, and to enhance communications among groups, an action database tool is needed to track action status.

Figure 2.6 shows this process schematically.

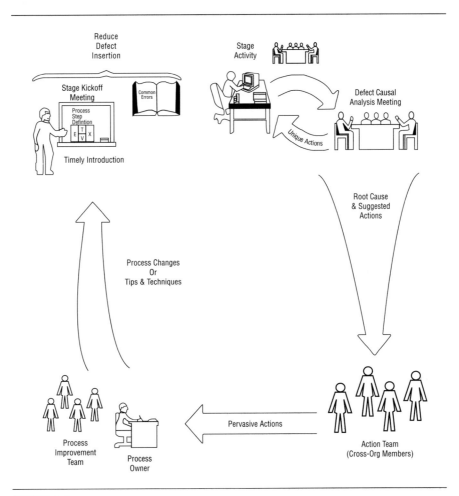

FIGURE 2.6
Defect Prevention Process

Different from postmortem analysis, the DPP is a real-time process, integrated into every stage of the development process. Rather than holding a postmortem after the entire project is completed, which has frequently been the case, DPP is incorporated into every subprocess and phase within that project. This helps ensure that meaningful discussion takes place when it is fresh in everyone's mind. It focuses on defect-related actions and process-oriented preventive actions, which is very important. Through the action teams and action tracking tools and methodology, DPP provides a systematic, objective, data-based mechanism for action implementation. It is a bottoms-up approach; causal analysis meetings are conducted by developers without management interference. However, the process requires management support and direct participation via the action teams.

For the past several years, DPP has been used successfully at IBM in Raleigh, North Carolina, on several software products. For example, their Network Communications Program had a 54% reduction in error injection during development and a 60% reduction in field defects after DPP was implemented. Also, the space shuttle onboard software control system developed by IBM Houston, Texas, has achieved zero defects for the past several releases. Causal analysis of defects along with actions aimed at eliminating the cause of defects are credited as the key factors for the successes (Mays *et al.,* 1990). Many sites and divisions in IBM are now implementing DPP. Indeed, the element of defect prevention has been incorporated as one of the "imperatives" of the software development process at IBM. Other companies, especially those in the software industry, have also begun implementing or investigating the process.

DPP can be applied to any development process, whether waterfall, prototyping, iterative, spiral, Cleanroom, or others. As long as the defects are recorded, causal analysis can be performed and preventive actions mapped and implemented. For example, the middle part of the waterfall process includes design, code, and test. After incorporating DPP at each stage, the process will look like Figure 2.7. The important role of DPP in software process improvement is widely recognized by the software community. In the SEI (Software Engineering Institute) software process maturity assessment model (Humphrey, 1989), the element of defect prevention must be present for a process to achieve the highest maturity level—Level 5. The SEI maturity model is discussed in more detail in the next section.

Finally, although the process has been initiated and implemented primarily in software development environments, it can be applied to any product or industry. Indeed, the international quality standard ISO 9000 has a major element of corrective action; DPP is often an effective vehicle employed by companies to address this element when they implement the ISO 9000 registration process. ISO 9000 is also covered in the next section on process maturity assessment and quality standards.

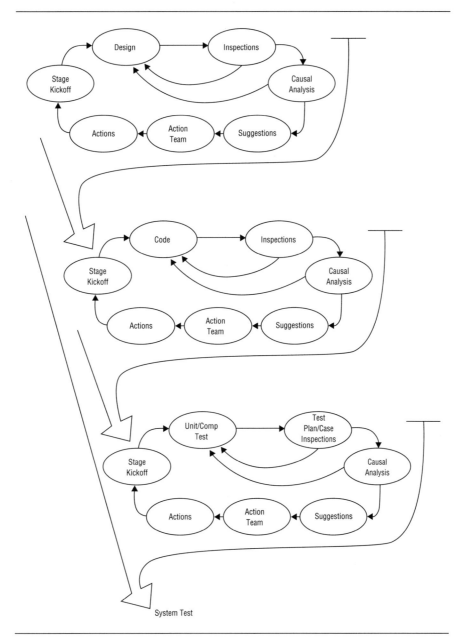

FIGURE 2.7
**Applying the Defect Prevention Process to the Waterfall Model**

## 2.8 Process Maturity Framework and Quality Standards

Regardless of which process is used, the degree to which it is implemented varies from organization to organization and even from project to project. Indeed, given the framework of a certain process model, the development team usually defines its specifics such as implementation procedures, methods and tools to be used, metrics and measurements, and so forth. Whereas certain process models are better for certain types of projects under certain environments, the success of a project depends heavily on the implementation maturity, regardless of the process model. Furthermore, in addition to the process model, there are questions related to the overall quality management system of the company, which are important to the outcome of the software projects.

In this section, we discuss the frameworks used to assess the process maturity of an organization or a project. We cover the SEI and the Software Productivity Research (SPR) process maturity assessment methods, the Malcolm Baldrige discipline and assessment processes, and the ISO 9000 registration process. Although the SEI and SPR methods are specific to software processes, the latter two frameworks are actually quality process and quality management standards that apply to all industries.

### 2.8.1 The SEI Process Capability Maturity Model (CMM)

The SEI at the Carnegie-Mellon University developed a framework of process maturity for software development (Humphrey, 1989). The framework includes five levels of process maturity (Humphrey, 1989, p. 56):

**Level 1: Initial**

Characteristics: chaotic; unpredictable cost, schedule, and quality performance.

**Level 2: Repeatable**

Characteristics: Intuitive; cost and quality highly variable, reasonable control of schedules, informal and *ad hoc* methods and procedures. The key elements to achieve level 2 maturity follow:

- ☐   Requirements management
- ☐   Software project planning and oversight
- ☐   Software subcontract management
- ☐   Software quality assurance
- ☐   Software configuration management

### Level 3: Defined

Characteristics: qualitative; reliable costs and schedules, improving but unpredictable quality performance. The key elements to achieve this level of maturity follow:

- Organizational process improvement
- Organizational process definition
- Training program
- Integrated software management
- Software product engineering
- Intergroup coordination
- Peer reviews.

### Level 4: Managed

Characteristics: quantitative; reasonable statistical control over product quality. The key elements to achieve this level of maturity follow:

- Process measurement and analysis
- Quality management.

### Level 5: Optimizing

Characteristics: quantitative basis for continued capital investment in process automation and improvement. The key elements to achieve this highest level of maturity follow:

- Defect prevention
- Technology innovation
- Process change management.

The SEI maturity assessment framework has been used by government agencies and companies in the software industry. The framework is to be used with an assessment methodology and a management system. The assessment methodology relies on an 85-item questionnaire, with yes or no answers. For each question, the SEI maturity level that the question is associated with is indicated. There are also special questions designated as key to each specific maturity level. To be qualified for a certain level, 90% of the key questions and 80% of all questions for that level must be answered yes. The maturity levels are hierarchical. Level 2 must be attained before the calculation for level 3 or higher is accepted. Levels 2 and 3 must be attained before level 4 calculation is accepted, and so forth. If an organization has more than one project, its ranking is determined by answering the questionnaire with a composite viewpoint—specifically, the answer to each question should be substantially true across the organization.

It is interesting to note that pervasive use of software metrics and models is a key characteristic of level 4 maturity, and for level 5 the element of defect prevention is key. In the following, we list the metrics-related topics that are addressed by the questionnaire.

- ☐ Profiles of software size maintained for each software configuration item over time
- ☐ Statistics on software design errors
- ☐ Statistics on software code and test errors
- ☐ Projection of design errors and comparison between projection and actuals
- ☐ Projection of test errors and comparison between projection and actuals
- ☐ Measurement of design review coverage
- ☐ Measurement of test coverage
- ☐ Tracking of design review actions to closure
- ☐ Tracking of testing defects to closure
- ☐ Database for process metrics data across all projects
- ☐ Analysis of review data gathered during design reviews
- ☐ Analysis of data already gathered to determine the likely distribution and characteristics of the errors remaining in the project
- ☐ Analysis of errors to determine their process-related causes
- ☐ Analysis of review efficiency for each project.

The several questions on defect prevention address the following topics:

- ☐ Mechanism for error cause analysis
- ☐ Analysis of error causes to determine the process changes that are required for prevention
- ☐ Mechanism for initiating error prevention actions.

The SEI maturity assessment has been conducted in software organizations on many projects, either carried out by SEI or by the organizations themselves in the form of self-assessment. The model has also been used as an evaluation vehicle for contract software by the U.S. Department of Defense. According to Humphrey (*American Programmer,* 1990), among the assessments conducted by SEI, about 75% of the projects were found to be at level 1. On the other hand, some level 4 and level 5 projects have been observed; their numbers are slim, but they do exist. At the organization level, however, it is even more difficult to achieve level 4 or above; at this point, we have no knowledge of whether any organizations have achieved such levels.

### 2.8.2 The SPR Assessment

Software Productivity Research, Inc. (SPR), developed the SPR assessment method in about the same time frame (Jones, 1986) during which the SEI process maturity model was developed. There is a large degree of similarity and some substantial differences between the SEI and SPR methods (Jones, 1992). Some leading U.S. software developers use both methods concurrently. While SEI's questions focus on software organization structure and software process, SPR's questions cover both strategic corporate issues and tactical project issues that affect quality, productivity, and user satisfaction. Compared to SEI's 85 questions, the total number of questions in the SPR questionnaire is about 400. Furthermore, the SPR questions are linked-multiple-choice questions with a five-point Likert scale for responses, whereas the SEI method uses a binary (yes/no) scale. The overall process assessment outcome by the SPR method is also expressed in the same five-point scale:

1. Excellent
2. Good
3. Average
4. Marginal
5. Poor.

Different from SEI's five maturity levels, which have predefined criteria, the SPR questions are structured so that a rating of "3" is the approximate average for the topic being explored. SPR has also developed an automated software tool (CHECKPOINT) for assessment and for resource planning and quality projection.

With regard to software quality and metrics, topics such as the following are addressed by the SPR questions:

- Quality and productivity measurements
- Pretest defect removal experience among programmers
- Testing defect removal experience among programmers
- Project quality and reliability targets
- Pretest defect removal at the project level
- Project testing defect removal
- Postrelease defect removal.

### 2.8.3 The Malcolm Baldrige Assessment

The Malcolm Baldrige National Quality Award (MBNQA) is the most prestigious quality award in the United States. Established in 1988 by the U.S. Department of Commerce (and named after Secretary Malcolm Baldrige), the award is given annually to recognize U.S. companies that excel in quality management and quality achievement. The examination criteria is divided into seven categories containing 28 examination items:

- ☐ Leadership
- ☐ Information and analysis
- ☐ Strategic quality planning
- ☐ Human resource utilization
- ☐ Quality assurance of products and services
- ☐ Quality results
- ☐ Customer satisfaction.

The system for scoring the examination items is based on three evaluation dimensions: approach, deployment, and results. Each item requires information relating to at least one of these dimensions. *Approach* refers to the methods the company is using to achieve the purposes addressed in the examination item. *Deployment* refers to the extent to which the approach is applied. *Results* refers to the outcomes and effects in achieving the purposes addressed and applied.

The purpose of the Malcolm Baldrige assessment approach (the examination items and their assessment) is fivefold:

1. Help elevate quality standards and expectations in the country.
2. Facilitate communication and sharing among and within organizations of all types based on a common understanding of key quality requirements.
3. Serve as a working tool for planning, training, assessment, and other uses.
4. Provide the basis for making the award.
5. Provide feedback to the applicants.

There are 1000 points available in the award criteria. Each examination item is given a percentage score (ranging from 0% to 100%). A candidate for the Baldrige award should be scoring in the 70% range. This would generally translate as follows:

- ☐ For an approach examination item, continuous refinement of approaches are in place and a majority of them are linked to each other.

☐    For a deployment examination item, deployment has reached all of the company's major business areas as well as many support areas.

☐    For a results examination item, the company's results in many of its major areas are among the highest in the industry. There should also be evidence that the results are caused by the approach.

While score is important, the most valuable output from an assessment is the feedback, which consists of the observed strengths and (most significant) the areas for improvement. It is not unusual for even the higher scoring enterprises to receive hundreds of improvement suggestions. By focusing on and eliminating the high-priority weaknesses, the company can be assured they are continuously improving.

To be the MBNQA winner, the four basic elements of the framework of the award criteria must be evident:

1. *Driver:* depicted by the leadership of the senior executive management team.

2. *System:* the set of well-defined and well-designed processes for meeting the company's quality and performance requirements.

3. *Measure of progress:* the results of the company's in-process quality measurements (aimed at improving customer value and company performance).

4. *Goal:* the basic aim of the quality process is the delivery of continuously improving value to customers.

Many U.S. companies have adopted the Malcolm Baldrige assessment and its discipline as the basis for their in-company quality program. IBM, for example, has taken the MBNQA assessment discipline with internal augments as a key ingredient of its total quality management system, the Market Driven Quality strategy and implementation.

In 1992, the European Foundation for Quality Management published The European Quality Award, which is awarded to the most successful proponents of total quality management in Western Europe. Its criteria are similar to the Baldrige award (i.e., 1000 maximum points; the areas of approach, deployment, results are scoring dimensions). Although there are nine categories (versus Baldrige's seven), they cover similar examination areas.

Unlike the SEI and SPR assessments, which focus on software organizations, projects, and processes, the Malcolm Baldrige National Quality Award and the European Quality Award encompass a much broader scope. They are actually a body of quality standards for overall quality management, regardless of industry. Indeed, the MBNQA covers three broad categories: manufacturing, service, and small business.

### 2.8.4 ISO 9000

ISO 9000, a set of standards and guidelines for a quality assurance management system, represents another body of quality standards. It was established by the International Organization for Standardization and has been adopted by the European Community. Many European Community companies are ISO 9000 registered. To better position their products to compete in the European market, many U.S. companies are working to have their development and manufacturing processes registered. There are 20 elements in the ISO guidelines. To obtain registration, a formal audit is involved and the outcome has to be positive. Guidelines for the application of the 20 elements to the development, supply, and maintenance of software are also specified in ISO 9000-3. The twenty elements are as follows:

1. Management responsibility
2. Quality system
3. Contract review
4. Design control
5. Document control
6. Purchasing
7. Purchaser-supplied product
8. Product identification and traceability
9. Process control
10. Inspection and testing
11. Inspection, measuring, and test equipment
12. Inspection and test status
13. Control of nonconforming product
14. Corrective action
15. Handling, storage, packaging, and delivery
16. Quality records
17. Internal quality audits
18. Training
19. Servicing
20. Statistical techniques.

Although many firms and companies are in the process of pursuing ISO 9000 registration, it is interesting to observe that many companies actually fail the audit during the first pass. The number of initial failures ranges from 60% to 70%. This is quite an interesting statistic and is probably explained by the complexity of the standards, their bureaucratic nature, the opportunity for omissions, and a lack of familiarity with what is actually required.

From the software standpoint, we observed that corrective actions and document control are the areas where most nonconformances were incurred. As we discussed earlier, implementation of the defect prevention process is a good vehicle to address the element of corrective action. It is important, however, to make sure that the process is fully implemented throughout the entire organization. If an organization does not implement the defect prevention process, a process for corrective action must be established to meet the ISO requirements.

With regard to document control, ISO 9000 has very strong requirements. Some examples of the implementation of this element (shown in the following) demonstrate a flavor:

☐ *Must be adequate for purpose:* The document must allow a person, properly trained, to adequately perform the duties described.

☐ *Owner must be identified:* The owner may be a person or department. The owner need not necessarily be the author.

☐ *Properly approved before issued:* Qualified approvers must be identified by the organization's title and approver's name.

☐ *Distribution must be controlled:* Control may be:
  Keeping a master hard copy with distribution on demand.
  Maintaining a distribution record.
  Having documents reside on line available to all authorized users, with the following control statement, "Master document is the on-line version."

☐ *Version identified:* The version level must be clearly identified by a version level or date.

☐ *Pages numbered:* All pages must be numbered to ensure sections are not missing.

☐ *Total pages indicated:* The total number of pages must be indicated, at a minimum, on the title page.

☐ *Promptly destroyed when obsolete:* When a controlled document is superseded, existing controlled copies must be recalled or otherwise destroyed. Individuals who receive controlled documents are responsible for prompt disposition of superseded documents.

From our perspective, what is more interesting to us are the requirements on software metrics, which are listed under the element of statistical techniques. The requirements address both product metrics and process metrics:

**1.** *Product metrics:* Measurements should be used for the following purposes:

☐   To collect data and report metric values on a regular basis.

☐   To identify the current level of performance on each metric.

☐   To take remedial action if metric levels grow worse or exceed established target levels.

☐   To establish specific improvement goals in terms of the metrics.

At a minimum, some metrics should be used that represent:

☐   Reported field failures.

☐   Defects from customer viewpoint.

Selected metrics should be described such that results are comparable.

**2.** *Process metrics*

☐   Are in-process quality objectives being met?

☐   Addresses how well development process is being carried out with checkpoints.

☐   Addresses how effective the development process is at reducing the probability that faults are introduced or go undetected.

The MBNQA criteria and the ISO 9000 quality assurance system can complement each other as an enterprise advances on its quality journey. However, note that Baldrige is a nonprescriptive assessment tool in which improvement items are illuminated; adherence to ISO 9000 requires passing (or failing) an audit. Furthermore, while the Malcolm Baldrige assessment focuses on both process and results, the ISO 9000 audit focuses on a quality management system and process control. Simply put, ISO 9000 can be described as "say what you do, do what you say, and prove it." But ISO 9000 does not examine the quality results and customer satisfaction, to which the Malcolm Baldrige assessment is heavily tilted. The two sets of standards thus actually complement each other. Development organizations that adopted them will see more rigor added to their processes. Figure 2.8 shows our view of ISO 9000 in comparison with the Baldrige scoring system. For the Baldrige system, the length of the arrow for each category is in proportion to the maximum score for that category. For ISO 9000, the lengths of the arrows are based on the perceived strength of focus from the IBM Rochester ISO 9000 audit experience, conducted by the British

Standard Institute (BSI) in 1992. As can be seen, if the strengths of ISO 9000 (process quality and process implementation) are combined with the strengths of the Baldrige discipline (quality results, customer focus and satisfaction, and broader issues such as leadership and human resource development), the quality system thus formed will have both broad-based coverage and deep penetration.

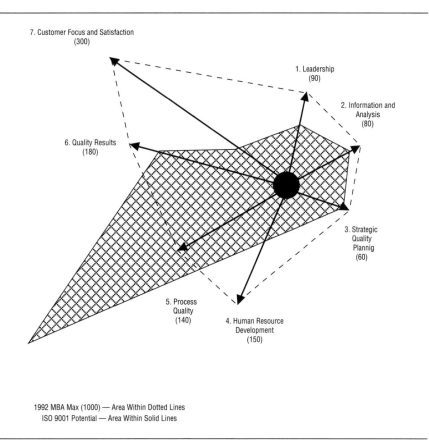

1992 MBA Max (1000) — Area Within Dotted Lines
ISO 9001 Potential — Area Within Solid Lines

FIGURE 2.8
Malcolm Baldrige Assessment and ISO 9000: A Comparison Based on the Baldrige Scoring

The Baldrige/ISO synergism comes from the following:

☐   The formal ISO documentation requirements (e.g., quality record), which facilitate addressing the Baldrige examination items.

☐   The formal ISO validation requirements (i.e., internal assessments, external audits, and periodic surveillance), which assist completeness and thoroughness.

☐   The heavy ISO emphasis on corrective action, which contributes to the company's continuous improvement program.

☐   The audit process itself, which results in additional focus on many of the Baldrige examination areas.

## 2.9  Summary

In this chapter we:

☐   Described the major process models and approaches in software development—the waterfall process, the prototyping approach, the spiral model, the iterative process, the object-oriented process, the Cleanroom methodology, and the defect prevention process.

☐   Discussed two methods of process maturity assessment—the SEI process capability maturity model and the SPR assessment method.

☐   Summarized two bodies of quality management standards—the Malcolm Baldrige National Quality Award assessment discipline and ISO 9000.

The waterfall process is time-proven and is most suitable for the development of complex system software with numerous interdependencies. This process yields clearly defined intermediate deliverables and enables strong project control.

The prototyping approach enables the development team and the customers to clarify the requirements and their interpretation early in the development cycle. It is not a process *per se;* it can be used with various process models. It has become widely used in application development. It can also be used with subsystems of system software when external interfaces are involved.

The iterative process and the spiral model have seen wide use in recent years, especially in application development. Coupled with risk management and prototyping, these new processes enhance the chance of the final product being able to satisfy user requirements and facilitate the reduction of cycle time.

In terms of the object-oriented development process, much has to be done; the proposed process discussed in this chapter is experimental. Among other issues, a sound object-oriented development process needs to address the reuse issue, from both standpoints of *developing with reuse* and *developing for reuse.*

The Cleanroom approach can be regarded as a process as well as a methodology. As a process, it is well defined. As a methodology, it can be used with other processes such as the waterfall and even object-oriented development. Since the early experimental projects in the late 1980s, the Cleanroom approach has seen increased use in recent years.

The defect prevention process is aimed at process development. When integrated with the development process, it facilitates process maturity because it enables the process to fine tune itself through the closed-loop learning process. It can be applied to software development as well as in other industries.

Whereas the process models deal with the issue of how to develop software, the SEI and SPR maturity models deal with how mature is the organization's development process, regardless of which process model is being used. They entail defining a set of ideal criteria and measuring the existing processes of organizations against these ideals. This concept has become very popular in the last decade and provides a mechanism for companies to be related with regard to process. The Malcolm Baldrige assessment and ISO 9000 are bodies of quality standards at an even broader scope. They pertain to the quality assurance management system at the company level regardless of industry. In sum, the specific development process that is being used, the maturity level of the process, and the company's quality management system certainly are all important factors affecting the quality of a software project.

In the next chapter we focus on some aspects of measurement theory that will set the stage for our discussions on software metrics.

## References

1. *American Programmer,* "An Interview with Watts Humphrey," September 1990, pp. 8–9.
2. Basili, V. R., and J. D. Musa, "The Future Engineering of Software: A Management Perspective," *IEEE Computer,* 1991, pp. 90–96.
3. Basili, V. R., and A. J. Turner, "Iterative Enhancement: A Practical Technique for Software Development," *IEEE Transactions on Software Engineering,* Vol. SE-1, No. 4, December 1975, pp. 390–396.
4. Boehm, B. W., "Software Engineering," *IEEE Transactions on Computer,* Vol. C-25, December 1976, pp. 1226–1241.
5. Boehm, B. W., "A Spiral Model of Software Development and Enhancement," *IEEE Computer,* May 1988, pp. 61–72.
6. Booch, G., *Object Oriented Design with Applications,* Redwood City, Calif.: Benjamin/Cummings, 1991.
7. Branson, M. J., and E. N. Herness, "Process for Building Object Oriented Systems from Essential and Constrained System Models: Overview," *Proceedings of the Fourth Worldwide MDQ Productivity and Process Tools Symposium: Volume 1 of 2,* Thornwood, N.Y.: International Business Machines Corp., March 1992, pp. 577–598.

**8.** Branson, M. J., and E. N. Herness, "The Object-Oriented Development Process," *Object Magazine,* Vol. 3, No. 4, Nov.–Dec. 1993, pp. 66–70.

**9.** Coad, P., and E. Yourdon, *Object-Oriented Analysis,* Englewood Cliffs, N.J.: Yourdon Press, 1990.

**10.** Davis, A. M., E. H. Bersoff, and E. R. Comer, "A Strategy for Comparing Alternative Software Development Life Cycle Models," *IEEE Transactions on Software Engineering,* Vol. 14, No. 10, October 1988, pp. 1453–1461.

**11.** Gomaa, H., and D. Scott, "Prototyping as a Tool in the Specification of User Requirements," *Proceedings 5th IEEE International Conference on Software Engineering,* March 1981, pp. 333–342.

**12.** Hausler, P. A., and C. J. Trammell, "Adopting Cleanroom Software Engineering with a Phased Approach," IBM Cleanroom Software Technology Center, Gaithersburg, Md., February 1993.

**13.** Henderson-Sellers, B., and Y. R. Pant, "Adopting the Reuse Mindset Throughout the Lifecycle: When Should We Generalize Classes to Make Them Reusable?" *Object Magazine,* Vol. 3, No. 4, Nov.–Dec. 1993, pp. 73–75.

**14.** Hough, D., "Rapid Delivery: An Evolutionary Approach for Application Development," *IBM Systems Journal,* Vol. 32, No. 3, 1993, pp. 397–419.

**15.** Humphrey, W. S., *Managing the Software Process,* Reading, Mass.: Addison-Wesley, 1989.

**16.** Jenkins, P., IBM Boca Raton, Fl., Private communication, 1992.

**17.** Jones, C. L., "A Process-Integrated Approach to Defect Prevention," *IBM Systems Journal,* Vol. 24, No. 2, 1985, pp. 150–167.

**18.** Linger, R. C., "Cleanroom Software Engineering for Zero-Defect Software," *Proceedings 15th International Conference on Software Engineering,* May 17–21, 1993, IEEE Computer Society Press.

**19.** Linger, R. C., and P. A. Hausler, "The Journey to Zero Defects with Cleanroom Software Engineering," *Creativity!,* IBM Corporation, September 1992.

**20.** Luckey, P. H., R. M. Pittman, and A. Q. LeVan, "Iterative Development Process with Proposed Applications," Technical Report, IBM Owego, New York, 1992.

**21.** Mays, Robert G., C. L. Jones, G. J. Holloway, and D. P. Studinski, "Experiences with Defect Prevention," *IBM Systems Journal,* Vol. 29, No. 1, 1990, pp. 4–32.

**22.** McMenamin, S. M., and J. F. Palmer, *Essential Systems Analysis,* Englewood Cliffs, N.J.: Yourdon Press, 1984.

**23.** Meyer, B., *Object-Oriented Software Construction,* Englewood Cliffs, N.J.: Prentice-Hall, 1988.

**24.** Radice, R. A., N. K. Roth, A. C. O'Hara, Jr., and W. A. Ciarfella, "A Programming Process Architecture," *IBM Systems Journal,* Vol. 24, No. 2, 1985, pp. 79–90.

**25.** Smith, D. J., and K. B. Wood, *Engineering Quality Software: A Review of Current Practices, Standards and Guidelines Including New Methods and Development Tools,* 2nd ed., New York: Elsevier Applied Science, 1989.

**26.** Wing, J. M., "A Specifier's Introduction to Formal Methods," *Computer,* Vol. 23, No. 9, September 1990, pp. 8–24.

# 3

## Fundamentals in Measurement Theory

This chapter discusses the fundamentals in measurement theory. We outline the relationships among theoretical concepts, definitions, and measurement and describe some basic measures that are used frequently. It is important to distinguish the different levels in the conceptualization process, from abstract concepts to definitions that are used operationally, and to actual measurements. Depending on the concept and the operational definition that is derived, different levels of measurement may be applied: nominal scale, ordinal scale, interval scale, and ratio scale. It is also beneficial to spell out the explicit differences among some basic measures such as ratio, proportion, percentage, and rate. In the software industry, confusion about these measurement fundamentals is frequently encountered. Significant amounts of wasted effort and resources can be avoided if these fundamentals are well understood.

We then focus on measurement quality. We discuss the most important issues in measurement quality, namely, reliability and validity, and their relationships with measurement errors. We then discuss the role of correlation in observational studies and the criteria for causality.

## 3.1 Definition, Operational Definition, and Measurement

It is an undisputed statement that measurement is crucial to the progress of all sciences. Scientific progress is made through observations and generalizations based on data and measurements, the derivation of theories as a result, and in turn the confirmation or refutation of theories via hypothesis testing based on further empirical data. As an example take the proposition "the more rigorously the front end of the software development process is executed, the better the quality at the back end." To confirm or refute this proposition, we first need to define the key concepts. For example, we define the software development process and distinguish the front-end process steps and activities from those for the back end. Assume that after the requirements-gathering process, our development process consists of the following phases:

- □   Design
- □   Design reviews and inspections
- □   Code
- □   Code inspection
- □   Debug and development test
- □   Integration (of components and modules to form the product)
- □   Formal machine testing
- □   Early customer programs.

Integration is the development phase in which various parts and components are integrated to form the entire software product, and usually after integration the product is under formal change control. Specifically, after integration every change of the software must have a specific reason (for example, to fix a bug uncovered during testing) and must be documented and tracked. Therefore, we may want to use integration as the cutoff point: The design to the debug phases are classified as the front end of the development process and after integration it is labeled the back end.

We then define what is rigorous implementation both in the general sense and in specific terms as they relate to the front end of the development process. Assuming the development process has been formally documented, we may define rigorous implementation as total adherence to the process: Whatever is described in the process documentation that needs to be executed, we plan to execute. However, this general definition is not sufficient for our purpose, which is to gather data to test our proposition. We need to further specify the indicator(s) of the definition and to make it (them) operational. For example, suppose the process documentation says all designs and code should be inspected. One of our operational definitions of rigorous implementation may be inspection coverage expressed in terms of the percentage of the estimated lines of code (LOC) that are actually inspected. Another indicator of good reviews and inspections could be the scoring of each inspection by the inspectors at the end of the inspection, based on a set of criteria. We may want to operationally use a five-point Likert scale to denote the degree of effectiveness (for example, 5 = very effective, 4 = effective, 3 = somewhat effective, 2 = not effective, 1 = poor inspection). There may also be other indicators in addition to these two.

In addition to design, design reviews, code implementation, and code inspections, development testing is also part of our definition of the front end of the development process. We also need to operationally define "rigorous execution" of this test. Two indicators that could be used are the percent coverage in terms of instructions executed (as measured by some test coverage measurement tools) and the defect rate expressed in terms of number of defects removed per thousand lines of source code (KLOC).

Likewise, we need to operationally define what is meant by quality at the back end and which measurement indicators are to be used. For the sake of simplicity let us use defects found per KLOC during formal machine testing as the indicator of back-end quality. From these metrics, we can then formulate several testable hypotheses such as the following:

- For software projects, the higher the percentage of the designs and code that are inspected, the lower the defect rate that will be encountered at the later phase of formal machine testing.

- The more effective the design reviews and the code inspections as scored by the inspection team, the lower the defect rate that will be encountered at the later phase of formal machine testing.

- The more thorough the development test (in terms of test coverage) done before integration, the lower the defect rate that will be encountered at the formal machine testing phase.

With the hypotheses formulated, we can set out to gather data and test the hypotheses. We also need to determine the unit of analysis for our measurement and data. In this case, it could be at the project level or at the component level of a large project. Suppose we are able to collect a number of data points that form a reasonable sample size (for example, 45 projects or components), we can then perform statistical analysis to test the hypotheses. We can classify projects or components into several groups according to the independent variable of each hypothesis, then compare the outcome of the dependent variable (defect rate during formal machine testing) across the groups. We can conduct simple correlation analysis. Or we can perform more sophisticated statistical analyses. If the hypotheses are substantiated by the data, we confirm the proposition. If they are rejected, we refute the proposition. If we have doubts or unanswered questions during the process (for example: Are our indicators valid? Are our data reliable? Are there other variables we need to control when we conduct the analysis for hypothesis testing? and so forth), then perhaps more research is needed. However, if the hypothesis(ses) or the proposition is confirmed, we can utilize the knowledge thus gained and take actions accordingly to improve our software development quality.

The example demonstrates the importance of measurement and data. It is measurement and data that really drive the progress of science and engineering. Without the empirical verification by data and measurement, theories and propositions will remain at the abstract level. The example also illustrates that from theory to testable hypothesis, and likewise from concepts to measurement, there are several steps with different levels of abstraction. Simply put, a theory consists of one or more propositional statements that describe the relationships among concepts—usually expressed in terms of cause and effect. From each proposition, one or more empirical hypotheses can be derived. The concepts are then formally defined and operationalized. The operationalization process produces metrics and indicators for which data can be collected. The hypotheses thus can be tested empirically. The hierarchy from theory to hypothesis and from concept to measurement indicators can be illustrated in Figure 3.1.

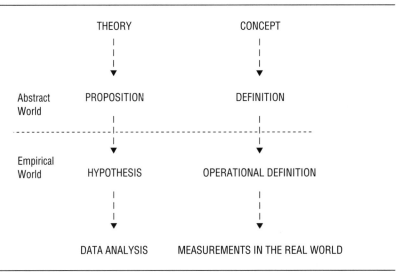

FIGURE 3.1
Abstraction Hierarchy

The building blocks of theory are concepts and definitions. In a theoretical definition a concept is defined in terms of other concepts that are already well understood. In the deductive logic system, certain concepts would be taken as undefined;

they are the primitives. All other concepts would be defined in terms of the primitive concepts. For example, the concepts point and line may be used as undefined and the concepts of triangle or rectangle can then be defined based on these primitives.

*Operational definitions,* in contrast, are definitions that actually spell out the metrics to be used and the procedures to be used to obtain data. An operational definition of "body weight" would indicate how the weight of a person is to be measured, what instrument is to be used, and what measurement unit is used to record the results. An operational definition of software product defect rate would indicate the formula for defect rate, what defect is to be measured (numerator), what denominator (for example, lines of code count, function point) to use, how to measure, and so forth.

## 3.2  Level of Measurement

We have seen that from theory to empirical hypothesis and from theoretically defined concepts to operational definitions, the process is by no means direct. As the example illustrates, when we operationalize a definition and derive measurement indicators, the scale of measurement needs to be considered. For instance, to measure the quality of software inspection we may use a five-point scale to score the inspection effectiveness or we may use percentage to indicate the inspection coverage. For some cases, more than one measurement scale is applicable; for others, the nature of the concept and the resultant operational definition can only be measured in a certain scale. In this section, we briefly discuss the four levels of measurement: nominal scale, ordinal scale, interval scale, and ratio scale.

### Nominal Scale

The most simple operation in science and the lowest level of measurement is classification. In classifying we attempt to sort elements into categories with respect to a certain attribute. For example, if the attribute of interest is religion, we may classify the subjects of the study into Catholics, Protestants, Jews, Buddhists, and so on. If we classify software products by the development process models through which the products were developed, then we may have categories such as waterfall development process, spiral development process, iterative development process, object-oriented programming process, and others. In a nominal scale, the two key requirements for the categories are that of jointly exhaustive and mutually exclusive. Mutually exclusive means a subject can be classified into one and only one category. Jointly exhaustive means that all categories together should cover all possible categories of the attribute. If the attribute has more categories than we are interested in, the use of the "other" category is needed to make the categories jointly exhaustive.

In a nominal scale, the names of the categories and their sequence order bear no assumptions about relationships between categories. For instance, we place the waterfall development process in front of spiral development process, but we do not imply that one is "better than" or "greater than" the other. As long as the requirements of mutually exclusive and jointly exhaustive are met, we have minimal conditions necessary for the application of statistical analysis. For example, we may want to compare the values of interested attributes such as defect rate, cycle time, and requirements defects across the different categories of software products.

**Ordinal Scale**

Ordinal scale refers to the measurement operations through which the subjects can be compared in order. For example, we may classify families according to socioeconomic status: upper class, middle class, and lower class. We may classify software development projects according to the SEI maturity levels, or according to a process rigor scale: totally adheres to process, somewhat adheres to process, does not adhere to process. Our earlier example of inspection effectiveness scoring is an ordinal scale.

The ordinal measurement scale is at a higher level than the nominal scale in the measurement hierarchy. Through it we are able not only to group subjects into separate categories, but also to order the categories. An ordinal scale is asymmetric in the sense that if $A > B$ is true then $B > A$ is false. It has the transitivity property in that if $A > B$ and $B > C$, then $A > C$.

We must recognize that in an ordinal scale there is no information about the magnitude of the differences between elements. For instance, for the process rigor scale we know only that "totally adheres to process" is better than "somewhat adheres to process" in terms of the quality outcome of the software product, and "somewhat adheres to process" is better than "does not adhere to process." However, we cannot say that the difference between the former pair of categories is the same as that between the latter pair. In customer satisfaction surveys of software products, the five-point Likert scale is often used with 1 = completely dissatisfied, 2 = somewhat dissatisfied, 3 = neutral, 4 = satisfied, and 5 = completely satisfied. We know only $5 > 4$, $4 > 3$, or $5 > 2$, and so forth, but we cannot say how much greater 5 is than 4. Nor can we say that the difference between categories 5 and 4 is equal to that between categories 3 and 2. Indeed, to make customers from satisfied (4) to very satisfied (5) versus from dissatisfied (2) to neutral (3), very different actions and types of improvements may be needed.

Therefore, when we translate order relations into mathematical operations, we cannot use operations such as addition, subtraction, multiplication, and division. We can use "greater than" and "less than." However, in real-world application for some specific types of ordinal scales (such as the Likert five-point, seven-point, or ten-point scales), the assumption of equal distance is often taken and operations such as averaging are applied to these scales. In such cases, the minimum we should do is to be aware that the measurement assumption is deviated, and then use extreme caution when interpreting the results of data analysis.

## Interval and Ratio Scales

An interval scale can indicate the exact differences between measurement points. The mathematical operations of addition and subtraction can be applied to interval scale data. For instance, if the defect rate of software product A is 5 defects per KLOC and product B's rate is 3.5 defects per KLOC, then we can say product A's defect level is 1.5 defects per KLOC higher than product B. An interval scale of measurement requires the establishment of a well-defined unit of measurement that can be agreed on as a common standard and that is repeatable. Given a unit of measurement, it is possible to say that the difference between two scores is 15 units or that one difference is the same as a second. Assuming product C's defect rate is 2 defects per KLOC, we can thus say the difference in defect rate between products A and B is the same as that between B and C.

When an absolute or nonarbitrary zero point can be located in an interval scale, it becomes a ratio scale. Ratio scale is the highest level of measurement and all mathematical operations can be applied to it, including division and multiplication. For example, we can say that product A's defect rate is twice as much as product C's because when the defect rate is zero, that means not a single defect exists in the product. Had the zero point been arbitrary, the statement would have been illegitimate. A good example of interval scale with arbitrary zero point is the traditional temperature measurement (Fahrenheit and centigrade scale). Thus we say that the difference between average summer temperature (80° F) and winter temperature (16° F) is 64° F, but we do not say that 80° F is five times as hot as 16° F. Fahrenheit and centigrade temperature scales are interval but not ratio scales. For this reason, scientists developed the absolute temperature scale (a ratio scale) for use in scientific activities.

Except for a few notable examples, for all practical purposes almost all interval measurement scales are also ratio scales. When the size of the unit is established, it is usually possible to conceive of zero unit.

For interval and ratio scales, the measurement can be expressed in both integer and noninteger data. Integer data are usually given in terms of frequency counts (for example, the total number of defects customers will encounter for a software product over a specified time length).

We should note that the measurement scales are hierarchical. Each higher level scale possesses all properties of the lower ones. The higher the level of measurement, the more powerful analysis can be applied to the data. Therefore, in our operationalization process we should devise metrics that can take advantage of the highest level of measurement as allowed by the nature of the concept and its definition. A higher level measurement can always be reduced to a lower one, but not vice versa. For example, in our defect measurement we can always make various types of comparisons if the scale is in terms of actual defect rate. However, if the scale is in terms of excellent, good, average, worse than average, and poor, as compared to an industrial standard, then our ability to perform additional analysis of the data is limited.

## 3.3  Some Basic Measures

Regardless of the measurement scale, when the data are gathered we need to analyze them so we can extract meaningful information. Various measures and statistics are available for summarizing the raw data and for making comparisons across groups. In this section we discuss some basic measures such as ratio, proportion, percentage, and rate, which are frequently used in our daily lives as well as in various activities associated with software development and software quality. These basic measures, while seemingly easy, are often misused. There are also numerous sophisticated statistical techniques and methodologies that can be employed in data analysis. However, such topics are not within the scope of this discussion.

**Ratio**

A ratio results from dividing one quantity by another. The numerator and denominator are from two distinct populations and are mutually exclusive. For example, in demography, sex ratio is defined as

$$\frac{\text{Number of males}}{\text{Number of females}} \times 100\%$$

If the ratio is less than 100, there are more females than males, otherwise there are more males than females.

In software metrics, ratios are also used. The one most often used, perhaps, is the ratio of number of people in an independent test organization to those in the development group. The test/development headcount ratio could range from 1:1 to 1:10 depending on the management approach to the software development process. For the large-ratio (e.g., 1:10) organizations, the development group usually is responsible for the complete development (including extensive development tests) of the product, and the test group conducts system-level testing in terms of customer environment verifications. For the small-ratio organizations, the independent group takes the major responsibility of testing (after debugging and code integration) and quality assurance.

**Proportion**

Proportion is different from ratio in that the numerator in a proportion is a part of the denominator:

$$p = \frac{a}{a+b}$$

Proportion also differs from ratio in that ratio is best used for two groups whereas proportion is used for multiple categories in one group. In other words, the denominator in the above formula can be more than just $a + b$. If

$$a + b + c + d + e = N$$

then we have

$$\frac{a}{N} + \frac{b}{N} + \frac{c}{N} + \frac{d}{N} + \frac{e}{N} = 1$$

When the numerator and the denominator are integers and represent counts of certain events, then $p$ is also referred to as a relative frequency. For example, the following gives the proportion of satisfied customers of the total customer set:

$$\frac{\text{Number of satisfied customers}}{\text{Total number of customers of a software product}}$$

The numerator and the denominator in a proportion need not be integers. They can be frequency counts as well as measurement units in continuous scale (for example, height in inches, weight in pounds). When the measurement unit is not integer, proportions are called fractions.

**Percentage**

A proportion or a fraction becomes a percentage when it is expressed in terms of per hundred units (the denominator is normalized to one hundred). The word *percent* means per hundred. A proportion $p$ is therefore equal to 100p percent (100p%).

Percentages are frequently used in reporting results, and as such are also frequently misused. First, because percentages represent relative frequencies, it is important that enough contextual information be given, especially the total number of cases, so that the readers have complete information. Jones (1992) observed that many reports and presentations in the software industry were careless in using percentages and ratios. For instance, the example he cited states:

> Requirements bugs were 15% of the total, design bugs were 25% of the total, coding bugs were 50% of the total, and other bugs made up 10% of the total.

Had the results been stated as follows, it would have been much more informative:

> The project consists of 8 thousand lines of code (KLOC).
> During its development a total of 200 defects were detected and
> removed, giving a defect removal rate of 25 defects per KLOC.
> Of the 200 defects, requirements bugs constituted 15%, design
> bugs 25%, coding bugs 50%, and other bugs made up 10%.

A second important rule of thumb is that the total number of cases must be sufficiently large enough in order to use percentages. Percentages computed from a small
total are not stable; they also convey an impression that a large number of cases are
involved. Some writers recommend that the minimum number of cases for which percentages can be calculated should be 50 or more. We recommend that, depending on
the number of categories, the minimum number should be no less than 30, the small-
est sample size required for parametric statistics. If the number of cases is too small,
the absolute numbers, instead of percentages, should be used. For instance,

> Of the total 20 defects for the entire project of 2 KLOC, there were
> 3 requirements bugs, 5 design bugs, 10 coding bugs, and 2 others.

| Type of Defect | Project A (%) | Project B (%) | Project C (%) |
|---|---|---|---|
| Requirements | 15.0 | 41.0 | 20.3 |
| Design | 25.0 | 21.8 | 22.7 |
| Code | 50.0 | 28.6 | 36.7 |
| Others | 10.0 | 8.6 | 20.3 |
| Total | 100.0 | 100.0 | 100.0 |
| (N) | (200) | (105) | (128) |

FIGURE 3.2
Percentage Distributions of Defect Type by Project

When presenting results in percentages in table format, usually both the percentages and actual numbers are shown when there is only one variable. When there
are more than two groups, such as the example in Figure 3.2, it is better just to show
the percentages and the total number of cases ($N$) for each group. With percentages and $N$ known, one can always reconstruct the frequency distributions. The total
of 100.0% should always be shown so that it is clear how the percentages are

computed. In a two-way table, the direction the percentages are computed depends on the purpose of the comparison. For instance, the percentages in Figure 3.2 are computed vertically (the total of each column is 100.0%), and the purpose is to compare the defect-type profile across different projects (for example, project B proportionally has more requirements defects than project A). In Figure 3.3, the percentages are computed horizontally. The purpose here is to compare the distribution of defects across projects for each type of defect. The interpretation of the two comparisons differ. Therefore, we should always carefully examine percentage tables to determine exactly how the percentages are calculated.

|                    |      | Project |      |       |      |
| ------------------ | ---- | ---- | ---- | ----- | ---- |
| Type of Defect     | A    | B    | C    | Total | (N)  |
| Requirements (%)   | 30.3 | 43.4 | 26.3 | 100.0 | (99) |
| Design (%)         | 49.0 | 22.5 | 28.5 | 100.0 | (102) |
| Code (%)           | 56.5 | 16.9 | 26.6 | 100.0 | (177) |
| Others (%)         | 36.4 | 16.4 | 47.2 | 100.0 | (55) |

FIGURE 3.3
Percentage Distributions of Defects Across Project by Defect Type

## Rate

Ratios, proportions, and percentages as discussed earlier are static summary measures. They provide a cross-sectional view of the phenomena of interest at a specific point in time. The concept of rate is associated with the dynamics (change) of the phenomena of interest; generally it can be defined as a measure of change in one quantity ($y$) per unit of another quantity ($x$) on which the former ($y$) depends. Usually the $x$ variable is time. It is important that the time unit always be specified when describing a rate associated with time. For instance, in demography the crude birth rate (CBR) is defined as:

$$\text{Crude birth rate} = \frac{B}{P} \times K$$

where $B$ is the total number of live births in a given calendar year, $P$ is the mid-year population, and $K$ is a constant, usually 1000.

The concept of *exposure to risk* is also central to the definition of rate, which distinguishes rate from proportion. Simply put, all elements or subjects in the denominator have to be at risk of becoming or producing the elements or subjects in the numerator. If we take a second look at the crude birth rate formula, we will note that the denominator is mid-year population and we know that not the entire population is subject to the risk of giving birth. Therefore the operational definition of CBR is not in compliance with the concept of population at risk, and for this reason, it is a "crude" rate. A better measurement is called the general fertility rate, in which the denominator is the number of women in the childbearing ages, usually defined as from age 15 to 44. In addition, there are other more refined measurements for birth rate.

In quality literature, the risk exposure concept is defined as opportunities for error (OFE). The numerator is the number of defects of interest. Therefore,

$$\text{Defect rate} = \frac{\text{Number of defects}}{\text{OFE}} \times K$$

In software, defect rate is usually defined as the number of defects per KLOC in a given time unit (for example, one year after the general availability of the product in the marketplace, or for the entire life of the product). Note that this defects per KLOC metric is also a crude measure. First, the opportunity for error is not known. Second, while any line of source code may be subject to error, a defect may involve many source lines. Therefore the metric is only a proxy measure of defect rate even assuming there are no other problems. Such limitations should be taken into account when analyzing results or interpreting data pertaining to software quality.

### Six Sigma

The term *six sigma* represents a stringent level of quality. It is a specific defect rate: 3.4 defective parts per million (ppm). It was made known in the industry by Motorola, Inc., in the late 1980s when Motorola won the first Malcolm Baldrige National Quality Award (MBNQA) and has become an industry standard as an ultimate quality goal.

Sigma ($\sigma$) is the Greek symbol for standard deviation. As Figure 3.4 indicates, the areas under the curve of normal distribution defined by standard deviations are constants in terms of percentages, regardless of the distribution parameters. The area under the curve as defined by plus and minus one standard deviation (sigma) from the mean is 68.26%. The area defined by plus/minus two standard deviations is 95.44%, and so forth. The area defined by plus/minus six sigma is 99.9999998%. The area outside the six sigma area is thus 100% − 99.9999998% = 0.0000002%.

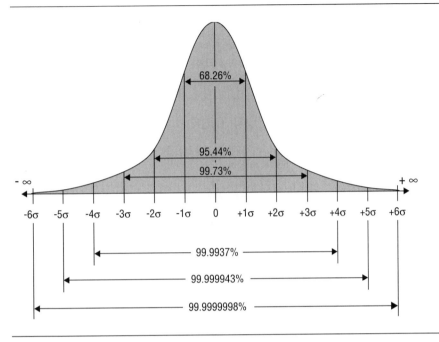

FIGURE 3.4
Areas Under the Normal Curve

If we take the area within the six sigma limit as the percentage of defect-free parts and the area outside the limit as the percentage of defective parts, we find that six sigma is equal to two defectives per billion parts or 0.002 defectives part per million (PPM). The interpretation of defect rate as it relates to the normal distribution will be clearer if we include the specification limits in the discussion, as shown in the top panel of Figure 3.5. Given the specification limits (which were derived from customers' requirements), our purpose is to produce parts or products within the limits. Parts or products outside the specification limits do not conform to requirements. If we can reduce the variations in the production process so that the six sigma (standard deviations) variation of the production process is within the specification limits, then we will have six sigma quality level.

The six sigma value of 0.002 ppm is from the statistical normal distribution. It assumes that each execution of the production process will produce the exact distribution of parts or products centered with regard to the specification limits. In reality, however, there are always process shifts and drifts due to variations in process execution. The maximum process shifts as indicated by research (Harry, 1989) is 1.5 sigma. If we account for this 1.5-sigma shift in the production process, we will get the value of 3.4 ppm. Such shifting is illustrated in the bottom two panels in Figure

3.5. Given fixed specification limits, the distribution of the production process may shift to the left or to the right. When the shift is 1.5 sigma, the area outside the specification limit on one end is 3.4 ppm, and on the other will be practically zero.

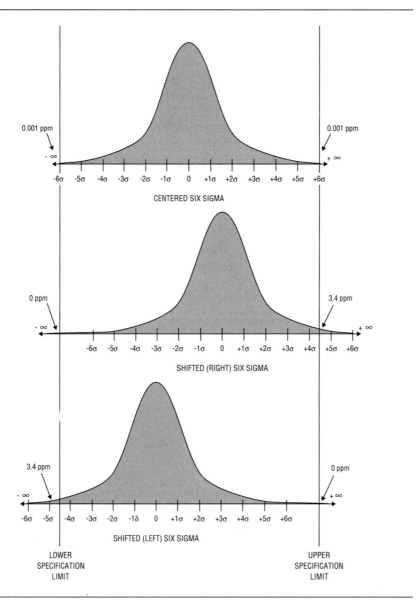

FIGURE 3.5
Specification Limits, Centered Six Sigma, and Shifted (1.5 Sigma) Six Sigma

The six sigma definition accounting for the 1.5-sigma shift (3.4 ppm) was proposed and used by Motorola, Inc. (Harry, 1989). It has now become the industry standard in terms of six sigma level quality (versus the normal distribution's six sigma of 0.002 ppm). Furthermore, when the production distribution shifts 1.5 sigma, the intersection points of the normal curve and the specification limits become 4.5 sigma at one end and 7.5 sigma at the other. Since for all practical purposes, the area outside 7.5 sigma is zero, one may say that the Motorola Six Sigma is equal to the one-tailed 4.5 sigma of the centered normal distribution.

The subtle difference between the centered six sigma and the shifted six sigma may imply something significant. The former is practically equivalent to zero defects and may invite the debate whether in reality it is feasible to achieve such a quality goal. The latter, while remaining at a very stringent level, does contain a sense of reality. As an example to illustrate the difference, assume we are to clean a 1500-ft$^2$ house. By centered six sigma, the area that we allow not to be clean enough is about the area of the head of a pin. By shifted six sigma, the area is about the size of the bottom of a soft drink can.

So far our discussion of six sigma has centered on the fact that it is a specific defect rate. Its concept, however, is much richer than that. As we touched on in the discussion, in order to reach six sigma, we have to improve the process—specifically reduce process variations so that the six sigma variation of the process is still within the specification limits. The notion of process improvement/process variation reduction is, therefore, an inherent part of the concept. Another notion is that of product design and product engineering. If failure tolerance is incorporated into the design of the product, that means it is a lot easier to meet the specifications of the finished product and, therefore, easier to achieve six sigma quality. The concept of process variation reduction also involves the theory and elaboration of process capability, which we do not discuss here. For details, see Harry and Lawson (1992) and other Motorola literature on the subject (for example, Smith, 1989).

In software, a defect is a binary variable (the program either works or does not), and it is difficult to relate to continuous distributions such as the normal distribution. However, for discrete distributions there is an equivalent approximation to the six sigma calculation in statistical theory. Moreover, the notions of process improvement and tolerance design cannot be more applicable. In the software industry, six sigma in terms of defect level is defined as 3.4 defects per million lines of code of the software product over its life. Interestingly, the original intent of using the sigma scale to measure quality was for easier comparisons across products or organizations. However, we have found that in reality this is not the case because the operational definition differs across organizations. For instance, the lines of code in the denominator are taken as the count of shipped source instructions by the International Business Machine Corporation regardless of the language type used to develop the software. Motorola, Inc., on the other hand, operationalized the denominator as the Assembler language equivalent instructions. In other words, the normalized lines of code (to Assembler language) is used. To achieve the normalization, the ratios of high-level language to Assembler by Jones (1986) were used (see Ref. 8). The difference between the two operational definitions can be orders of magnitude. For example, according to Jones' conversion table, one line of PL/I code is equivalent to four lines of Assembler statements, and one line of SMALLTALK is equivalent to 15 lines of Assembler.

## 3.4  Reliability and Validity

In our discussion of the abstraction hierarchy earlier, concepts and definitions have to be operationally defined before actual measurements can be taken. Assuming operational definitions are derived and measurements are taken, the logical question to ask is how good are the operational metrics and the actual measurement data? Do they really accomplish their task—measuring the concept that we want them to with good quality? There are many criteria of measurement quality. Reliability and validity are the two most important ones.

Reliability refers to the consistency of a number of measurements taken using the same measurement method on the same subject. If repeated measurements are highly consistent or even identical, then there is a high degree of reliability with the measurement method or the operational definition. If the variations among repeated measurements are large, then reliability is low. For example, if an operational definition of a body height measurement of children (for example, between ages 3 and 12) includes specifications of the time of the day to take measurements, the specific scale to use, who takes the measurements (for example, trained nurses), whether the measurements should be taken barefooted, etc., it is likely that reliable data will be obtained. If the operational definition is very vague in terms of these considerations, the data reliability may be low. Measurements taken in the early morning may be greater than those taken in the late afternoon as children's bodies tend to be more stretched after a good night's sleep and become somewhat compacted after a tiring day. By the same token, different scales used, trained versus untrained personnel, with or without shoes on, etc., are factors that can contribute to the variations of the measurement data.

The measurement of any phenomenon always contains a certain amount of chance error. The goal of error-free measurement, while laudable and widely recognized, is never attained in any discipline of scientific investigation. The amount of measurement error and therefore the degree of reliability, may be large or small, but it is universally present to some extent. The goal is of course to achieve the best possible reliability. Reliability can be expressed in terms of the size of the standard deviations of the repeated measurements. When different variables are compared, usually the index of variation (IV) is used. IV is simply a ratio of the standard deviation to the mean:

$$IV = \frac{\text{Standard deviation}}{\text{Mean}}$$

The smaller the IV, the more reliable the measurements.

Validity refers to whether the measurement or metric really measures what we intend it to measure. In other words, it refers to the extent to which an empirical measure adequately reflects the real meaning of the concept under consideration. In cases where the measurement involves no higher level of abstraction, for example, the measurements of body height and weight, validity is simply accuracy. However, validity is different from reliability. Measurements that are reliable may not necessarily be valid, and vice versa. For example, a new bathroom scale for body weight may give identical results upon five consecutive measurements (for example, 160 lb.) and therefore it is reliable. However, the measurements may not be valid to reflect the person's body weight if the offset of the scale was at 10 lb. instead of at zero.

For abstract concepts, validity can be a very difficult issue. For instance, the use of church attendance for measuring religiousness in a community may have low validity because religious persons may or may not always go to church. Often, it is difficult to recognize that a certain metric is invalid in measuring a concept; it is even more difficult to improve it or to invent a new metric.

Researchers tend to classify validity into several types. The type of validity we have discussed so far is called *construct validity,* which refers to the validity of the operational measurement or metric representing the theoretical construct. In addition, there are *criterion-related validity* and *content validity.* Criterion-related validity is also referred to as predictive validity. For example, the validity of a written driver's test is determined by the relationship between the scores people get on the test and how well they drive. Predictive validity is also applicable to modeling, which we will discuss in later chapters on software reliability models. Content validity refers to the degree to which a measure covers the range of meanings included within the concept. For instance, a test of mathematical ability for elementary pupils cannot be limited to addition alone but would also need to cover subtraction, multiplication, division, and so forth.

Given a theoretical construct, the purpose of measurement is to measure the construct validly and reliably. Figure 3.6 graphically portrays the difference between validity and reliability. If the purpose of the measurement is to hit the center of the target, we see that reliability looks like a tight pattern regardless of where it hits, because reliability is a function of consistency. Validity, on the other hand, is a function of shots being arranged around the bull's eye. In statistical terms, if the expected value (or the mean) is the bull's eye, then it is valid; if the variations are small relative to the entire target, then it is reliable.

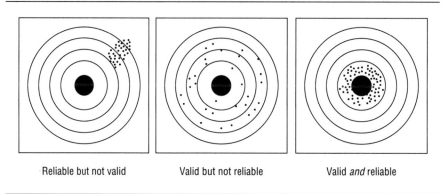

|  Reliable but not valid  |  Valid but not reliable  |  Valid *and* reliable  |

FIGURE 3.6
An Analogy to Validity and Reliability

(*Source:* Babbie, E., *The Practice of Social Research,* Belmont, Calif.: Wadsworth Publishing Co., 1986, p. 113. Copyright © 1986 Wadsworth Publishing Co., with permission to reprint.)

Note that there is some tension between validity and reliability. For the data to be reliable, the measurement must be specifically defined and in such an endeavor, the risk of being not able to represent the theoretical concept validly may be high. On the other hand, for the definition to have good validity, it may be quite difficult to define precisely the measurements. For example, the measurement of church attendance may be quite reliable because it is specific and observable. However, it may not be valid to represent the concept of religiousness. On the other hand, to derive valid measurements for the religiousness concept is quite difficult. In the real world of measurements and metrics, it is not uncommon for a certain trade-off or balance to be made between validity and reliability.

Validity and reliability issues come about when we try to use metrics and measurements to represent abstract theoretical constructs. In traditional quality engineering where measurements are frequently physical and usually do not involve abstract concepts, the counterparts of validity and reliability are termed *accuracy* and *precision* (Juran and Gryna, 1970). Much confusion surrounds the terminology for accuracy and precision despite the two terms having distinctly different meanings. If we want a much higher degree of precision in measurement (for example, accuracy up to three digits after the decimal point when measuring height), then our chance of getting all measurements accurate may be reduced. In contrast, if accuracy is required only at the level of integer inch (less precise), then it is a lot easier to meet the accuracy requirement.

Reliability and validity are the two most important issues of measurement quality. These two issues should be well thought through before a metric is proposed, used, and analyzed. In addition, there are other desirable attributes for software metrics to achieve. For instance, the draft of the IEEE standard for a software quality metrics methodology even includes factors such as correlation, tracking, consistency, predictability, and discriminative power (Schneidewind, 1991).

## 3.5  Measurement Errors

In this section we discuss validity and reliability in the context of measurement error. There are two types of measurement errors: *systematic* and *random*. Systematic measurement error is associated with validity; random error is associated with reliability. Let us revisit our example about the bathroom weight scale with an offset of 10 lb. Using the scale, each time we weigh, we will get a measurement that is 10 lb. more than our actual body weight, in addition to the slight variations among measurements. Therefore, the expected value of the measurements from the scale does not equal the true value due to the systematic deviation of 10 lb. In simple formula:

> Measurement from the scale =
> True body weight + 10 lb. + Random variations

In a general case:

$$M = T + s + e$$

where $M$ is the observed/measured score, $T$ is the true score, $s$ is systematic error, and $e$ is random error.

The presence of $s$ (systematic error) is what makes the measurement invalid. Now let us assume the measurement is valid and the $s$ term is not in the equation. We have the following:

$$M = T + e$$

The equation still states that any particular observed score is not equal to the true score because of random disturbance—the random error $e$. These disturbances mean that on one measurement, a person's score may be higher than his true score while on another occasion the measurement may be lower than the true score. However, since the disturbances are random, it means that the positive errors are just as likely to occur as the negative errors and these errors are expected to cancel each other in the long run. In other words, the average of these errors in the long run, or the expected value of $e$, is zero: $E(e) = 0$. Furthermore, from statistical theory about random error, we can also assume the following:

&#9633;   The correlation between the true score and the error term is zero.

&#9633;   There is no serial correlation between the true score and the error term.

&#9633;   The correlation between errors on distinct measurements is zero.

From these assumptions, we find that the expected value of the observed scores is equal to the true score:

$$\begin{aligned} E(M) &= E(T) + E(e) \\ &= E(T) + 0 \\ &= E(T) \\ &= T \end{aligned}$$

The question now is to assess the impact of $e$ on the reliability of the measurements (observed scores). Intuitively, the smaller the variations of the error term, the more reliable the measurements. This intuition can be observed in Figure 3.6 as well as expressed in statistical terms:

$$M = T + e$$
$$\text{var}(M) = \text{var}(T) + \text{var}(e) \qquad \text{(var represents variance. This relationship is due to the assumptions on error terms)}$$

$$\begin{aligned} \text{Reliability} = \rho m &= \text{var}(T)/\text{var}(M) \\ &= [\text{var}(M) - \text{var}(e)]/\text{var}(M) \\ &= 1 - [\text{var}(e)/\text{var}(M)]. \end{aligned}$$

Therefore, the reliability of a metric varies between 0 and 1. In general, the larger the error variance relative to the variance of the observed score, the poorer the reliability. If all variance of the observed scores is due to random errors, then the reliability is zero $[1 - (1/1) = 0]$.

### 3.5.1 Assessing Reliability

Thus far we have discussed the concept and meaning of validity and reliability and their interpretation in the context of measurement errors. Validity is associated with systematic error and the only way to get rid of systematic error is through a better understanding of the concept we try to measure, and through deductive logic and reasoning to derive better definition. Reliability is associated with random error. To reduce random error, we need good operational definitions, and based on them, good execution of measurement operations and data collection. In this section, we discuss how to assess the reliability of empirical measurements.

There are several ways to assess the reliability of empirical measurements including the test/retest method, the alternative-form method, the split-halves method, and the internal consistency method (Carmines and Zeller, 1979). Because our purpose is to illustrate how to utilize our understanding of reliability in interpreting software metrics rather than in-depth statistical examination of the subject, we take the easiest method, the retest method. The retest method is simply taking a second measurement of the subjects sometime after the first measurement is taken and then computing the correlation between the first and the second measurements. For instance, if we are to evaluate the reliability of a blood pressure machine, we would take the first measurement of a group of people and, after everyone is done, we would take the second set of measurements. The second measurement could be taken one day later at the same time, or we could simply take two measurements the first time. Either way, each person will have two scores. For the sake of simplicity let us confine ourselves to just one measurement, either the systolic or the diastolic score. We then calculate the correlation between the first and second score and the correlation coefficient is the reliability of the blood pressure machine. A schematic representation of the test/retest method for estimating reliability is shown in Figure 3.7.

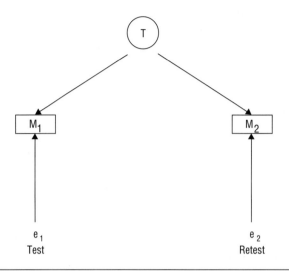

FIGURE 3.7
Test/Retest Method for Estimating Reliability

The equations for the two tests can be represented as follows:

$$M_1 = T + e_1$$
$$M_2 = T + e_2$$

From the assumptions about the error terms as we briefly stated before, it can be shown that

$$\rho_m = p_{m1m2} = \operatorname{var}(T)/\operatorname{var}(M)$$

in which $\rho_m$ is the reliability measure.

As an example in software metrics, let us try to assess the reliability of the reported number of defects found at design inspection. Assume that the inspection is formal in that an inspection meeting was held and the participants include the design owner, the inspection moderator, and the inspectors. At the meeting, each defect is agreed to by the whole group and the record keeping is done by the moderator. The test/retest method may involve using two record keepers and, at the end of the inspection, each turns in their recorded number of defects. If this method is applied to a series of inspections in a development organization, we will have two reports for each inspection over a sample of inspections. We then calculate the correlation between the two series of reported numbers and we can estimate the reliability of the reported inspection defects.

### 3.5.2 Correction for Attenuation

One of the important uses of reliability assessment is to adjust or correct correlations for unreliability due to random errors in measurements. Correlation is perhaps one of the most important methods in software engineering and other disciplines for analyzing relationships between metrics. For us to substantiate or refute a hypothesis, we have to gather data for both the independent variable and dependent variable and examine the correlation of the data. Let us revisit our hypothesis testing example at the beginning of this chapter: The more effective the design reviews and the code inspections as scored by the inspection team, the lower the defect rate encountered at the later phase of formal machine testing. As we mentioned before, we first need to operationally define the independent variable (inspection effectiveness) and the dependent variable (defect rate during formal machine testing). Then we gather data on a sample of components or projects and calculate the correlation between the independent variable and dependent variable. However, due to random errors in the data, the resultant correlation often is lower than the true correlation. With knowledge about the estimate of the reliability of the variables of interest, we can adjust the observed correlation to get a more accurate picture of the relationship under consideration. In software development, we observed that a key reason for some theoretically sound hypotheses not being supported by actual project data is because the operational definitions of the metrics are poor and there are too many noises in the data.

Given that we know the observed correlation and the reliability estimates of the two variables, the formula for correction for attenuation (Carmines and Zeller, 1979) is as follows:

$$\rho(x_t y_t) = \rho(x_i y_i) / \sqrt{\rho_{xx^1} \rho_{yy^1}}$$

where

$\rho(x_t\ y_t)$ is the correlation corrected for attenuation, in other words, the estimated true correlation

$\rho(x_i\ y_i)$ is the observed correlation, calculated from the observed data

$\rho_{xx'}$ is the estimated reliability of the $X$ variable

$\rho_{yy'}$ is the estimated reliability of the $Y$ variable

For example, if the observed correlation between two variables was 0.2 and the reliability estimates were 0.5 and 0.7, respectively, for $X$ and $Y$, then the correlation corrected for attenuation would be

$$\rho(x_t y_t) = 0.2 / \sqrt{0.5 \times 0.7}$$
$$= 0.34$$

This means that the correlation between $X$ and $Y$ would be 0.34 if both were measured perfectly without error.

---

## 3.6 Be Careful with Correlation

Correlation is probably the most widely used statistical method in assessing relationships among observational data (versus experiment data). However, caution must be exercised when using correlation, otherwise the true relationship under investigation may be disguised or misrepresented. There are several points about correlation that one has to know before using it. First, although there are special types of nonlinear correlation analysis available in statistical literature, most of the time when one mentions correlation, it means linear correlation. Indeed, the most well-known Pearson correlation coefficient assumes a linear relationship. Therefore, if a correlation coefficient between two variables is weak, it simply means there is no linear relationship between the two variables. It doesn't mean there is no relationship of any form. Let us look at the five types of relationships shown in Figure 3.8. Panel A represents a positive linear relationship and panel B a negative linear relationship. Panel C shows a curvilinear convex type of relationship, and panel D a concave relationship. In panel E, a cyclical relationship (such as the Fourier series representing frequency waves) is shown. Because correlation assumes linear relationships, when the correlation coefficients (Pearson) for the five relationships are calculated, the results will accurately show that panels A and B have significant correlation. However, for the other three relationships the correlation coefficients will be very weak or will show no relationship at all. For this reason, it is highly recommended that when we use correlation we always look at the scattergrams. If the scattergram shows a particular type of nonlinear relationship, then we need to pursue analyses or coefficients other than linear correlation.

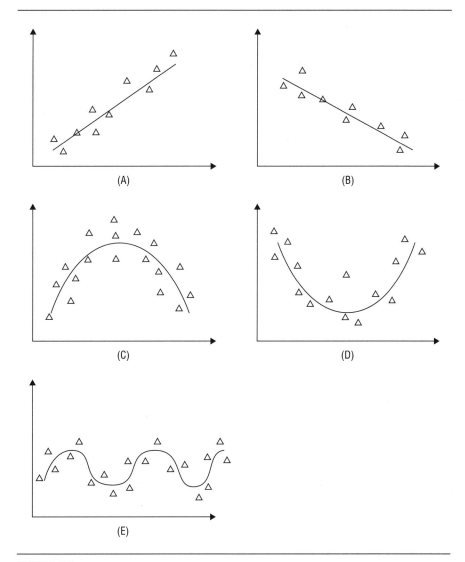

FIGURE 3.8
Five Types of Relationships Between Two Variables

Secondly, if the data contain noise (due to unreliability in measurement) or if the range of the data points is large, more likely than not the correlation coefficient (Pearson) will show no relationship. In such a situation, we recommend using the rank-order correlation method, such as Spearman's rank-order correlation. The Pearson correlation (the correlation we usually refer to) requires interval scale data, whereas rank-order correlation requires only ordinal data. If there is too much noise in the interval data, the Pearson correlation coefficient thus calculated will be greatly attenuated. As we discussed in the last section, if we know the reliability of the variables involved, we can adjust the resultant correlation. However, if we have no knowledge about the reliability of the variables, rank-order correlation will be more likely to detect the underlying relationship. Specifically, if the noises of the data did not affect the original ordering of the data points, then rank-order correlation will be more successful in representing the true relationship. Since both Pearson's correlation and Spearman's rank-order correlation are covered in basic statistics textbooks and are available in most statistical software packages, we do not get into the calculation details here.

Thirdly, the method of linear correlation (least-squares method) is very vulnerable to extreme values. If there are a few extreme outliers in the sample, the correlation coefficient may be seriously affected. For example, Figure 3.9 shows a moderate negative relationship between $X$ and $Y$. However, due to a couple of extreme outliers at the northeast coordinates, the correlation coefficient will become positive. This outlier susceptibility reinforces our earlier point that when correlation is used, one should also look at the scatter diagram of the data.

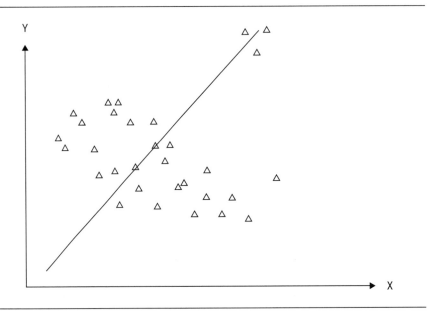

FIGURE 3.9
Effect of Outliers on Correlation

Finally, while a significant correlation demonstrates that an association exists between the two variables, it does not automatically imply a cause-and-effect relationship. Although it is an element of causality, correlation alone is inadequate to show the existence of causality. In the next section, we discuss the criteria for establishing causality.

## 3.7  Criteria for Causality

The isolation of cause and effect in controlled experiments is relatively easy. For example, a headache medicine was administered to a sample of subjects who are having headaches. A placebo was administered to another group with headaches (who were statistically not different from the first group). If after a certain time of taking the headache medicine and the placebo, the headaches of the first group were reduced or disappeared while they still persisted among the second group, then the curing effect of the headache medicine is clear.

For analysis with observational data, the task is much more difficult. Researchers (for example, Babbie, 1986) have identified three criteria:

1. The first requirement in a causal relationship between two variables is that the cause precedes the effect in time or as shown clearly in logic.

2. The second requirement in a causal relationship is that the two variables be empirically correlated with one another.

3. The third requirement for a causal relationship is that the observed empirical correlation between two variables is not because of a spurious relationship.

The first and second requirements simply state that in addition to empirical correlation, the relationship has to be examined in terms of sequence of occurrence or deductive logic. Correlation is a statistical tool and could be misused without the guidance of a logic system. For instance, it is possible to correlate the outcome of a Super Bowl (National Football League versus American Football League) to some interesting artifacts such as fashion (length of skirt, popular color, and so forth) and weather. However, logic tells us that coincidence or spurious association cannot substantiate causation.

The third requirement is a difficult one. There are several types of spurious relationships, as shown in Figure 3.10, and sometimes it may be a formidable task to show that the observed correlation is not due to a spurious relationship. For this reason, it is much more difficult to prove causality in observational data than in experimental data. Nonetheless, examining for spurious relationships is a must for scientific reasoning and as a result, our conclusion or findings from the data will be of higher quality.

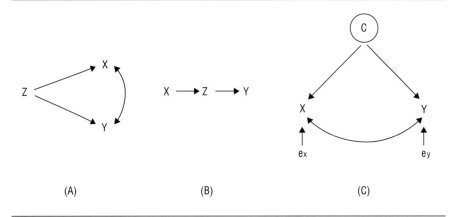

(A)                          (B)                          (C)

FIGURE 3.10
Spurious Relationships

In Figure 3.10, case A is the typical spurious relationship between *X* and *Y* in which both *X* and *Y* are caused by a common cause *Z*. Case B is called the case of the *intervening variable*, in which the real cause of *Y* is an intervening variable *Z* instead of *X*. In the strict sense, *X* is not a direct cause of *Y*. However, since *X* causes *Z* and *Z* in turn causes *Y*, one could still claim causality if the sequence is not too indirect. Case C is somewhat similar to case A. However, instead of both *X* and *Y* being caused by a common cause as in case B here, both *X* and *Y* are indicators (operational definitions) of the same concept C. It is logical that there is a correlation between them, but in no way should causality be inferred.

An example of the spurious causal relationship due to two indicators measuring the same concept is Halstead's (1977) software science formula for program length:

$$N = n_1 \times \log_2 n_1 + n_2 \times \log_2 n_2$$

where

$N$ = estimated program length

$n_1$ = number of unique operators

$n_2$ = number of unique operands.

Researchers have reported high correlations between actual program length (actual lines of code count) and the predicted length based on the formula, sometimes as high as 0.95 (Fitzsimmons and Love, 1978). However, as Card and Agresti (1987) showed, both the formula and actual program length are functions of $n_1$ and $n_2$, so correlation exists by definition. In other words, both the formula and the actual lines of code counts are operational measurements of the concept of program length. One has to conduct an actual $n_1$ and $n_2$ count for the formula to work. However, $n_1$ and $n_2$ counts are not available until the actual program is complete or almost complete. Therefore, the relationship is not a cause-and-effect relationship and the usefulness of the formula's predictability is limited in that prediction cannot be made in advance.

## 3.8 Summary

Measurement is related to the concept or entity of interest and the operational definition of the concept. Depending on the operational definition, different levels of measurement can be applied: nominal scale, ordinal scale, interval scale, and ratio scale. The measurement scales are hierarchical; each scale at a higher level possesses all properties of the lower ones.

Basic measures such as ratio, proportion, percentage, and rate all have specific purposes. Care should be exercised to avoid misuse. The concept of six sigma not only represents a stringent level of quality, it also includes the notions of process-variation reduction and product-design improvement. Its definition as used in the industry (shifted six sigma) is different from the statistical definition based on normal distribution (centered six sigma). Although meant for comparisons across differing measurement units, in software the sigma levels may not be compared across companies due to differences in operational definitions.

Validity and reliability are the two most important criteria of measurement quality. Validity refers to whether the metric really measures what it is intended to. Reliability refers to the consistency of measurements of the metric and measurement method. Validity is associated with systematic measurement error and reliability with random measurement errors. Unreliability of measurements leads to an attenuation of correlation between two variables. When the measurement reliabilities of the variables are known, correction for such attenuation can be made.

Correlation is widely used with observational data, including software measurements. Correlation alone, however, cannot establish causality. To establish a cause-and-effect relationship based on observational data, three criteria must be met: (1) the cause precedes the effect in time or logically, (2) significant correlation exists, and (3) the observed correlation is not due to a spurious relationship.

Measurement is the key to making software development a true engineering discipline. Yet examples of misuses and abuses of measurement in the software industry are numerous. To improve the practice of software measurement, it is important to have a good understanding of the fundamentals in measurement theory.

# References

1. Babbie, E., *The Practice of Social Research,* 4th ed., Belmont, Calif.: Wadsworth Publishing Co., 1986.
2. Card, D. N., and W. W. Agresti, "Resolving the Software Science Anomaly," *Journal of Systems and Software*, Vol. 7, March 1987, pp. 29–35.
3. Carmines, E. G., and R. A. Zeller, *Reliability and Validity Assessment*, Beverly Hills, Calif.: Sage Publications, 1979.
4. Fitzsimmons, A., and T. Love, "A Review and Evaluation of Software Science," *ACM Computing Surveys,* Vol. 10, No. 1, March 1978, pp. 3–18.
5. Halstead, M. H., *Elements of Software Science,* New York: Elsevier, 1977.
6. Harry, M. J., "The Nature of Six Sigma Quality," Government Electronics Group, Motorola, Inc., Schaumberg, Il., 1989.
7. Harry, M. J., and J. R. Lawson, *Six Sigma Producibility Analysis and Process Characterization*, Reading, Mass.: Addison-Wesley, 1992.
8. Information obtained from Motorola when the author was a member of a software benchmarking team at Motorola, Schaumberg, Il., on February 9, 1990.
9. Jones, C., *Applied Software Measurement: Assuring Productivity and Quality,* New York: McGraw-Hill, 1986.
10. Jones, C., "Critical Problems in Software Measurement," Version 1.0, Burlington, Mass.: Software Productivity Research (SPR), August 1992.
11. Juran, J. M., and F. M. Gryna, Jr., *Quality Planning and Analysis: From Product Development Through Use,* New York: McGraw-Hill, 1970.
12. Schneidewind, N. F., "Report on IEEE Standard for a Software Quality Metrics Methodology (Draft) P1061, with Discussion of Metrics Validation," *Proceedings IEEE Fourth Software Engineering Standards Application Workshop,* 1991, pp. 155–157.
13. Smith, W. B., "Six Sigma: TQC, American Style," presented at the National Technological University television series on October 31, 1989.

# 4

---

# Software Quality Metrics

Software metrics can be classified into three categories: product metrics, process metrics, and project metrics. Product metrics are those that describe the characteristics of the product such as size, complexity, design features, performance, and quality level. Process metrics are those that can be used for improving the software development and maintenance process. Examples include the effectiveness of defect removal during development, the pattern of testing defect arrival, and the response time of the fix process. Project metrics are those that describe the project characteristics and execution. Examples include the number of software developers, the staffing pattern over the life cycle of the software, cost, schedule, and productivity.

Software quality metrics are a subset of software metrics that focus on the quality aspects of the product, process, and project. In general, software metrics are more closely associated with process and product metrics than with project metrics. Nonetheless, the project parameters such as the number of developers and their skill levels, the schedule, the size, and the organization structure certainly affect the quality of the product. Software quality metrics can further be divided into end-product quality metrics and in-process quality metrics. The essence of software quality engineering is to investigate the relationships among in-process metrics, project characteristics, and end-product quality; and, based on the findings, to engineer improvements in both process and product quality. Moreover, we should view quality from the entire software life-cycle perspective and, in this regard, we should include metrics that measure the quality level of the maintenance process as another category of software quality metrics. In this chapter we discuss several metrics in each of three groups of software quality metrics. In the last sections we also describe the key metrics used by several major software developers and discuss software metrics data collection.

## 4.1  Product Quality Metrics

In this section we discuss several metrics of product quality. As discussed in Chapter 1, the *de facto* definition of software quality consists of two levels: intrinsic product quality and customer satisfaction. The metrics we discuss here cover both levels:

- ☐   Mean time to failure
- ☐   Defect density
- ☐   Customer problems
- ☐   Customer satisfaction.

Intrinsic product quality is usually measured by the number of "bugs" (functional defects) in the software or by how long the software can run before encountering a "crash." In operational definitions, the two metrics are defect density (rate) and mean time to failure (MTTF). The MTTF metric is most often used with safety-critical systems such as the airline traffic control systems, avionics, and weapons. For instance, the U.S. government mandates that its new air traffic control system cannot be unavailable for more than three seconds a year. In civilian airliners, the probability of certain catastrophic failures must be no worse than $10^{-9}$ per hour (Littlewood and Strigini, 1992). The defect density metric, in contrast, is used in many commercial software systems.

The two metrics are correlated but are different enough to merit close attention. First, one measures the *time* between failures, the other measures the *defects* relative to the software size (lines of code, function points, etc.). Second, although it is difficult to separate defects and failures in actual measurements and data tracking, failures and defects (or faults) have different meanings. According to the IEEE/American National Standards Institute (ANSI) standard (982.2):

- ☐   An error is a human mistake that results in incorrect software.
- ☐   The resulting fault is an accidental condition that causes a unit of the system to fail to function as required.
- ☐   A defect is an anomaly in a product.
- ☐   A failure occurs when a functional unit of a software-related system can no longer perform its required function or cannot perform it within specified limits.

From these definitions, the difference between a fault and a defect is unclear. For practical purposes, there is no difference between the two terms. Indeed, in many development organizations the two terms are used synonymously. In this book we also use the two terms interchangeably with the same meaning.

Simply put, when an error occurs, a fault or a defect is caused in the software. In operational mode, failures are caused by faults or defects, or failures are materializations of faults. Sometimes a fault may cause more than one failure situation and, on the other hand, some faults may not materialize until the software has been executed for a long time with some particular scenarios. Therefore, defect and failure do not have a one-to-one correspondence.

Third, the defects that cause higher failure rates are usually encountered and removed early. The probability of failure associated with a latent defect is called its size, or "bug size." For special-purpose software systems such as the air traffic control systems or the Space Shuttle control systems, the operations profile and scenarios are better defined and, therefore, the time to failure metric is appropriate. For general-purpose computer systems or commercial-use software, for which there is no typical user profile of the software, the MTTF metric is more difficult to implement and may not be representative for all customers.

Fourth, from the data-gathering perspective, time between failures data are much more expensive. It requires the failure occurrence time for each software failure recorded. It is sometimes quite difficult to record the time for all the failures observed during test or operation. To be useful, time between failures data also requires a high degree of accuracy. This is perhaps the reason the MTTF metric is not widely used by commercial developers.

Finally, the defect rate metric (or for that matter, the number of estimated defects) has another appeal to commercial developers. The defect rate of a product or the expected number of defects over a certain time period is important for cost and resource estimates of the maintenance phase of the software life cycle.

Regardless of their differences and similarities, MTTF and defect density are the two key metrics for intrinsic product quality. Accordingly, there are two main types of software reliability growth models—the time between failures models and the defect count (defect rate) models. We discuss the two types of models and provide several examples of each type in Chapter 8.

### 4.1.1 The Defect Density Metric

Although seemingly straightforward, many issues should be taken into consideration when comparing the defect rates of software products. In this section we try to articulate the major points. To define a rate, we first have to operationalize the numerator and the denominator, and specify the time frame. As we discussed in Chapter 3, the general concept of defect rate is the number of defects over the opportunities for errors during a specific time frame. We have just discussed the definitions of software defect and failure. Because failures are defects materialized, we can use the number of unique causes of observed failures to approximate the number of defects in the software. The denominator is the size of the software, usually expressed in thousand lines of code (KLOC). In terms of time frames, various operational definitions are used for the life of product (LOP) of a software, ranging from one year to many years after the general availability of the software product to the market. In our experience with operating systems, usually more than 95% of the defects are found within four years of the software release (the LOP definition used by IBM Rochester is four years).

The denominator, the lines of code (LOC) metric, is everything but simple and straightforward. The major problem comes from the ambiguity of the operational definition, the actual counting. In the early days of Assembler programming, in which one physical line was the same as one instruction, the LOC definition was clearly understood. With the availability of high-level languages the one-to-one correspondence broke down. Differences between physical lines and instruction statements and differences among languages contribute to the huge variations existing with regard to LOC counting. Even within the same language, the methods and algorithms used by different counting tools can cause significant differences in the final counts. Jones (1986) has described several variations in counting lines of code:

- ☐ Count only executable lines.
- ☐ Count executable lines plus data definitions.
- ☐ Count executable lines, data definitions, and comments.
- ☐ Count executable lines, data definitions, comments, and job control language.
- ☐ Count lines as physical lines on an input screen.
- ☐ Count lines as terminated by logical delimiters.

To illustrate the variations in LOC count practices, let us look at a few examples by authors of software metrics. In Boehm's well-known book *Software Engineering Economics* (1981), the LOC counting method counts lines as physical lines and includes executable lines, data definitions, and comments. In *Software Engineering Metrics and Models* by Conte *et al.* (1986), LOC is defined as follows:

> A line of code is any line of program text that is not a comment or blank line, regardless of the number of statements or fragments of statements on the line. This specifically includes all lines containing program headers, declarations, and executable and non-executable statements.

Thus their method is to count physical lines including prologues and data definitions (declarations) but not comments. The method used by IBM is to count source instructions (versus physical lines) including executable lines and data definitions but excluding comments and program prologues. In *Programming Productivity* by Jones (1986), the IBM method is used. Indeed, to maintain consistent programming size metrics and productivity and quality data across its divisions, IBM developed its own LOC counting tools. These tools are widely used throughout the corporation.

The resultant differences in program size between counting physical (or logical card image) lines and counting instruction statements are difficult to assess. It is not even known which method will result in a larger number. In some languages such as BASIC, PASCAL, and C, several instruction statements can be entered on one physical line. On the other hand, some instruction statements and data declarations may span several physical lines, especially when the programming style aims for easy maintenance in the future, which is not necessarily done by the original code owner. Languages that have a fixed column format such as FORTRAN may have the physical-lines-to-source-instructions ratio closest to one. According to Jones (1992), the difference between physical lines and instruction statements can be as large as 500%; and the average difference is about 200%, with logical statements outnumbering physical lines. In contrast, for COBOL the difference is about 200% in the opposite direction, with physical lines outnumbering instruction statements.

Therefore, extreme caution should be exercised when comparing the defect rates of two products if the operational definition (counting) of LOC, defects, and time frame are not identical. To reduce and eventually eliminate the LOC count variations now existing in the industry, industry-wide standards and counting conventions must be established. It is not necessary to have just one standard. Multiple standards can be defined as long as specific criteria are established and recognized. When any data on size of program products, their productivity, or quality are presented, the standard that is used for LOC count should always be required. Furthermore, as we discussed in Chapter 3, some companies may use the straight LOC count (whatever LOC count method is used) as the denominator for calculating defect rate (for example, IBM), whereas others may use the normalized count (normalized to Assembler equivalent

LOC based on some conversion ratios) for the denominator (for example, Motorola). Therefore, industry-wide standards should include the conversion ratios from high-level language to assembler. So far, very little research on this topic has been published. The conversion ratios published by Jones (1986) are the most well known in the industry. As more and more high-level languages become available for software development, more research will be needed in this area.

When a software product is released to the market for the first time, and when a certain LOC count method is specified, it is relatively easy to state its quality level (projected or actual). For example, statements such as the following can be made: "This product has a total of 50 KLOC; the latent defect rate for this product during the next four years is 2.0 defects per KLOC." However, when enhancements are made and subsequent releases of the product are available, the situation becomes more complicated. One needs to measure the quality of the entire product for the new release as well as the portion of the product that is new. The latter is the measurement of true development quality—the defect rate of the new and changed code. While the defect rate for the entire product will improve from release to release due to aging, the defect rate of the new and changed code will not improve unless there is real improvement in the development process. To calculate defect rate for the new and changed code, the following must be done:

- ☐ *LOC count:* The entire software product as well as the new and changed code must be counted for each release of the product.
- ☐ *Defect tracking:* Defects must be tracked to the release origin—the portion of the code that contains the defects and at what release the portion was added, changed, or enhanced. When calculating the defect rate of the entire product, all defects are used; when calculating the defect rate for the new and changed code, only defects of the release origin of the new and changed code are included.

These tasks are enabled by the practice of change flagging. Specifically, when a new function is added or an enhancement is made to an existing function, the new and changed lines of code are flagged with a specific identification (ID) number through the use of comments. The ID is linked with the requirements number, which is usually briefly described in the module prologue. Therefore, any changes in the program modules can be linked to a certain requirement. This type of linkage procedure is part of the software configuration management mechanism and is usually practiced by organizations that have an established process. (As discussed in Chapter 3, configuration management is a key element for achieving level 2 in the SEI process capability maturity model.) If the change-flagging IDs and requirements IDs are further linked to the release number of the product, the LOC counting tools can utilize the linkages to count the new and changed code for the new releases. The change-flagging practice is also important to the developers from the problem determination and maintenance point of view. When a defect is reported and the fault zone determined, the developer can determine in which function or enhancement pertaining to what requirements at what release origin the defect was injected.

The new and changed LOC counts can also be obtained via the delta-library method. By comparing program modules in the original library with the new versions in the current release library, the LOC count tools can determine the amount of new and changed code for the new release. This method does not involve the change-flagging method. However, change flagging remains very important for maintenance. In many software development environments, tools for automatic change-flagging are also available.

### An Example: IBM Rochester

Now that we have addressed the key issues related to the defect rate metric, we should look at IBM Rochester's defect rate metrics as an example. Similar to other IBM divisions, IBM Rochester counts lines of code as instruction statements (instead of physical lines) and includes executable code and data definitions but excludes comments. LOC counting for each release is done for the total product as well as the new and changed code. Because the LOC count is based on source instructions, the two size metrics are called *shipped source instructions* (SSI) and new and *changed source instructions* (CSI), respectively. The relationship between the SSI count and the CSI count can be expressed in the following formula:

SSI (current release) = SSI (previous release)
+ CSI (new and changed code insructions for
current release)
− deleted code (usually very small)
− changed code (to avoid double count in both
SSI and CSI)

Defects identified after the release of the product are called APARs (Authorized Program Analysis Reports). APARs opened because of customer problems are called field APARs, whereas APARs opened internally are called internal APARs. The LOP defect tracking for any given release is four years. The several defect rate metrics for a given release are:

TVUA/KSSI (all APARs that are reported on the release)

TFVUA/KSSI (all field APARs that are reported on the release)

TVUA/KCSI (APARs determined by release origin)

TFVUA/KCSI (field APARs determined by release origin)

where

TVUA   = total valid unique APARs

TFVUA = total field valid unique APARs

KSSI    = thousand shipped source instructions

KCSI    = thousand new and changed source instructions.

TVUA/KSSI measures the total release code quality, and TVUA/KCSI measures the quality of the new and changed code. For the initial release where the entire product is new, the two metrics are the same. Thereafter, TVUA/KSSI is affected by aging and the improvement (or deterioration) of TVUA/KCSI. Strong focus has been placed on release-to-release TVUA/KCSI improvement as a key driving factor for quality improvement for each release. TVUA/KSSI and TVUA/KCSI are process measures, their TFVUA counterparts represent the customer's perspective. Given an estimated defect rate (KCSI or KSSI), software developers can minimize the impact to customers by finding and fixing the defects before customers encounter them.

## Customer's Perspective

The defect rate metrics measure code quality on a per unit basis. It is useful to drive quality improvement from the development team's point of view. Good practice in software quality engineering, however, also needs to consider the customer's perspective. Assume that we are to set the defect rate goal for release-to-release improvement of the same product. From the customer's point of view, the defect rate is not as relevant as the total number of defects he/she is going to encounter. Therefore, we have to ensure that the total number of defects decreases from release to release regardless of size. If the size of a new release is much larger than its predecessors, it means the defect rate goal for the new and changed code has to be significantly better than the previous release in order to reduce the total number of defects.

Consider the following hypothetical example:

*Initial Release of Product Y:*

KCSI = KSSI = 50 KLOC

Defects/KCSI = 2.0

Total number of defects = 2.0 × 50 = 100

*Second Release:*

KCSI = 20

KSSI = 50 + 20 (new and changed code) – 4 (changed code) = 66

Defect/KCSI = 1.8 (representing 10% improvement over the first release)

Total number of additional defects = 1.8 × 20 = 36

*Third Release:*

KCSI = 40

KSSI = 66 + 40 – 10 = 96

Total number of additional defects = 36

Defect rate target: 36/40 = 0.9 defects/KCSI or lower

From the initial release to the second release the defect rate improved by 10%. However, customers experienced a 64% reduction [(100 – 36)/100] in the number of defects because the second release is smaller. The size factor works against the third release because it is much larger than the second release. Its defect rate must be 50% better than that of the second release so the total number of new defects does not exceed that of the second release.

## 4.1.2 Customer Problems Metric

Another product quality metric that is used by major developers in the software industry measures the problems customers encounter when using the product. For the defect rate metric, the numerator is the number of valid defects. However, from the customers' standpoint, all problems they encounter while using the software product, not just the valid defects, are problems with the software. Problems that are not valid defects may be usability problems, unclear documentation or information, duplicates of valid defects (defects that were reported by other customers and fixes were available but the current customers were not aware of), or even user errors. These so-called "non-defect-oriented" problems, together with the defect problems, constitute the total problem space of the software from the customers' perspective.

The problems metric is usually expressed in terms of problems per user month (PUM):

> PUM = Total problems that customers reported (true defects and
> non-defect-oriented problems) for a time period/
> Total number of license-months of the software during
> the period

where

> Number of license-months = Number of install licenses
> of the software × Number of months in the calculation period

PUM is usually calculated for each month after the software is released to the market, and also to arrive at a yearly average. Note that the denominator is the number of license-months instead of KLOC and the numerator is all problems customers encountered. Basically this metric relates problems to usage. To achieve a low PUM, one can take several approaches:

1.  Improve the development process and reduce the product defects.
2.  Reduce the non-defect-oriented problems by improving all aspects of the products (such as usability, documentation), customer education, and support.
3.  Increase the sale (the number of installed licenses) of the product.

The first two approaches serve to reduce the numerator of the PUM metric, and the third increases the denominator. The result of any of these courses of action is that the PUM metric will have a lower value. All three approaches make good sense for quality improvement and business goals for any organization. The PUM metric, therefore, is a good metric. The only minor drawback is that when the business is in excellent condition and the number of software licenses is rapidly increasing, the PUM metric will look extraordinarily good (low value) and, hence, the need to continue to reduce the number of customers' problems (the numerator of the metric) may be undermined. Therefore, the total number of customer problems should also be monitored and aggressive year-to-year or release-to-release improvement goals set as the number of installed licenses increases. However, unlike valid code defects, customer problems are not totally under the control of the software development organization. Hence it may not be feasible to set a constraint for PUM goal setting that the total customer problems cannot increase from release to release, especially when the sale of the software is expanding.

The key points of the defect rate metric and the customer problems metric are briefly summarized in Table 4.1.

|  | **Defect/KLOC** | **PUM** |
|---|---|---|
| Numerator | Valid and unique product defects | All customer problems (defects and nondefects, first time and repeated) |
| Denominator | Size of product (KLOC) | Customer usage of the product (user-months) |
| Measurement perspective | Producer—software development organization | Customer |
| Scope | Intrinsic product quality | Intrinsic product quality plus other factors |

TABLE 4.1
Defect Rate Metric and Customer Problems Metric

The two metrics, therefore, represent two perspectives of product quality. For each metric the numerator and denominator match each other well: Defects relate to source instructions, and problems encountered relate to usage of the product. If the numerator and denominator are mixed up, poor metrics will result. Such metrics could even become a disservice to the quality improvement effort because they will cause confusion and wasted resources. In practice many ill-defined metrics are being used in the software industry. As an example, the metric relating total customer problems to the size of the product (problems per MSSI—million shipped source instructions) is being used by some software developers.

The customer problems metric can be regarded as an intermediate measurement between defects measurement and customer satisfaction. To reduce customer problems, one has to reduce the functional defects in the products and, in addition, improve other factors (usability, documentation, problem rediscovery, and so forth). To improve customer satisfaction, one has to reduce defects and overall problems and, in addition, manage other factors of broader scope such as timing and availability of the product, company image, services, total customer solutions, and so forth. From the definition of software quality standpoint, the relationship of the scopes of the three metrics can be represented by the Venn diagram in Figure 4.1.

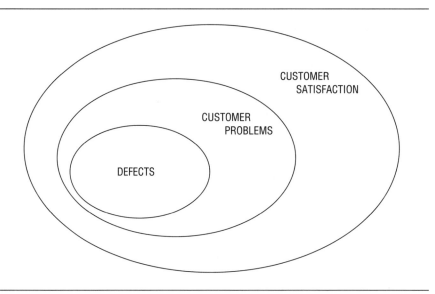

FIGURE 4.1
Scopes of Three Quality Metrics

### 4.1.3  Customer Satisfaction Metrics

Customer satisfaction is often measured by customer survey data via the five-point scale:

- ☐  Very satisfied
- ☐  Satisfied
- ☐  Neutral
- ☐  Dissatisfied
- ☐  Very dissatisfied.

Satisfaction with the overall quality of the product and its specific dimensions is usually obtained through various methods of customer surveys. For example, the specific parameters of customer satisfaction in software monitored by IBM include the CUPRIMDSO categories (capability, functionality, usability, performance, reliability, installability, maintainability, documentation/information, service, and overall); for Hewlett-Packard they are FURPS (functionality, usability, reliability, performance, and service).

Based on the five-point-scale data, several metrics with slight variations can be constructed and used, depending on the purpose of analysis. For example:

1. Percent of completely satisfied customers
2. Percent of satisfied customers (satisfied and completely satisfied)
3. Percent of dissatisfied customers (dissatisfied and completely dissatisfied)
4. Percent of nonsatisfied (neutral, dissatisfied, and completely dissatisfied).

Usually the second metric, percent satisfaction, is used. In some practices where the focus is on reducing the percentage of nonsatisfaction, much like reducing product defects, metric 4 is used.

In addition to forming percentages for various satisfaction or dissatisfaction categories, the weighted index approach can also be used. For instance, some companies use the *net satisfaction index* (NSI) to facilitate comparisons across product. The NSI has the following weighting factors:

☐   Completely satisfied—100%
☐   Satisfied—75%
☐   Neutral—50%
☐   Dissatisfied—25%
☐   Completely Dissatisfied—0%.

NSI ranges from 0% (all customers are completely dissatisfied) to 100% (all customers are completely satisfied). If all customers are satisfied (but not completely satisfied), NSI will have a value of 75%. This weighting approach, however, may be masking the satisfaction profile of one's customer set. For example, if half of the customers are completely satisfied and half are neutral, NSI's value is also 75%, which is equivalent to the scenario that all customers are satisfied. If satisfaction is a good indicator of product loyalty, then half completely satisfied and half neutral is certainly less positive than all satisfied. Furthermore, we are not sure of the rationale behind giving a 25% weight to those who are dissatisfied. Therefore, this example of NSI is not a good metric; it is inferior to the simple approach of calculating percentage of specific categories. If the entire satisfaction profile is desired, one can simply show the percent distribution of all categories. A weighted index is for data summary when multiple indicators are too cumbersome to be shown. For example, if customers' purchase decisions can be expressed as a function of their satisfaction with specific dimensions of a product, then a purchase decision index could be useful. In contrast, if simple indicators can do the job, then the weighted index approach should be avoided.

### 4.1.4 Function Points

In the defect density metric discussed earlier, the size measure used is the LOC count. LOC count is only one of the operational definitions of size. Due to the lack of standardization in LOC counting and the resulting variations in actual practices, alternative measures were investigated; one such measure is the *function point*. In recent years the function point has been gaining acceptance in application development in terms of both productivity (e.g., function points per person-year) and quality (e.g., defects per function point). In this section we provide a concise summary of the subject.

A function can be defined as a collection of executable statements that performs a certain task, together with declarations of the formal parameters and local variables manipulated by those statements (Conte *et al.*, 1986). The ultimate measure of software productivity is how many functions a development team can produce given a certain amount of resource, regardless of the size of the software in lines of code. The defect rate metric, ideally, should be indexed on the number of functions a software provides. If defects per unit of functions is low, then the software should have better quality even though the defects per KLOC value could be higher—when the functions were implemented by fewer lines of code. However, measuring functions is theoretically promising but realistically very difficult.

The function point metric, originated by Albrecht and his colleagues at IBM in the mid-1970s, however, is something of a misnomer because the technique does not measure functions explicitly (Albrecht, 1979). It does address some of the problems associated with LOC counts in size and productivity measures, especially the differences in LOC counts due to different levels of languages used. It is a weighted total of five major components that comprise an application:

- ☐  Number of external inputs (for example, transaction types) × 4
- ☐  Number of external outputs (for example, report types) × 5
- ☐  Number of logical internal files (files as the user might conceive them, not physical files) × 10
- ☐  Number of external interface files (files accessed by the application but not maintained by it) × 7
- ☐  Number of external inquiries (types of on-line inquiries supported) × 4.

These are the average weighting factors. There are also low and high weighting factors, depending on the complexity assessment of the application in terms of the five components (Sprouls, 1990; Kemerer and Porter, 1992):

- ☐ External input: low complexity, 3; high complexity, 6
- ☐ External output: low complexity, 4; high complexity, 7
- ☐ Logical internal file: low complexity, 7; high complexity, 15
- ☐ External interface file: low complexity, 5; high complexity, 10
- ☐ External inquiry: low complexity, 3; high complexity, 6.

The complexity classification of each component is based on a set of standards that define complexity in terms of objective guidelines. For instance, for the external output component, if the number of data element types is 20 or more and the number of file types referenced is two or more, then complexity is high. If the number of data element types is 5 or fewer and the number of file types referenced is two to three, then complexity is low.

With the weighting factors, the first step is to calculate the function counts (FCs) based on the following formula:

$$FC = \sum_{i=1}^{5} \sum_{j=1}^{3} w_{ij} \times x_{ij}$$

where

$w_{ij}$ are the weighting factors of the five components by complexity level (low, average, high) and $x_{ij}$ are the numbers of each component in the application. The second step involves using a scale from 0 to 5 to assess the impact of 14 general system characteristics in terms of their likely effect for the application. The 14 characteristics are:

1. Data communications
2. Distributed functions
3. Performance
4. Heavily used configuration
5. Transaction rate
6. On-line data entry

7. End-user efficiency
8. On-line update
9. Complex processing
10. Reusability
11. Installation ease
12. Operational ease
13. Multiple sites
14. Facilitation of change.

The scores (ranging from 0 to 5) for these characteristics are then summed, based on the following formula, to form the value adjustment factor (VAF)

$$VAF = 0.65 + 0.01 \sum_{i=1}^{14} c_i$$

where $c_i$ is the score for general system characteristic $i$. Finally, the number of function points is obtained by multiplying function counts and the value adjustment factor:

$$FP = FC \times VAF$$

This equation is a simplified description of the calculation of function points. One should consult the fully documented methods, such as the International Function Point User's Group (IFPUG) Standard, Release 3.0 (Sprouls, 1990), for a complete treatment.

Over the years the function point metric has gained acceptance as a key productivity measure in the application world. In 1986 the IFPUG was established. The IFPUG counting practices committee is the *de facto* standards organization for function point counting methods (Jones, 1992). Classes and seminars on function points counting and applications are frequently available from consulting firms and at software conferences. In application contract work, the function point is often used as a unit to measure the amount of work, and quality is expressed as defects per function point.

In system software, however, function point has been slow to gain acceptance. This is perhaps simply because it is not quite applicable to system software as it was originally developed for applications. System software is also much more complex, and to have accurate function point counts, the effort is likely much more than counting accurate lines of code. Intriguingly, the same observation can be made about function point use in academic research. While it appears to be better than the LOC count metric, the function point metric is not without measurement problems. For instance, research indicated that there are variations in counting function points in the industry (Kemerer, 1991) and there are several major methods other than the IFPUG standard. More fundamentally, the meaning of function point and the derivation algorithm and its rationale apparently need more research and more theoretical groundwork.

## 4.2  In-Process Quality Metrics

Since our goal is to understand the programming process and to learn to engineer quality into the process, in-process quality metrics play an important role. However, compared to end-product metrics, in-process quality metrics are less formally defined, and their practices vary greatly among software developers. On the one hand, in-process quality metrics simply means the tracking of defect arrival during formal machine testing for some organizations. On the other hand, there are some software organizations with well-established software metrics programs that cover various parameters in each phase of the development cycle. In this section we briefly discuss several metrics that are needed as a minimum for in-process quality management. In later chapters on modeling we will examine some of them in greater detail and discuss others within the context of models.

### 4.2.1  Defect Density During Machine Testing

Defect rate during formal machine testing (testing after code is integrated into the system library) is usually positively correlated with the defect rate experienced in the field. Higher defect rates found during testing is an indicator that the software has experienced higher error injection during its development process, unless the higher testing defect rate is due to an extraordinary testing effort—additional testing or a new testing approach that was deemed more effective in detecting defects. The rationale for the positive correlation is simple: Software defect density never follows the uniform distribution. If a piece of code or a product has higher testing defects, either it is due to more effective testing or it is because of higher latent defects in the code. In *The Art of Software Testing,* Myers (1979) discusses a counterintuitive principle that the more defects found during testing, the more defects will be found later. That principle is another expression of the positive correlation between defect rates during testing and in the field or between defect rates between phases of testing.

This simple metric of defects per KLOC (or other denominator), therefore, is a good indicator of quality while the software is still under testing. It is especially useful to monitor subsequent releases of the same product within the same development organization. Therefore, release-to-release comparisons are not contaminated by other extraneous factors. The development team or the project manager can use the following scenarios to derive their judgment of the release quality:

□ If the defect rate during testing is the same or lower than that of the previous release (or a similar product), then ask: Does the testing for the current release deteriorate?

If the answer is no, the quality perspective is positive.

If the answer is yes, you need to do extra testing (for example, add more test cases to increase coverage, blitz test, customer testing, stress testing, and so forth).

□ If the defect rate during testing is substantially higher than that of the previous release (or a similar product), then ask: Did we plan for and actually improve testing effectiveness?

If the answer is no, the quality perspective is negative. Ironically, the only remedial approach that can be taken at this stage of the life cycle is to do more testing, which will yield even higher defect rates.

If the answer is yes, then the quality perspective is the same or positive.

### 4.2.2  Defect Arrival Pattern During Machine Testing

Overall defect density during test is a summary indicator. The pattern of defect arrivals (or for that matter, times between failures) gives more information. Even with the same overall defect rate during test, different patterns of defect arrivals indicate different quality levels in the field. Figure 4.2 shows two contrasting patterns for both the defect arrival rate and the cumulative defect rate. Data were plotted from 44 weeks before code-freeze until the week prior to code-freeze. The second pattern, represented by the charts on the right-hand side, obviously indicates that testing started late, the test suite was not sufficient, and that the testing ended prematurely.

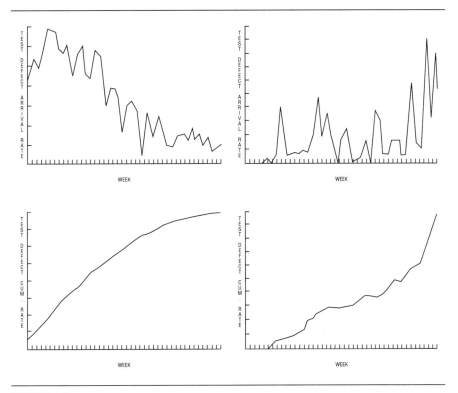

FIGURE 4.2
Two Contrasting Defect Arrival Patterns During Test

The objective is always to look for defect arrivals stabilizing at a very low level, or the times between failures becoming far apart, before ending the testing effort and releasing the software to the field. Such declining patterns of defect arrival during test are indeed the basic assumption of many software reliability models. The time unit for observing the arrival pattern is usually in weeks and occasionally in months. For reliability models that require execution time data, the time interval is in terms of units of CPU time.

When we talk about the defect arrival pattern during test, there are actually three slightly different metrics and they should be looked at simultaneously:

☐　The defect arrivals (defects reported) during the testing phase by time interval (for example, week). These are the raw number of arrivals, not all of which are valid defects.

☐   The pattern of valid defect arrivals—when problem determination is done on the reported problems. This is the true defect pattern.

☐   The pattern of defect backlog overtime. This metric is needed because development organizations cannot investigate and fix all reported problems immediately. This metric is a workload statement as well as a quality statement. If the defect backlog is large at the end of the development cycle and a lot of fixes have to be integrated into the system, the stability of the system (hence its quality) will be affected. Retesting (regression test) is needed to ensure that product quality levels are reached.

### 4.2.3 Phase-Based Defect Removal Pattern

The phase-based defect removal pattern is an extension of the test defect density metric. In addition to testing, it requires the tracking of defects at all phases of the development cycle, including the design reviews, code inspections, or formal verifications before testing. Because a large percentage of programming defects is related to design problems, conducting formal reviews or functional verifications to enhance the defect removal capability of the process at the front end helps reduce the error injection. The pattern of phase-based defect removal reflects the overall defect removal ability of the development process.

With regard to the metrics for the design and coding phases, in addition to defect rates, many development organizations also use metrics such as inspection coverage and inspection effort for in-process quality management. Some companies even set up "model values" and "control boundaries" for various in-process quality indicators. For example, Cusumano (1992) reported the specific model values and control boundaries for metrics such as review coverage rate, review manpower rate (review work hours/number of design work hours), defect rate, etc., which were used by NEC's Switching Systems Division.

Figure 4.3 shows the patterns of defect removal of two IBM development projects: project A was front-end loaded and project B was heavily testing-dependent for removing defects. In the figure, the various phases of defect removal are high-level design review (I0), low-level design review (I1), code inspection (I2), unit test (UT), component test (CT), and system test (ST). As expected, the field quality of project A outperformed project B significantly.

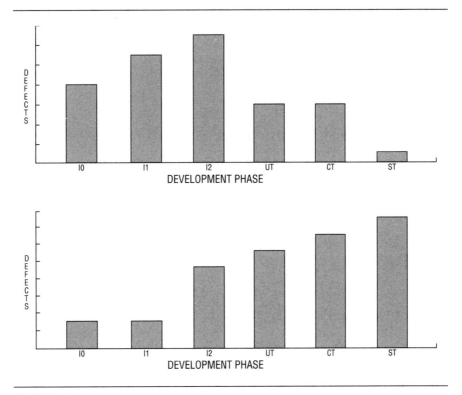

FIGURE 4.3
Defect Removal by Phase for Two Products

### 4.2.4 Defect Removal Effectiveness

Defect removal effectiveness (or efficiency as used by some writers) can be defined as follows:

$$\text{DRE} = \frac{\text{Defects removed during a development phase}}{\text{Defects latent in the product}} \times 100\%$$

Because the total number of latent defects in the product at any given phase is not known, the denominator of the metric can only be approximated. It is usually estimated by:

Defects removed during the phase + defects found later

The metric can be calculated for the entire development process, for the front end (before code integration), and for each phase. It is called *early defect removal* and *phase effectiveness* when used for the front end and for specific phases, respectively. The higher the value of the metric, the more effective the development process and the fewer the defects that escaped to the next phase or to the field. This metric is a key concept of the defect removal model for software development. (In Chapter 6 we give this subject a detailed treatment.) Figure 4.4 shows the DRE by phase for a software project with which we have experience. The weakest phases were unit test (UT), code inspections (I2), and component test (CT). Based on this metric, action plans to improve the effectiveness of these phases were established and deployed.

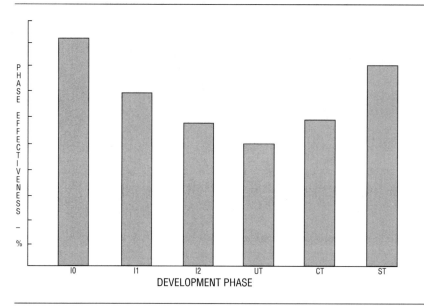

FIGURE 4.4
Phase Effectiveness of a Software Project

## 4.3 Metrics for Software Maintenance

When a software product has completed its development and is released to the market, it enters into the maintenance phase of its life cycle. During this phase the defect arrivals by time interval and customer problem calls (which may or may not be defects) by time interval are the *de facto* metrics. However, the number of defect or problem arrivals is largely determined by the development process before the maintenance phase. Not much can be done to alter the quality of the product during this phase. Therefore, these two *de facto* metrics, while important, do not reflect the quality of software maintenance. What can be done during the maintenance phase is to fix the defects as soon as possible and with excellent fix quality. Such actions, although still not able to improve the defect rate of the product, can improve customer satisfaction to a large extent. The following metrics are hence very important:

☐  Fix backlog and backlog management index
☐  Fix response time
☐  Percent delinquent fixes
☐  Fix quality.

### 4.3.1  Fix Backlog and Backlog Management Index

Fix backlog is a work load statement for software maintenance. It is related to both the rate of defect arrivals and the rate at which fixes for reported problems become available. It is a simple count of reported problems that remain opened at the end of each month or each week. Using it in the format of a trend chart, this metric can provide meaningful information for managing the maintenance process. Another metric to manage the backlog of open problems is the backlog management index (BMI).

$$\text{BMI} = \frac{\text{Number of problems closed during the month}}{\text{Number of problem arrivals during the month}} \times 100\%$$

As a ratio of number of closed problems to number of newly opened problems, if BMI is larger than 100, it means the backlog is reduced. If BMI is less than 100, then backlog increases. With enough data points, the techniques of control charting can be used to calculate the backlog management capability of the maintenance process. If the value of BMI exceeds the control limits, then more investigation and analysis should be triggered. Of course, the goal is always to strive for a BMI larger than 100. A BMI trend chart or control chart should be examined together with trend charts of defect arrivals, defects fixed (closed), and the number of problems in the backlog. Figure 4.5 shows a trend chart for the numbers of monthly opened and closed problems of a software product, and a pseudo-control chart for the BMI. The latest release of the product was available to customers in September 1992; this explains the rise and fall of the problem arrivals and closures. The mean BMI was 102.9%, indicating that the capability of the fix process was functioning normally. The lower

BMI for September 1992 was because that month was the first month of the new release, and that for July 1993 was due to vacations around Independence Day. Nonetheless, all BMI values were within the upper (UCL) and lower (LCL) control limit—the backlog management process was in control. (*Note:* We call the BMI chart a pseudo-control chart because the BMI data are autocorrelated and therefore the assumption of independence for control charts is violated. Despite not being "real" control charts in statistical terms, however, we found pseudo-control charts such as the BMI chart quite useful in software quality management. In Chapter 5 we provide more discussions and examples.)

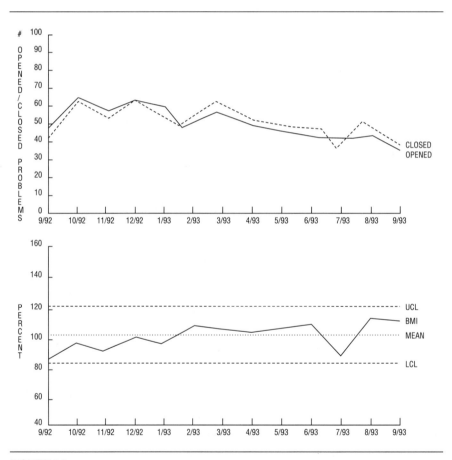

FIGURE 4.5
Monthly Opened Problems, Closed Problems, and Backlog Management Index

### 4.3.2  Fix Response Time

For many software development organizations, guidelines are established on the time limit within which the fixes should be available for the reported defects. Usually the criteria are set in accordance with the severity of the problems. For the critical situations where the customers' businesses are at risk due to the defects encountered in the software product, software developers or the software change teams work around the clock to fix the problems. For less severe defects for which circumventions are available, the fix response time requirement is more relaxed. The fix response time metric is usually calculated as follows for all problems as well as by severity level:

> Mean time of all problems from open to closed

If there are data points with extreme values, medians should be used instead of mean. Such cases could occur for less severe problems for which customers may be satisfied with the circumvention and didn't demand a fix. Therefore the problem may remain open for a long time in the tracking report.

### 4.3.3  Percent Delinquent Fixes

The mean (or median) response time metric is a central tendency measure. Another more sensitive metric is the percentage of delinquent fixes. For each fix, if the turnaround time exceeds the response time criteria by severity, then it is classified as delinquent:

Percent delinquent fixes =

$$\frac{\text{Number of fixes that exceeded the fix response time criteria by severity level}}{\text{Total number of fixes delivered in a specified time}} \times 100\%$$

This metric, however, is not a metric for real-time delinquent management because it is for closed problems only. Problems that are still open must be factored into the calculation for a real-time metric. Assuming the time unit is a week, we propose that the percent delinquent of all problems in the active backlog be used. *Active backlog* refers to all opened problems for the week, which is the sum of the existing backlog at the beginning of the week and new problem arrivals during the week. In other words, it contains the total number of problems to be processed for the week—the total work load. The number of delinquent problems is checked at the end of the week. Figure 4.6 shows the index diagrammatically.

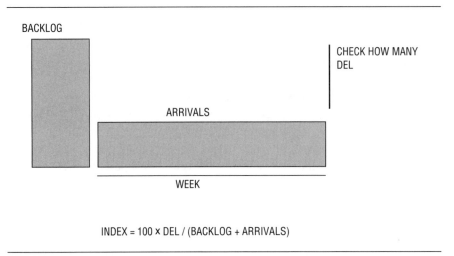

INDEX = 100 × DEL / (BACKLOG + ARRIVALS)

FIGURE 4.6
Real-Time Delinquency Index

It is important to note that the metric of percent delinquent fixes is a cohort metric. Its denominator refers to a cohort of problems (problems closed in a given period of time, or problems to be processed in a given week). The cohort concept is important because if it is operationalized as a cross-sectional measure, then invalid metrics will result. For example, we have seen practices in which at the end of each week the number of problems in backlog (opened problems that were still to be fixed) and the number of delinquent open problems were counted, and the percent delinquent problems was calculated. This cross-sectional counting approach neglects those problems that were processed and closed before the end of the week, and will create a high delinquent index when significant improvement (reduction in problems backlog) is made.

### 4.3.4  Fix Quality

Fix quality or the number of defective fixes is another important quality metric for the maintenance phase. From the customer's perspective, it is bad enough to encounter functional defects when they are running their business on the software. It is even worse if the fixes turn out to be defective. For mission-critical software, defective fixes are detrimental to customer satisfaction. The metric of percent defective fixes is simply the percentage of all fixes in a time interval (for example, month) that are defective. A fix is defective if it did not fix the problem that was reported, or if it fixed the original problem but injected a new defect.

A defective fix can be recorded in two ways: Record it in the month it was discovered or record it in the month when the fix was delivered. The first is a customer measure, the second is a process measure. The difference between the two dates is the latent period of the defective fix. It is meaningful to keep track of the latency data and other information such as the number of customers who were affected by the defective fix. Usually the longer the latency the more customers are affected because there is more time for customers to apply that defective fix to their software system.

There is an argument against using percentage for defective fixes. If the number of defects and, hence, the fixes is large, then the small value of the percentage metric will show an optimistic picture, although the number of defective fixes could be quite large. This metric, therefore, should be a straight count of the number of defective fixes. The quality goal for the maintenance process, of course, is zero defective fixes without delinquency.

## 4.4  Examples of Metrics Programs

### 4.4.1  Motorola

Motorola's software metrics program is well articulated by Daskalantonakis (1992). By following the Goal/Question/Metric paradigm of Basili and Weiss (1984), goals were identified, questions were formulated in quantifiable terms, and metrics were established. The goals and measurement areas identified by the Motorola Quality Policy for Software Development (QPSD) are listed in the following.

*Goals:*

- ☐  Goal 1: Improve project planning
- ☐  Goal 2: Increase defect containment
- ☐  Goal 3: Increase software reliability
- ☐  Goal 4: Decrease software defect density
- ☐  Goal 5: Improve customer service
- ☐  Goal 6: Reduce the cost of nonconformance
- ☐  Goal 7: Increase software productivity.

*Measurement Areas:*

- ☐  Delivered defects and delivered defects per size
- ☐  Total effectiveness throughout the process
- ☐  Adherence to schedule
- ☐  Estimation accuracy
- ☐  Number of open customer problems
- ☐  Time that problems remain open
- ☐  Cost of nonconformance
- ☐  Software reliability.

For each goal the questions to be asked and the corresponding metrics were also formulated. In the following, we list the questions and metrics for each goal (*Source:
pp. 1001–1004 in Daskalantonakis, M. K., "A Practical View of Software
Measurement and Implementation Experiences Within Motorola," IEEE Transactions
on Software Engineering, Vol. 18, No.11, November 1992, pp. 998–1010. Copyright ©
1992, IEEE, with permission to reprint.*):

*Goal 1: Improve Project Planning*

   Question 1.1: What was the accuracy of estimating the actual value of
   project schedule?

   Metric 1.1 : Schedule Estimation Accuracy (SEA)

$$SEA = \frac{\text{Actual project duration}}{\text{Estimated project duration}}$$

   Question 1.2: What was the accuracy of estimating the actual value of
   project effort?

   Metric 1.2 : Effort Estimation Accuracy (EEA)

$$EEA = \frac{\text{Actual project effort}}{\text{Estimated project effort}}$$

*Goal 2: Increase Defect Containment*

   Question 2.1: What is the currently known effectiveness of the defect
   detection process prior to release?

   Metric 2.1: Total Defect Containment Effectiveness (TDCE)

$$TDCE = \frac{\text{Number of prerelease defects}}{\text{Number of prerelease defects} + \text{Number of postrelease defects}}$$

Question 2.2: What is the currently known containment effectiveness of faults introduced during each constructive phase of software development for a particular software product?

Metric 2.2: Phase Containment Effectiveness for phase $i$ (PCEi)

$$PCEi = \frac{\text{Number of phase } i \text{ errors}}{\text{Number of phase } i \text{ errors} + \text{Number of phase } i \text{ defects}}$$

*Note:* From Daskalantonakis' definition of error and defect, it appears that Motorola's use of the two terms differs from what we discussed earlier in this chapter. To understand the preceding metric, consider Daskalantonakis' definitions:

☐ *Error:* A problem found during the review of the phase where it was introduced.

☐ *Defect:* A problem found later than the review of the phase where it was introduced.

☐ *Fault:* Both errors and defects are considered faults.

*Goal 3: Increase Software Reliability*

Question 3.1: What is the rate of software failures, and how does it change over time?

Metric 3.1: Failure Rate (FR)

$$FR = \frac{\text{Number of failures}}{\text{Execution time}}$$

*Goal 4: Decrease Software Defect Density*

Question 4.1: What is the normalized number of in-process faults, and how does it compare with the number of in-process defects?

Metric 4.1a: In-process Faults (IPF)

$$IPF = \frac{\text{In-process faults caused by incremental software development}}{\text{Assembly-equivalent delta source size}}$$

Metric 4.1b: In-process Defects (IPD)

$$IPF = \frac{\text{In-process defects caused by incremental software development}}{\text{Assembly-equivalent delta source size}}$$

Question 4.2: What is the currently known defect content of software delivered to customers, normalized by assembly-equivalent size?

Metric 4.2a: Total Released Defects total (TRD total)

$$\text{TRD total} = \frac{\text{Number of released defects}}{\text{Assembly-equivalent total source size}}$$

Metric 4.2b: Total Released Defects delta (TRD delta)

$$\text{TRD delta} = \frac{\text{Number of released defects caused by}}{\text{Assembly-equivalent total source size}}$$

Question 4.3: What is the currently known customer-found defect content of software delivered to customers, normalized by assembly-equivalent source size?

Metric 4.3a: Customer-Found Defects total (CFD total)

$$\text{CFD total} = \frac{\text{Number of customer-found defects}}{\text{Assembly-equivalent total source size}}$$

Metric 4.3b: Customer-Found Defects delta (CFD delta)

$$\text{CFD delta} = \frac{\text{Number of customer-found defects caused by}}{\text{Assembly-equivalent total source size}}$$

*Goal 5: Improve Customer Service*

Question 5.1 What is the number of new problems that were opened during the month?

Metric 5.1: New Open Problems (NOP)

NOP =
Total new postrelease problems opened during the month

Question 5.2 What is the total number of open problems at the end of the month?

Metric 5.2: Total Open Problems (TOP)

> TOP = Total new postrelease problems that remain open
> at the end of the month

Question 5.3: What is the mean age of open problems at the end of the month?

Metric 5.3: Mean Age of Open Problems (AOP)

> AOP = (Total time postrelease problems remaining open
> at the end of the month have been open)/(Number of open post
> release problems remaining open at the end of the month)

Question 5.4: What is the mean age of the problems that were closed during the month?

Metric 5.4: Mean Age of Closed Problems (ACP)

> ACP = (Total time postrelease problems closed within
> the month were open)/(Number of open postrelease
> problems closed within the month)

*Goal 6: Reduce the Cost of Nonconformance*

Question 6.1: What was the cost to fix postrelease problems during the month?

Metric 6.1: Cost of Fixing Problems (CFP)

> CFP = Dollar cost associated with fixing postrelease
> problems within the month

*Goal 7: Increase Software Productivity*

Question 7.1: What was the productivity of software development projects (based on source size)?

Metric 7.1a: Software Productivity total (SP total)

$$\text{SP total} = \frac{\text{Assembly-equivalent total source size}}{\text{Software development effort}}$$

Metric 7.1b: Software Productivity delta (SP delta)

$$\text{SP delta} = \frac{\text{Assembly-equivalent delta source size}}{\text{Software development effort}}$$

From the preceding goals one can see that metrics 3.1, 4.2a, 4.2b, 4.3a, and 4.3b are metrics for end-product quality, metrics 5.1 to 5.4 are metrics for software maintenance, and metrics 2.1, 2.2, 4.1a, and 4.1b are in-process quality metrics. The others are for scheduling, estimation, and productivity.

In addition to the preceding metrics, which are defined by the Motorola Software Engineering Process Group (SEPG), Daskalantonakis also described additional in-process metrics that can be used for schedule, project, and quality control. Without getting into too many details, we list these additional in-process metrics in the following. [For details and other information about Motorola's software metrics program, see Daskalantonakis' original article (1992).] As can be seen, items 1 to 4 are for project status/control and 5 to 7 are really in-process quality metrics that can provide information about the status of the project and for possible actions for further quality improvement.

1. *Life-cycle phase and schedule tracking metric:* Track schedule based on life-cycle phase comparing actual to plan.
2. *Cost/earned value tracking metric:* Track actual cumulative cost of the project versus budgeted cost, and actual cost of the project so far, with continuous update throughout the project.
3. *Requirements tracking metric:* Track the number of requirements change at the project level.
4. *Design tracking metric:* Track the number of requirements implemented in design versus the number of requirements written.
5. *Fault-type tracking metric:* Track fault cause.
6. *Remaining defect metrics:* Track faults per month for the project and use Rayleigh curve to project the number of faults assumed to be found in the months ahead during development.

**7.** *Review effectiveness metric:* Track error density by stages of review and use control chart methods to flag the exceptionally high or low data points.

## 4.4.2 Hewlett-Packard

The book *Software Metrics: Establishing A Company-Wide Program* by Grady and Caswell (1986) contains a good description of Hewlett-Packard's software metric program. It lists both the primitive metrics and computed metrics that are widely used at HP. Primitive metrics are those that are directly measurable and accountable such as control token, data token, defect, total operands, LOC, and so forth. Computed metrics are metrics that are mathematical combinations of two or more primitive metrics. The following is an excerpt of HP's computed metrics (*Source:* Grady, R. B., and D. L. Caswell, *Software Metrics: Establishing A Company-Wide Program,* Englewood Cliffs, N.J.: Prentice-Hall, pp. 225–226. Copyright © 1986 Prentice-Hall, Inc., with permission to reprint.):

Average fixed defects/working day: self-explanatory.

Average engineering hours/fixed defect: self-explanatory.

Average reported defects/working day: self-explanatory.

Bang: "a quantitative indicator of net usable function from the user's point of view" (DeMarco, 1982). There are two methods for computing Bang. Computation of Bang for function-strong systems involves counting the tokens entering and leaving the function multiplied by the weight of the function. For data-strong systems it involves counting the objects in the database weighted by the number of relationships of which the object is a member.

Branches covered/total branches: when running a program, this metric indicates what percentage of the decision points were actually executed.

Defects/KNCSS: self-explanatory.

Defects/LOD: self-explanatory.

(Note: LOD—Lines of documentation not included in program source code; KNCSS—Thousand noncomment source statements.)

Defects/testing time: self-explanatory.

Design weight: "Design weight is a simple sum of the module weights over the set of all modules in the design" (DeMarco, 1982). Each module weight is a function of the token count associated with the module and the expected number of decision counts which are based on the structure of data.

NCSS/engineering month: self-explanatory.

Percent overtime: average overtime/40 hours per week.

(Phase) engineering months/total engineering months: self-explanatory.

Of these metrics, defects/KNCSS and defects/LOD are end-product quality metrics. Defects/testing time is a statement of testing effectiveness and branches covered/total branches is testing coverage in terms of decision points. Therefore, both are meaningful in-process quality metrics. Bang is a measurement of functions and NCSS/engineering month is a productivity measure. Design weight is an interesting measurement but its use is not clear. The others are metrics for work load, schedule, project control, and cost of defects.

As Grady and Caswell pointed out, this list represents the most widely used computed metrics in HP, but it may not be comprehensive. For instance, many others are discussed in other sections of their book. For example, customer satisfaction measurements in relation to software quality attributes are a key area in HP's software metrics. As mentioned earlier in this chapter, the software quality attributes defined by HP are called FURPS (functionality, usability, reliability, performance, and supportability). Goals and objectives for FURPS are set for software projects. Furthermore, to achieve the FURPS goals of the end product, measurable objectives using FURPS for each life-cycle phase are also set (Grady and Caswell, 1986, pp. 159–162).

More recently, MacLeod (1993) describes the implementation and sustenance of a software inspection program in a HP division. The metrics used include average hours per inspection, average defects per inspection, average hours per defect, and defect causes. These inspection metrics, when appropriately used in the proper context (for example, comparing the current project with previous projects), can be used to monitor the inspection phase (front end) of the software development process.

### 4.4.3 IBM Rochester

Because many examples of the metrics used at IBM Rochester have already been discussed or will be elaborated on later, here we give just a brief overview. Furthermore, we list only selected quality metrics; metrics related to project management, productivity, scheduling, costs, and resources are not included.

For the software community within IBM, a set of standard 5-UP software quality metrics is defined by the IBM corporate software measurement council. The 5-UP metrics include the following:

☐ Overall customer satisfaction as well as satisfaction with the CUPRIMDS parameters.

☐ Postrelease defect rate for three-year LOP tracking: TVUA/MSSI based on the release the defects are reported.

☐ Customer problem calls.

☐ Fix response time.

☐ Number of defective fixes.

IBM Rochester uses the corporate 5-UP metrics. In addition, other product quality metrics and many in-process metrics are also used. The following gives a sample of these metrics, some of which have been discussed in early sections, and some which will entail more in-depth discussions in later chapters:

☐ TVUA/KSSI based on whether the release contains the defect or not (regardless of which reported release) for four-year LOP tracking

☐ TVUA/KCSI based on release origin for four-year LOP tracking

☐ Customer reported problems per user month

☐ Backlog management index

☐ Postrelease arrival patterns for defects and problems (both defects and non-defect-oriented problems)

☐ Defect removal model for the software development process with target defect removal rate for each phase

☐ Phase effectiveness (for each phase of inspection and test)

☐ Inspection coverage, effort, and defect rates

☐ In-process inspection escape rate

☐ Compile failures and build/integration defects

☐ Driver stability index

☐ Weekly defect arrivals and backlog during testing

☐ Defect severity

☐ Defect cause

☐ Reliability: mean time to initial program loading (IPL) during test

☐ Models for postrelease defect estimation

☐ S curves for project progress comparing actual to plan for each phase of development such as number of inspections conducted by week, LOC integrated by week, number of test cases attempted and succeeded by week, and so forth.

## 4.5  Collecting Software Engineering Data

The challenge of collecting software engineering data is to make sure that the data can provide useful information for project, process, and quality management and, at the same time, that the data collection process will not be a burden on the development teams. Therefore, it is important to consider carefully what data to collect. The data must be based on well-defined metrics and models, which are used to drive improvements. Therefore, the goals of the data collection methodology should be established and the questions of interest be defined before attempting any data collection. Data classification schemes to be used and the level of precision must be carefully specified. The collection form or template and data fields should be pretested. The amount of data to be collected and the number of metrics to be used need not be overwhelming. It is more important that the information extracted from the data be focused, accurate, and useful. Without being metrics driven there is a tendency for overcollection of data, which could be wasteful. Overcollection of data is quite common when people start to measure software without an *a priori* specification of purpose, of objectives, of profound versus trivial issues, and of metrics and models.

Gathering software engineering data can be expensive, especially if it is done as part of a research program, For example, the NASA Software Engineering Laboratory spent about 15% of their development costs on gathering and processing data on hundreds of metrics for a number of projects (Shooman, 1983). For large commercial development organizations, the relative cost of data gathering and processing should be much lower because of economy of scale and a smaller number of metrics. However, the cost of data collection will never become insignificant. Nonetheless, data collection and analysis, which yields intelligence about the project and the development process, is vital for business success. Indeed, in many organizations, a tracking and data collection system is often an integral part of the software configuration or the project management system, without which the chance of success of large and complex projects will be reduced.

Basili and Weiss (1984) proposed a data collection methodology that could be applicable anywhere. The schema consists of six steps with considerable feedback and iteration occurring at several places:

1. Establish the goal of the data collection
2. Develop a list of questions of interest
3. Establish data categories
4. Design and test data collection forms
5. Collect and validate data
6. Analyze data.

The importance of the validation element of a data collection system or a development tracking system cannot be overemphasized. In their study of NASA's Software Engineering Laboratory projects, Basili and Weiss (1984) found that software data are error-prone and that special validation provisions are generally needed. Validation should be performed concurrently with software development and data collection, based on interviews with those people supplying the data. In cases where data collection is part of the configuration control process and automated tools are available, data validation routines (for example, consistency check, range limits, conditional entries, etc.) should be an integral part of the tools. Furthermore, training, clear guidelines and instructions, and an understanding of how the data are used by people who enter or collect the data enhance data accuracy significantly.

The actual collection process can take several basic formats: reporting forms, interviews, and automatic collection using the computer system. For data collection to be efficient and effective, it should be merged with the configuration management or change control system. In most large development organizations, this is usually the case. For example, at IBM Rochester the change control system covers the entire development process, and on-line tools are used for plan change control, development items and changes, integration, and change control after integration (defect fixes). The tools capture data pertinent to schedule, resource, and project status, as well as quality indicators. In general, change control is more prevalent after the code is integrated. This is one of the reasons that in many organizations defect data are usually available for the testing phases but not for the design and coding phases.

With regard to defect data, testing defects are generally more reliable than inspection defects. During testing, a "bug" exists when a test case cannot execute or when the test results deviate from the expected outcome. During inspections, the determination of a defect is based on the judgment of the inspectors. Therefore, it is important to have a clear definition of an inspection defect. The following provides an example of such a definition:

> Inspection defect: A problem found during the inspection process which, if not fixed, would cause one or more of the following to occur:

1. a defect condition in a later inspection phase
2. a defect condition during testing
3. a field defect
4. nonconformance to requirements and specifications
5. nonconformance to established standards such as performance, national language translation, and usability.

For example, misspelled words are not counted as defects, but would be if they were found on a screen that customers use. Using nested IF-THEN-ELSE structures instead of a SELECT statement would not be counted as a defect unless some standard or performance reason dictated otherwise.

Figure 4.7 shows an example of an inspection summary form. The form records the total number of inspection defects and the LOC estimate for each part (module), as well as defect data classified by defect origin and defect type. The following guideline pertains to the defect type classification by development phase:

☐ *Interface defect:* An interface defect is a defect in the way two separate pieces of logic communicate. These are errors in communication between:

Components

Products

Modules and subroutines within a component

User interface (e.g., messages, panels).

Examples of interface defects per development phase follow:

*High-Level Design (I0):*

Use of wrong parameter

Inconsistent use of function keys on user interface (e.g., screen)

Incorrect message used

Presentation of information on screen not usable.

*Low-Level Design (I1):*

Missing required parameters (e.g., missing parameter on module)

Wrong parameters (e.g., specified incorrect parameter on module)

Intermodule interfaces: input not there, input in wrong order

Intramodule interfaces: passing values/data to subroutines

Incorrect use of common data structures

Misusing data passed to code.

*Code (I2):*

> Passing wrong values for parameters on macros, application program interfaces (API), modules

> Setting up a common control block/area used by another piece of code incorrectly

> Not issuing correct exception to caller of code.

☐ *Logic defect:* A logic defect is one that would cause incorrect results in the function to be performed by the logic. High-level categories of this type of defect are as follows:

> Function: capability not implemented or implemented incorrectly

> Assignment: initialization

> Checking: validate data/values before use

> Timing: management of shared/real-time resources

> Data Structures: static and dynamic definition of data.

Examples of logic defects per development phase follow:

*High-Level Design (I0):*

> Invalid or incorrect screen flow

> High-level flow through component missing or incorrect in the review package

> Function missing from macros you are implementing

> Using a wrong macro to do a function that will not work (e.g., using XXXMSG to receive a message from a program message queue, instead of YYYMSG).

> Missing requirements

> Missing parameter/field on command/in database structure/on screen you are implementing

> Wrong value on keyword (e.g., macro, command)

> Wrong keyword (e.g., macro, command).

*Low-Level Design (I1):*

Logic does not implement I0 design

Missing or excessive function

Values in common structure not set

Propagation of authority and adoption of authority (lack of or too much)

Lack of code page conversion

Incorrect initialization

Not handling abnormal termination (conditions, cleanup, exit routines)

Lack of normal termination cleanup

Performance: too much processing in loop that could be moved outside of loop.

*Code (I2):*

Code does not implement I1 design

Lack of initialization

Variables initialized incorrectly

Missing exception monitors

Exception monitors in wrong order

Exception monitors not active

Exception monitors active at the wrong time

Exception monitors set up wrong

Truncating of double-byte character set data incorrectly (e.g., truncating before shift in character)

Incorrect code page conversion

Lack of code page conversion

Not handling exceptions/return codes correctly.

☐   *Documentation defect*:

A documentation defect is a defect in the description of the function (e.g., prologue of macro) that causes someone to do something wrong based on this information. For example, if a macro prologue contained an incorrect description of a parameter that caused the user of this macro to use the parameter incorrectly, this would be a documentation defect against the macro.

Examples of documentation defects per development phase follow:

*High-Level Design (I0):*

Incorrect information in prologue (e.g., macro)

Misspelling on user interface (e.g., screen)

Wrong wording (e.g., messages, command prompt text)

Using restricted words on user interface

Wording in messages, definition of command parameters is technically incorrect.

*Low-Level Design (I1):*

Wrong information in prologue (e.g., macros, program, etc.)

Missing definition of inputs and outputs of module, subroutines, etc.

Insufficient documentation of logic (comments tell what but not why).

*Code (I2):*

Information in prologue not correct or missing

Wrong wording in messages

Second-level text of message technically incorrect

Insufficient documentation of logic (comments tell what but not why)

Incorrect documentation of logic.

Product: _____    Component: _____         Release: _____

Inspection Type: _____      (RQ SD I0 I1 I2 U1 U2)

Description: _____

D e f e c t   C o u n t s

| Tot for inspection / Part Name | LOC | By Defect Origin | | | | | By Defect Type | | | Tot. |
|---|---|---|---|---|---|---|---|---|---|---|
| | | RQ | SD | I0 | I1 | I2 | LO | IF | DO | |
| | | | | | | | | | | |
| | | | | | | | | | | |
| | | | | | | | | | | |
| | | | | | | | | | | |
| | | | | | | | | | | |
| | | | | | | | | | | |
| | | | | | | | | | | |
| | | | | | | | | | | |

LO ( Logic)     IF (Interface)     DO (Documentation)

Total Prep Hrs: __.__     Total Insp Hrs: __.__
Total persons attended: __   Inspection Date: __/__/__
Reinspection required? __ (Y/N)

Defect types:           Defect origins and inspection types:
DO = Documentation      RQ = Requirements
IF = Interface          SD = System Design
LO = Logic              I0 = High-Level Design
                        I1 = Low-Level Design
                        I2 = Code

FIGURE 4.7
An Example of an Inspection Summary Form

## 4.6 Summary

Software quality metrics focus on the quality aspects of the product, process, and project. They can be grouped into three categories in accordance with the software life cycle: end-product quality metrics, in-process quality metrics and maintenance quality metrics. This chapter gave several examples for each category, summarized the metrics programs at Motorola, Hewlett-Packard, and IBM Rochester, and discussed data collection.

- Product quality metrics:

    Mean time to failure

    Defect density

    Customer-reported problems

    Customer satisfaction.

- In-process quality metrics:

    Phase-based defect removal pattern

    Defect removal effectiveness

    Defect density during formal machine testing

    Defect arrival pattern during formal machine testing.

- Maintenance quality metrics:

    Fix backlog

    Backlog management index

    Fix response time

    Percent delinquent fixes

    Defective fixes.

With regard to in-process data, generally those at the back end (for example, testing defects) are more reliable than those at the front end (for example, design reviews and inspections). To improve data reliability, it is important to establish definitions and examples (for example, what constitutes a defect during design reviews). Furthermore, validation must be an integral part of the data collection system and should be performed concurrently with software development and data collection.

# References

1. Albrecht, A. J., "Measuring Application Development Productivity," *Proceedings of the Joint IBM/SHARE/GUIDE Application Development Symposium,* October 1979, pp. 83–92.

2. Basili, V. R., and D. M. Weiss, "A Methodology for Collecting Valid Software Engineering Data," *IEEE Transactions on Software Engineering,* Vol. SE-10, 1984, pp. 728–738.

3. Boehm, B. W., *Software Engineering Economics*, Englewood Cliffs, N.J.: Prentice-Hall, 1981.

4. Conte, S. D., H. E. Dunsmore, and V. Y. Shen, *Software Engineering Metrics and Models,* Menlo Park, Calif.: The Benjamin/Cummings Publishing Company, 1986.

5. Cusumano, M. A., "Objectives and Context of Software Measurement, Analysis and Control," Massachusetts Institute of Technology Sloan School of Management Working Paper 3471-92, October 1992.

6. Daskalantonakis, M. K., "A Practical View of Software Measurement and Implementation Experiences Within Motorola," *IEEE Transactions on Software Engineering,* Vol. SE-18, 1992, pp. 998–1010.

7. DeMarco, T., *Controlling Software Projects,* New York: Yourdon Press, 1982.

8. Grady, R. B., and D. L. Caswell, *Software Metrics: Establishing A Company-Wide Program,* Englewood Cliffs, N.J.: Prentice-Hall, 1986.

9. Jones, C., *Programming Productivity*, New York: McGraw-Hill, 1986.

10. Jones, C., "Critical Problems in Software Measurement," Burlington, Mass.: Software Productivity Research, 1992.

11. Kemerer, C. F., "Reliability of Function Point Measurement: A Field Experiment," Massachusetts Institute of Technology Sloan School of Management Working Paper 3193-90-MSA, January 1991.

12. Kemerer, C. F., and B. S. Porter, "Improving the Reliability of Function Point Measurement: An Empirical Study," *IEEE Transactions on Software Engineering,* Vol. 18, No.11, November 1992, pp. 1011–1024.

13. Littlewood, B., and L. Strigini, "The Risks of Software," *Scientific American,* November 1992, pp. 62–75.

14. MacLeod, J. M., "Implementing and Sustaining a Software Inspection Program in an R&D Environment," *Hewlett-Packard Journal,* June 1993, pp. 60–63.

15. Myers, G. J., *The Art of Software Testing,* New York: John Wiley and Sons, 1979.

16. Shooman, M. L., *Software Engineering: Design, Reliability, and Management,* New York: McGraw-Hill, 1983.

17. Sprouls, J., *IFPUG Function Point Counting Practices Manual,* Release 3.0, Westerville, Ohio: International Function Point Users Group, 1990.

# 5

---

# Applying the Seven Basic Quality Tools in Software Development*

The basic statistical tools for quality control as promoted by Ishikawa (1989) are widely used in manufacturing productions. They have indeed become an integral part of the quality control literature, and have been known as Ishikawa's seven basic tools. This chapter describes the application of these tools for quality control in software development. There are many ways to analyze software metrics; the applications of Ishikawa's seven tools represent a set of basic operations. Keep in mind that these statistical tools are for project and quality control at the project level and, hence, are useful for project leaders and product managers, especially in medium and large development organizations. In contrast, they do not provide specific information to software developers on how to improve the quality of their designs or implementation. Also, they may be less useful for small projects where statistical patterns of parameters of the development process are less obvious, hence the benefits of statistics may not be realized. Second, although the benefits of these tools have long been proven in manufacturing operations, the use of these tools and their role in software development has not been widely recognized. For instance, the use

*An earlier version of this chapter was presented at the International Software Quality Exchange conference (ISQE 92, March 10–11, 1992, San Francisco), which was sponsored by the Juran Institute. *ISQE 92 Conference Proceedings,* Wilton, Conn.: Juran Institute, Inc., pp. 4A-35–4A-51.

of control charts in manufacturing production can ensure a certain end-product quality once the process is defined and the control limits are set. In software development, however, the process is complex and involves a high degree of creativity and mental activity. It is extremely difficult, if not impossible, to define the process capability of software development in statistical terms. Therefore, achieving statistical process control in software development may mean a lot more than control charting (for example, new development technology, CASE tools, and the use of defect models and reliability estimating techniques). However, good use of the seven basic tools can lead to positive results for quality management in software development.

In the following sections, we begin with a brief description of the tools. We then discuss each tool separately and give specific examples of applications. Where appropriate, the influences these tools have on quality improvement and on decision making are also described. The examples are either from software engineering literature or from the development of the IBM Application System/400 (AS/400) at IBM Rochester, Minnesota.

## 5.1  Ishikawa's Seven Basic Tools

Ishikawa's seven basic tools for quality control are checklist (or check sheet), Pareto diagram, histogram, scatter diagram, run chart, control chart, and cause-and-effect diagram. Figure 5.1 shows a simple representation of the tools.

A check sheet is a paper form with printed items to be checked. Its main purposes are to gather data easily and to arrange data while collecting it so the data can be easily used later. Another type of check sheet is the check-up confirmation check sheet. It is concerned mainly with the quality characteristics of a process or a product. To distinguish this confirmation check sheet from the ordinary data-gathering check sheet, we use the term *checklist*. In most software development environments, the data-gathering aspect is automated electronically and goes far beyond the data-gathering checksheet approach, which has been used in manufacturing production. Our discussion on this tool, therefore, is confined to checklists.

A Pareto diagram is a frequency bar chart in descending order in which the frequency bars are usually associated with types of problems. It is named after a nineteenth-century Italian economist named Vilfredo Pareto (1848–1923), who expounded his principle in terms of the distribution of wealth—that a large share of the wealth is owned by a small percentage of the population. In 1950 Juran applied the principle to the identification of quality problems—that most of the quality problems are due to a small percentage of the possible causes. In software development, the $X$-axis for a Pareto diagram is usually the defect cause and the $Y$-axis the defect count. By arranging the causes based on defect frequency, a Pareto diagram can identify the few causes that account for the majority of defects. It indicates which problems should be solved first in eliminating defects and improving the operation. Pareto analysis is commonly referred to as the 80–20 principle (20% of the causes account for 80% of the defects), although the cause-defect relationship is not always in a 80–20 distribution.

The histogram is a graphic representation of frequency counts of a sample or a population. The $X$-axis lists the unit intervals of a parameter (for example, severity level of software defects) ranked in ascending order from left to right, and the $Y$-axis contains the frequency counts. In a histogram, the frequency bars are shown by the order of the $X$ variable, whereas in a Pareto diagram the frequency bars are shown by order of the frequency counts. The purpose of the histogram is to show the distribution characteristics of the parameter such as overall shape, central tendency, dispersion, skewness, and so forth. It enhances a better understanding about the parameter of interest.

A scatter diagram vividly portrays the relationship of two interval variables. In a cause-effect relationship, the $X$-axis is for the independent variable and the $Y$-axis for the dependent variable. Each point in a scatter diagram represents an observation of both the dependent and independent variables. Scatter diagrams aid data-based decision making (for instance, if action is planned on the $X$ variable and some effect is expected on the $Y$ variable). One should always look for a scatter diagram when the correlation coefficient of two variables is presented. As we discussed in Chapter 3, this is because the method for calculating the correlation coefficient is highly sensitive to outliers, and a scatter diagram can clearly tell whether there are outliers in the relationship. Secondly, the most commonly used correlation coefficient is Pearson's product moment correlation coefficient, which assumes a linear relationship. If the relationship is nonlinear, the Pearson correlation coefficient may show no relationship, hence it may convey the wrong information.

A run chart tracks the performance of the parameter of interest over time. The $X$-axis is time and the $Y$-axis is the value of the parameter. A run chart is best used for trend analysis, especially if historical data are available for comparisons with the current trend. In Ishikawa's book (1989), he also included various graphs such as the pie chart, bar graph, compound bar graph, and circle graph under the section that discusses run charts. An example of a run chart in software is the weekly number of open problems in the backlog; it shows the work load of software fixes for the development team.

A control chart can be regarded as an advanced form of a run chart for situations where the process capability can be defined. It consists of a central line, a pair of control limits (and sometimes a pair of warning limits within the control limits), and values of the parameter of interest plotted on the chart, which represent the state of a process. The $X$-axis is real time. If all values of the parameter are within the control limits without any particular tendency, the process is regarded as being in a controlled state. If they fall outside the control limits or show a particular trend, the process is considered to be out of control. In such cases, causal analysis and corrective actions are to be taken.

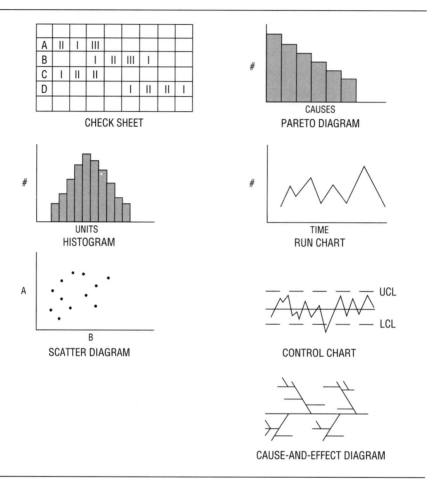

FIGURE 5.1
Ishikawa's Seven Basic Tools for Quality Control

The cause-and-effect diagram, also known as the fishbone diagram, was developed by Ishikawa and associates in the early 1950s in Japan. It was first used to explain factors affecting the production of steel. It was included in the Japanese Industrial Standards terminology for quality control (Kume, 1989). It shows the relationship between a quality characteristic and factors affecting that characteristic. Its layout resembles a fishbone, with the quality characteristic of interest labeled at the fish head position, and factors affecting the characteristics placed where the bones are located. While the scatter diagram describes a specific bivariate relationship in detail, the cause-and-effect diagram identifies all causal factors of a quality characteristic in one chart.

## 5.2 Checklist

The checklist plays a significant role in software development. As a senior software development manager at a major software organization observed, checklists that summarize the key points of the process are much more effective than the lengthy process documents (Bernstein, 1992). At IBM Rochester, the software development process consists of multiple phases, for example, requirements (RQ), system architecture (SD), high-level design (HLD), low-level design (LLD), code development (CODE), unit test (UT), integration and build (I/B), component test (CT), system test (ST), and early customer programs (EP). Each phase has a set of tasks to complete and has entry and exit criteria. Checklists help developers/programmers ensure that all tasks are complete, and for each task the important factors or quality characteristics are covered. Several examples of checklists are code inspection checklist, moderator (for design review and code inspection) checklist, and pre-integration checklist.

The use of checklists is pervasive. Checklists, used daily by the entire development community, are developed and revised based on accumulated experience. Checklists are often a part of the process documents. Their daily use also keeps the processes alive.

Another type of checklist is the common error list, which is part of the stage kickoff of the defect prevention process (DPP). As discussed in Chapter 2, DPP involves three key steps: (1) analysis of defects to trace the root causes, (2) action teams to implement suggested actions, and (3) stage kickoff meetings as the major feedback mechanism. Stage kickoff meetings are conducted by the technical teams at the beginning of each development phase. Reviewing lists of common errors and brainstorming on how to avoid them is one of the focus areas (Mays *et. al.,* 1990)

Perhaps the most outstanding checklist at IBM Rochester software development is the PTF checklist. PTF is the abbreviation for program temporary fix, which is the fix delivered to customers when they encounter defects in the software system. Defective PTFs are detrimental to customer satisfaction and have always been a strong focus area within IBM. By implementing an automated PTF checklist and other action items (such as formal inspection on software fixes, root cause analysis of defective fixes, regular stage kickoff sessions on the fix process so that developers can be kept up to date when they need to develop and deliver a fix, and so forth), IBM Rochester has reduced the already very low percentage of defective fixes to a single-digit number for the entire year. As there are more than 20 million lines of source code in the AS/400 software system and there are more than 250,000 licenses, this achievement is very significant. Note that the PTF checklist is just one part of the fix quality improvement approach; however, there is no doubt it played an important role in IBM Rochester's fix quality.

The PTF checklist was developed based on analysis of vast experiences accumulated over the years and is being reexamined and revised on a continuous basis. Starting out as an on-line checklist, it has now evolved into an automated expert system that is ingrained with the software fix process. When the fix process is invoked, the expert system automatically provides the advice and step-by-step guidance to software developers. The process discipline is, therefore, enforced as a result. Figure 5.2 shows several items on the PTF checklist.

---

\_\_\_ Qn (Y,N) It is critical that you fix the exact problem described in the APAR/PTR problem description. If the problem description is vague, you can't be sure that you are indeed fixing the specific problem that the customer reported. Is the problem description in the APAR/PTR specific and are you fixing that specific problem?

\_\_\_ Qn (Y,N) Did this PTF require a change to a macro or include? If yes, WARN-ING: Don't change the size or offsets of an include. There are probably hard-coded references to the various offsets and you may introduce a defect.

— a. (Y,N) Is the macro/include a CUE, Common Use Element?

☐ Every effort must be made to develop PTFs that do not require changes to a CUE.

☐ If a change is required, the change must be made such that only the changed modules need to be recompiled and all other modules function correctly with the unchanged CUE.

☐ If a change is required to the CUE that cannot be isolated to the changed modules, then a temporary restriction should be considered based on APAR severity and availability of a circumvention.

If you must still PTF a CUE,

1. (Y,N) Has this fix been released and approved by the CUE coordinator? Contact XXX.

— b. (Y,N) Is the macro or include used by more than one module/component?

To help you determine if the macro or include is used by more than one module/component, do the following:

☐ If possible, ask the originator of the code.

☐ Use the YYY command to search for occurrences. Make sure you scan all affected versions for the release you are PTFing.

☐ Use the YYY1 command to see what other modules use this macro or include.

---

FIGURE 5.2 (Continued on Next Page)
**Example Items of the PTF Checklist**

If yes,

_____ 1. (Y,N) Is it necessary to recompile all the modules that use the macro(s) or include(s) for this PTF?

_____ 2. (Y,N) Have all affected modules been PUT with the correct PTR number?

_____ 3. (Y,N) WARNING: Have you gotten approval from all component owners that the change is OK and won't cause a problem? Send a note to all affected component owners explaining the change and asking for an OK. When you think of it, if you change a macro/include, and this changed part gets to the build level, all future PTFs containing modules that use this macro/include will get your code, and they won't even know it unless you tell them. This could cause a defective PTF.

Note: Qn stands for specific question number.

FIGURE 5.2 (Continued from previous page)
**Example Items of the PTF Checklist**

## 5.3 Pareto Diagram

Pareto analysis helps by identifying focus areas that cause most of the problems, which normally means you get the best return on investment when you fix them. It is most applicable in software quality because software defects or defect density never follow a uniform distribution. Rather, almost as a rule of thumb, there are always patterns of clusterings—defects cluster in a minor number of modules or components, a few causes account for the majority of defects, some tricky installation problems account for most of the customer complaints, and so forth. It is, therefore, not surprising to see Pareto charts in software engineering literature. For example, Daskalantonakis (1992) shows an example of Motorola's Pareto analysis for identifying major sources of requirement changes that enabled in-process corrective actions to be taken. Grady and Caswell (1986) showed a Pareto analysis of software defects by category for four Hewlett-Packard software projects. The top three types (new function or different processing required, existing data need to be organized/presented differently, and user needs additional data fields) account for more than one-third of the defects. By focusing on these more prevalent defect types, determining probable causes, and instituting process improvements, Hewlett-Packard was able to achieve significant quality improvements. Figure 5.3 shows an example of a Pareto analysis of the cause of defects for an AS/400 product. Interface problems (INTF) and data initialization problems (INIT) were found to be the most dominant causes for defects for that product. By focusing on the two areas throughout the design, implementation, and test processes, and by conducting technical education by peer experts, significant improvement was observed. The other defect causes in the figure include complex logical problems (CPLX), translation-related national language problems (NLS), problems related to addresses (ADDR), and data definition problems (DEFN).

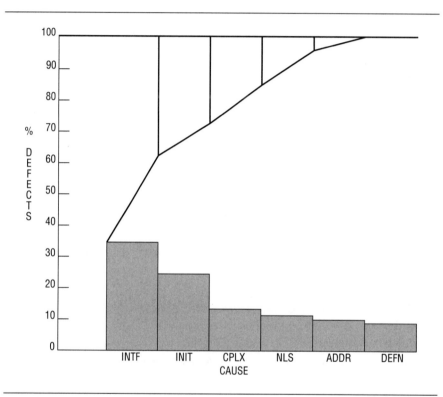

FIGURE 5.3
Pareto Analysis of Software Defects

Another example of Pareto analysis is the problem component analysis conducted at IBM Rochester. The AS/400 software system consists of many products and components. To ensure good return on investment in quality improvement resources, for the past several years a component problem index based on three indicators was calculated for each release of the AS/400 software system, and for

significant improvements strong focus was placed on the problem components. The
problem index is a composite index of three indicators:

☐  Postrelease defects from the new and changed code of the release per thousand new and changed source instructions (defects of current release origin per KCSI). If the components defect rate is

   the same or less than the system target, then score = 0.
   higher than system target but less than twice of system target, then
   score = 1.
   higher than or equal to twice the system target but less than three
   times of system target, then score = 2.
   three times or more of system target, then score = 3.

☐  All postrelease defects are normalized to the total shipped source instructions of the component (all defects per KSSI). This is the defect rate for the
   entire component including base code from previous releases, ported code,
   and new and changed code. The scoring criteria are the same as above.

☐  Actual number of defects categorized by quartiles. If the component is in
   the first quartile, then score = 0, and so forth. This indicator is from the
   customers' perspective because customers may not care about the lines of
   code for the functions and the normalized defect rates. The number of
   defects they encounter is what counts. This indicator may not be fair to
   large components that will have a greater number of defects even if their
   defect density is the same as others. However, the purpose of the index is
   not for quality comparison, but for guiding the improvement effort. Thus
   this indicator was included.

The composite component problem index ranges from 0 to 9. Components with
an index of 5 and higher are considered problem components. From a Pareto analysis of a product 27% of the components had an index of 5 and higher; they accounted
for about 70% of field defects (Figure 5.4). As a result of this type of Pareto analysis,
formal line items for improving problem components (for example, component
restructure, module breakup, complexity measurement and test coverage, intramodule cleanup, and so forth) were included in the development plan and have effected
significant positive results.

(Note that Figure 5.4 is not a Pareto chart in its strict sense because the frequencies are not rank ordered. For a Pareto chart, the frequencies are always in strictly
descending order, and the cumulative percentage line is a piecewise convex curve. If
we take a two-category view (5* + components versus others), then it is a Pareto chart.)

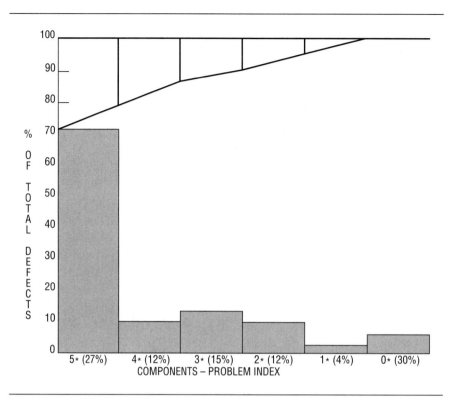

FIGURE 5.4
Pareto Diagram of Defects by Component Problem Index

## 5.4 Histogram

Figure 5.5 shows two examples of histograms used for software project and quality management. Panel A shows the defect frequency of a product by severity level (from 1 to 4 with 1 being the most severe and 4 the least). Defects with different severity levels differ in their impact on customers. Less severe defects usually have circumventions available and to customers they mean inconvenience. In contrast, high severity defects may cause system downtime and affect customers' business. Therefore, given the same defect rate (or number of defects), the defect severity histogram tells a lot more about the quality of the software. Panel B shows the frequency of defects during formal machine testing by number of days the defect reports have been opened (1–7 days, 8–14, 15–21, 22–28, 29–35, and 36+). It reflects the response time in fixing defects during the formal testing phases, hence it is also a workload statement. In Figure 5.6, the customer satisfaction profile of a software product in terms of very satisfied, satisfied, neutral, dissatisfied, and very dissatisfied is shown. Although one can construct various metrics with regard to the categories of satisfaction level, a simple histogram conveys the complete information at a glance.

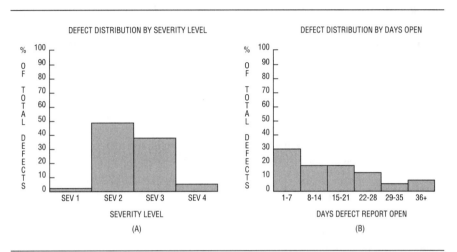

FIGURE 5.5
Examples of Histogram

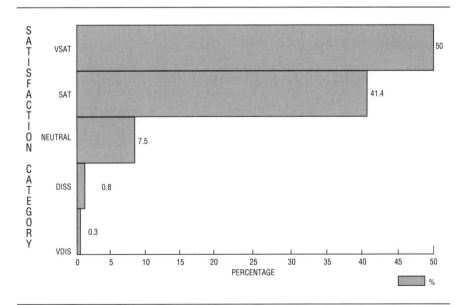

FIGURE 5.6
Profile of Customer Satisfaction of a Software Product

## 5.5 Run Charts

Run charts are also frequently used for software project management; numerous real-life examples can be found in books and journals on software engineering. For example, the weekly arrival of defects and defect backlog during the formal machine testing phases can be monitored via run charts. These charts serve as real-time statements of quality as well as work load. Often these run charts are compared to the projection models and historical data so that the interpretation can be placed into proper perspectives. Another example is tracking the percentage of software fixes that exceed the fix response time criteria. The goal is to ensure timely deliveries of fixes to customers.

Figure 5.7 shows a run chart for the weekly percentage of delinquent open reports of field defects (defect reports that were not yet closed with fixes by the response time criteria) of AS/400 products. The horizontal line (denoted by the letter T) is the target delinquency rate. The dashed vertical line denotes the time when special remedial actions were rolled out to combat the high delinquency rate. For each delinquent defect report, causal analysis was done and corresponding actions implemented. In Figure 5.8, a sample of the cause categories and the actions implemented are shown. As a result, the delinquent-defect report rate was brought down to target in about one month. The rate fluctuated around the target for about four months and eventually was brought under control. (The acronym APAR in Figure 5.8 stands for Authorized Programming Analysis Report, which refers to postrelease problem reports.)

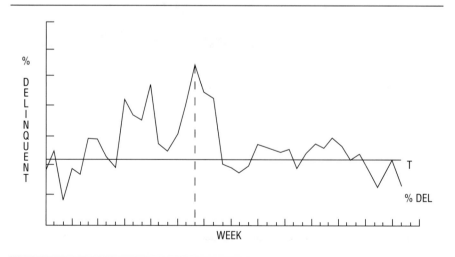

FIGURE 5.7
Run Chart of Percentage of Delinquent Fixes

Another type of run chart that is used by almost all software development organizations for project and schedule management is the S curve, which tracks the cumulative progress of the parameter of interest over time versus the plan. At IBM Rochester, parameters that are tracked for every project in terms of actual versus planned include:

- Completion of design review over time
- Completion of code inspection over time
- Completion of code integration over time
- Completion of component test in terms of number of test cases attempted and successful over time
- Completion of system test in terms of number of test cases attempted and successful over time
- Other parameters related to project and quality management.

| Cause | Increase Delinquency Awareness | Delinquency Highest Priority | Work Load No Excuse | Emphasis on Complete and Quality Fix | Use Test Fix; Provide Circumvention | Internal Screen Team/APAR Coordinator | Active Communication to Secure Info. | Guideline for Awaiting Customer Info. | Internal APAR Procedure | World Trade APAR Routing | New Function APAR Process |
|---|---|---|---|---|---|---|---|---|---|---|---|
| New Function | | | | | | | | | | | X |
| Complex Problem or Fix | | | | X | X | X | | | | | |
| Procedural Problem | X | | | | | | | X | X | X | |
| Not Reproducible | | | | | X | | | | | | |
| Waiting for Cust. Response | | | | | | | X | X | | | |
| Serialized on Other Fix | | | | X | | | | | | | |
| Received Late | | X | | | | | | | | | |
| Waiting on Ext. IBM Group | | | | | | | X | X | | X | |
| Work Load | X | X | X | | | X | | | | | |
| Mishandled | X | X | | | | X | | | X | X | |
| IBM Internal | | X | | | | | | | X | | |

FIGURE 5.8

Causes and Improvement Actions to Reduce Percentage of Delinquent Fixes

## 5.6  Scatter Diagram

Compared to other tools, the scatter diagram is more difficult to apply. It usually relates to investigative work and requires precise data. It is often used together with other techniques such as correlational analysis, regression, and statistical modeling.

Figure 5.9 shows an example of the scatter diagram illustrating the relationship between McCabe's complexity index and defect level. Each data point represents a program module with the $X$ coordinate being its complexity index and the $Y$ coordinate its defect level. Because program complexity can be measured as soon as the program is complete, whereas defects are discovered over a long period of time, the positive correlation between the two allows us to use program complexity to predict defect level. Furthermore, we can reduce the program complexity when it is developed (as measured by McCabe's index), therefore reducing the chance for defects. Reducing complexity can also make programs easier to maintain. Some component teams of the AS/400 operating system adopt this approach as their strategy for quality and maintainability improvement. Program modules with high-complexity indexes are the targets for analysis and possible module breakup, encapsulation, intramodule cleanup, and other actions. Of course, modules with low-complexity indexes but high defects reported are clear indications of poor design or implementation and should also be scrutinized.

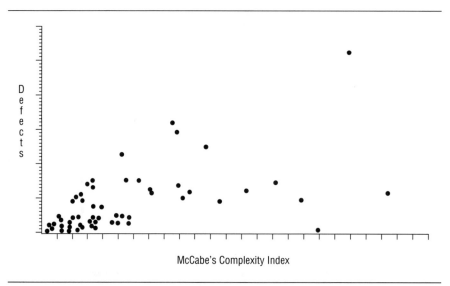

McCabe's Complexity Index

FIGURE 5.9
Scatter Diagram of Program Complexity and Defect Level

Other examples of the scatter diagram include the relationships among defects, fan-in and fan-out, quality index of the same components between the current and previous releases, the relationship between testing defect rates and field defect rates, and so forth. We have gained insights in software quality engineering through the investigations of such relationships.

In software development, reuse is perhaps the most significant factor in improving productivity. The quality of the new software, however, is often constrained by the latent defects or design limitations in the legacy code. For the AS/400 software system, some products were developed by reusing components of existing products on the IBM System/38 platform. To examine the relationship of the defect rate of the reused components between the two platforms, we utilized the scatter diagram. Figure 5.10 shows an example of a product. In the figure, each data point represents a component, with the $X$ coordinate indicating its defect rate in the System/38 platform and the $Y$ coordinate indicating its defect rate in the AS/400 platform. Although there are changes and modifications to the AS/400 product and additional reviews and testing were conducted, clearly the correlation (0.69) is quite strong. Also shown are both the linear regression line (the diagonal line) and the 95% confidence interval (area between the two broken lines).

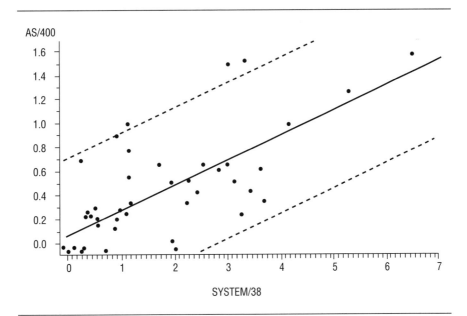

FIGURE 5.10

Correlation of Defect Rates of Reused Components Between Two Platforms

We then proceeded to classify the scattergram into four quadrants according to the medians of the component defect rates on the AS/400 and System/38 platforms (Figure 5.11). Such classification allows different analysis and improvement strategies to be applied to different groups of components.

☐ The components in the upper right-hand quadrant (indicated by stars) are the chronic problem components. The fact that these components sustained high defect rates in spite of years of aging on the System/38 platform implies that significant actions (such as examination of the design structure, a rewrite of error-prone modules, etc.) need to be considered.

☐ The components in the upper left-hand quadrant (denoted by triangles) are components with low defect rates on System/38 but high on AS/400. The improvement strategy should focus on the nature of the enhancements on AS/400 and the process the development teams used.

☐ Those in the lower right-hand quadrant (denoted by circles) are the components that had high defect rates on System/38 but low on AS/400. The changes made to these components for AS/400 and the actions taken during the AS/400 development should be examined to shed light for other components.

☐ In the lower left-hand quadrant (denoted by darkened circles) are components that have low defect rates in both platforms. The focus of analysis should be on their usage and if the usage is not low, on their design structure.

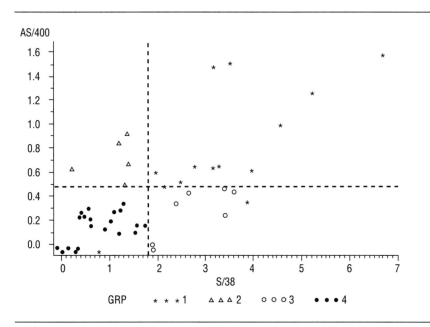

FIGURE 5.11

Grouping of Reused Components Based on Defect Rate Relationship

## 5.7 Control Chart

The control chart is a powerful tool for achieving statistical process control (SPC). However, in software development it is difficult to use control charts in the formal SPC manner. It is a formidable task, if not impossible, to attempt to define the process capability of a software development process. Process capability is the inherent variation of the process in relation to the specification limits. The smaller the process variation, the better the process's capability. Defective parts are parts that are produced with values of specified parameters outside the specification limits. Therefore, the smaller the process variations, the better the product quality.

In statistical terms, process capability is defined as:

$$C_p = \frac{|USL - LSL|}{6 \text{ sigma}}$$

where USL and LSL are the upper and lower engineering specification limits, respectively, sigma is the standard deviation of the process, and 6 sigma represents the overall process variation.

If a unilateral specification is affixed to some characteristics, the capability index may be defined as:

$$C_p = \frac{|USL - u|}{3 \text{ sigma}}$$

where $u$ is the process mean, or

$$C_p = \frac{|u - LSL|}{3 \text{ sigma}}$$

In manufacturing environments where many parts are produced daily, process variation and process capability can be calculated in statistical terms and control charts can be used on a real-time basis. Software differs from manufacturing in several aspects and such differences make it almost impossible to estimate the process capability of a software development organization.

- [ ] Specifications for most metrics defined are nonexistent or poorly related to real customer needs. Well-defined specifications based on customer requirements that can be expressed in terms of metrics are lacking for practically all software projects (more accurately, they are extremely difficult to derive).

- [ ] Software is development (not production) and it takes various phases of activity (architecture, design, code, test, and so forth) and a long time in order to complete one project.

&#9633;   Even with the same development process, differences in execution rigor result in different levels of quality.

&#9633;   Yet to be investigated are reliable models that can quantify the relationships between the various activities in each phase of the development to the end-product quality level.

&#9633;   Within a software development organization, multiple processes are often used.

&#9633;   Technology and development processes are fast changing.

Despite these issues, control charts are useful for software quality improvement—when they are used in a more relaxed manner. That means that control chart use in software is not in terms of formal statistical process control and process capability. Rather, they are used as a tool for improving consistency and stability. On many occasions, they are not used on a real-time basis and are more appropriately called pseudo-control charts.

There are many types of control charts. The most common are the X-bar and S charts for sample averages and standard deviation. There are also median charts, charts for individuals, the $p$ chart for proportion nonconforming, the $np$ chart for number nonconforming, the $c$ chart for number of nonconformities, the $u$ chart for nonconformities per unit, and so forth. The most approximate ones for software applications are the $p$ chart, when percentages are involved, and the $u$ chart, when defect rates are used. The control limits are calculated as the value of the parameter of interest (X-bar or $p$, for example) plus/minus three standard deviations. One can also increase the sensitivity of the chart by adding a pair of warning limits, which are calculated as the value of the parameter plus/minus two standard deviations. As the calculation of standard deviations differs among types of parameters, the formulas for control limits (and warning limits) also differ. For example, control limits for defect rates ($u$ chart) can be calculated as follows:

$$\text{Upper limit} = \mu + 3\sqrt{\frac{\mu}{n}}$$

$$\text{Lower limit} = \mu - 3\sqrt{\frac{\mu}{n}}$$

where $\mu$ is the cumulative defect rate from historical data (weighted average of defect rates) and $n$ is the average number of lines of source code.

Control limits for percentages (for example, effectiveness metric) can be calculated as follows:

$$\text{Upper limit} = p + 3\sqrt{\frac{p(1-p)}{n}}$$

$$\text{Lower limit} = p - 3\sqrt{\frac{p(1-p)}{n}}$$

where $p$ is the weighted average of percentages from historical data and $n$ is the average sample size.

Various metrics from the software development process can be control charted, for instance, inspection defects per KLOC, testing defects per KLOC, phase effectiveness, defect backlog management index (as discussed in Chapter 4), and so forth. Figure 5.12 shows an example of a pseudo-control chart on testing defects per KLOC by component for a project at IBM Rochester, from which error-prone components were identified for further in-depth analysis and actions. In this case, the use of the control chart involved more than one iteration. In the first iteration, components with defect rates outside the control limits (particularly high) were identified. (It should be noted that in this example the control chart is one-sided with only the upper control limit.) In the second iteration, the components that were previously identified were removed and the data were plotted again, with a new control limit (Figure 5.13). This process of "peeling the onion" permitted the identification of the next set of potentially defect-prone components, some of which may have been masked on the initial set of charts. This process can continue for a few iterations. Priority of improvement actions as they relate to available resources can also be determined based on the order of iteration in which problem components are identified (Craddock, 1988). At each iteration, the out-of-control points should only be removed from the analysis when their causes have been understood and prevented from recurring.

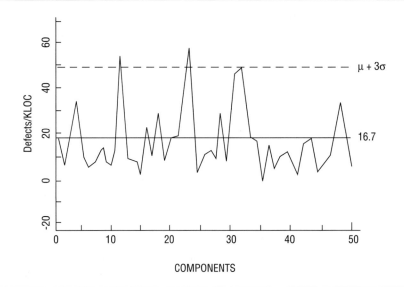

FIGURE 5.12
Pseudo-Control Chart of Test Defect Rate—First Iteration

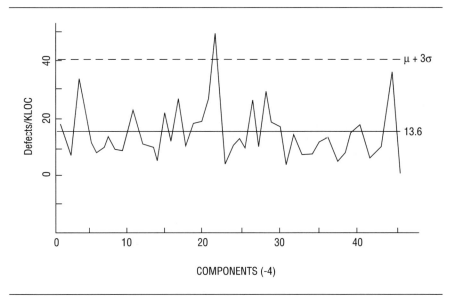

FIGURE 5.13
Pseudo-Control Chart of Test Defect Rate—Second Iteration

Another example, also from IBM Rochester, is charting inspection effectiveness by area for the several phases of reviews and inspections, as shown in Figure 5.14. Effectiveness is a relative measure in percentage, with the numerator being the number of defects removed in a development phase and the denominator the total number of defects found in that phase, plus defects found later. In the figure, each data point represents the inspection effectiveness of a second-line level development area. The four panels represent high-level design review (I0), low-level design review (I1), code inspection (I2), and overall effectiveness combining all three phases (lower right). Areas with low effectiveness (below the warning and control limits) as well as those with the highest effectiveness were studied and contributing factors identified. As a result of this control charting and subsequent work, the inspection effectiveness of the AS/400 development process was improved.

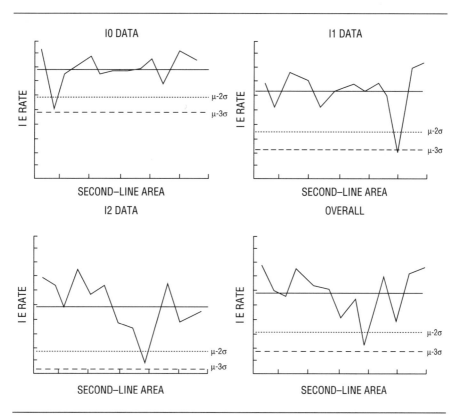

FIGURE 5.14
Pseudo-Control Chart of Inspection Effectiveness

## 5.8 Cause-And-Effect Diagram

The cause-and-effect diagram is perhaps the least used tool for software development. Among the several fishbone diagrams that we encountered, perhaps the best example is the one given by Grady and Caswell (1986) on a Hewlett-Packard project. The development team, in their quality improvement effort, first used a Pareto diagram and found that defects associated with register allocation were the most prevalent in their project. With the help of a cause-and-effect diagram, they then conducted brainstorming sessions on those problems. As Figure 5.15 shows, they found side effects of register usage and incorrect register usage to be the two primary causes. Ultimately both were caused by incomplete knowledge of the operation of the registers. With this finding, that HP division took aggressive steps to provide proper training and documentation regarding registers and processors prior to subsequent projects.

As another example, Figure 5.16 shows a fishbone diagram relating the key factors to effective inspections. Such a diagram was part of the process education material for a project with which we have had experience.

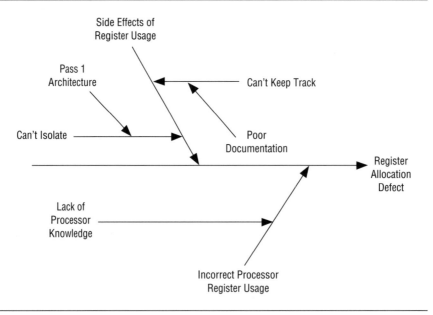

FIGURE 5.15

Cause-and-Effect Diagram

*(Source:* Grady, R. B., and D. L. Caswell, *Software Metrics: Establishing A Company-Wide Program,*
Englewood Cliffs, N.J.: Prentice-Hall, Inc., 1986, p. 127, Fig. 9–8. Copyright © Prentice-Hall with permission
to reprint.)

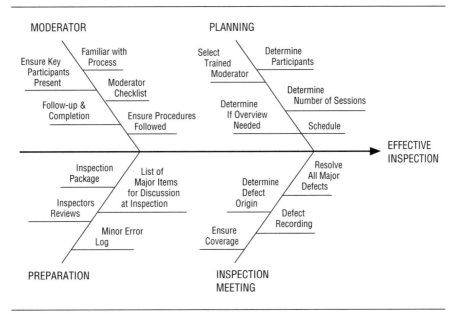

FIGURE 5.16
Cause-and-Effect Diagram of Design Inspection

## 5.9  Summary

In recent years, there has been an emerging trend in the software industry to use scientific methods to achieve precision in managing software projects. Many quality engineering and statistical tools that have been used widely in manufacturing are gaining acceptance in software development environments. In this chapter we discussed the possible applications of the seven basic tools with real-life examples. In many instances, analysis based on these tools has yielded significant effects on software process improvement.

The degree of application of individual tools varies. While some have been used extensively on a daily basis (such as the checklist and run chart), others are just now being recognized (such as the cause-and-effect diagram). The tools can be used together (with each other) or with other more advanced methods. For instance, the Pareto diagram, cause-and-effect diagram, and scatter diagram can be used together for identifying the dominant problems and their root causes. Control charts can be put in place to monitor process stability, or to determine whether improvements really occur after corrective actions are taken.

The seven basic tools indeed are basic tools. They may not be appealing from a researcher's standpoint. Their real value lies in the consistent and pervasive use by development teams for process improvement. Their impact can be enormous, especially when they are automated and become ingrained in the software development process, as demonstrated by the example of the automated fix checklist at IBM Rochester.

Finally, Ishikawa's seven basic tools in recent years are also called the seven old tools or the seven quality control tools. In recent years there emerged the seven new quality planning/management tools (which are mostly qualitative), which are the affinity diagram, the relations diagram, the tree diagram, the metric chart, the matrix data analysis chart, the process decision program chart (PDPC), and the arrow diagram. Although discussion of these seven new planning tools are not in the scope of this book, we would be remiss not to mention that they are also gaining usage in software engineering. For instance, a large software development company has automated these seven new tools in its CASE environment to facilitate the quality function deployment approach in software development (especially in gathering and verifying customers' requirements) and has gained positive experience (Rudisill, 1992).

## References

1. Bernstein, L., "Notes on Software Quality Management," presented at the *International Software Quality Exchange,* San Francisco, March 10–11, 1992, sponsored by the Juran Institute, Wilton, Conn.
2. Craddock, L. L., "Control Charting in Software Development," *Proceedings Sixth Annual Pacific Northwest Software Quality Conference,* Portland, Oregon, September 1988, pp. 53–70.
3. Daskalantonakis, M. K., "A Practical View of Software Measurement and Implementation Experiences within Motorola," *IEEE Transactions on Software Engineering,* Vol. SE-18, 1992, pp. 998–1010.
4. Grady, R. B., and D. L. Caswell, *Software Metrics: Establishing A Company-Wide Program,* Englewood Cliffs, N.J.: Prentice-Hall, 1986.
5. Ishikawa, Kaoru, *Guide to Quality Control,* White Plains, N.Y.: Quality Resource, 1971, 1989.
6. Kume, Hitoshi, *Statistical Methods for Quality Improvement,* Tokyo: The Association for Overseas Technical Scholarship, 1985, 1989.
7. Mays, R. G., C. L. Jones, G. J. Holloway, and D. P. Studinski, "Experiences with Defect Prevention," *IBM Systems Journal,* Vol. 29, No.1, February 1990, pp. 4–32.
8. Rudisill, D., "QCASE: A New Paradigm for Computer Aided Software Engineering," *International Software Quality Exchange 92 Conference Proceedings,* San Francisco, Calif., March 10–11, 1992, sponsored by the Juran Institute, Wilton, Conn., pp. 4A-19–4A-34.

# 6

# Defect Removal Effectiveness

The concept of defect removal effectiveness and its measurement are central to software development. Defect removal is one of the top expense elements in any software project and also affects project scheduling. Effective defect removal can lead to reductions in the development cycle time and good product quality. For improvements in quality, productivity, and cost, as well as schedule, it is important to utilize better defect prevention and defect removal technologies to maximize the effectiveness of the project. For any project and development organization, it is important to measure the effectiveness of their defect removal process.

In Chapter 4 we briefly touched on the metrics of defect removal effectiveness and fault containment. In this chapter we further elaborate on the concept, its measurements, and its use in the phase-based defect removal model. Before we begin, a point on terminology is in order. In the literature some writers use the terms *defect removal efficiency, error detection efficiency, fault containment, defect removal effectiveness*, and the like. In this book we prefer using the term *effectiveness* rather than *efficiency*. *Efficiency* implies the element of time, *effectiveness* is related to the extent of impact and we think the latter is more appropriate. In the following sections we may sometimes use the two terms interchangeably, especially when we have to refer to the definitions and metrics by other writers.

## 6.1 Literature Review

In the 1960s and before, when software development was simply "code and test" and software projects were characterized by cost overruns and schedule delays, the only defect removal step was test. In the 1970s, formal reviews and inspections were being recognized as important to productivity and product quality, and thus were adopted by development projects. As a result, defect removal within the development process strengthened. In his classic article on design and code inspections, Fagan (1976) touched on the concept of defect removal effectiveness. He defined error detection efficiency as:

$$\frac{\text{Errors found by an inspection}}{\text{Total errors in the product before inspection}} \times 100\%$$

In an example of a COBOL application program Fagan cited in his article, the total error detection efficiency for both design and code inspection was 82%. From our observation and experience, such a degree of efficiency was outstanding. Specifically, the project found 38 defects per KNCSS (thousand noncommentary source statements) via design and code inspections, and 8 defects per KNCSS via unit test and preparation for acceptance test. There were no defects found during acceptance test or in actual usage in a six-month period. From this example we know that defects found in the field (actual usage of the software) were also included in the denominator in Fagan's calculation of defect removal efficiency.

Intriguingly, the concept of defect removal effectiveness and its measurements were seldom discussed in the literature, as its importance merits, until the mid-1980s (Jones, 1986). Not surprisingly, Jones' definition, stated here, is very similar to Fagan's:

$$\text{Removal efficiency} = \frac{\text{Defects found by removal operation}}{\text{Defects present at removal operation}} \times 100\%$$

$$= \frac{\text{Defect found}}{\text{Defects found } + \text{Defects not found}} \times 100\%$$
$$\text{(found later)}$$

In Jones' definition, defects found in the field are also included in the denominator of the formula.

IBM's Federal Systems Division in Houston, Texas, develops mission-unique Space Shuttle flight software systems for the National Aeronautics and Space Administration (NASA) and is well known for its high product quality. The Space Shuttle is "fly-by-wire"; all of the astronaut's commands are sent from flight deck controls to the computers, which then send out electronic commands to execute a given function. There are five computers onboard the shuttle. The Primary Avionics Software System (onboard software) is responsible for vehicle guidance, navigation, flight control, and numerous systems management and monitoring functions, and also provides the interface from the vehicle to crew and ground communications systems. There are about 500,000 lines of source code in the onboard software. In addition, there are about 1.7 million lines of code for the ground software systems that are used to develop and configure the onboard system for shuttle missions (Kolkhorst and Macina, 1988).

IBM Houston has won many quality awards from NASA and from the IBM Corporation for its outstanding quality in the Space Shuttle flight systems. For example, it received the first NASA Excellence Award for Quality and Productivity in 1987 (Ryan, 1987), and in 1989 it won the first Best Software Laboratory Award from the IBM Corporation. Its shuttle onboard software (PASS) has achieved defect-free quality since 1985, and the defect rate for the support systems has been reduced to an extraordinarily low level. IBM Houston has taken several key approaches to improve its quality, and one of them is the focus on rigorous and formal inspections. Indeed, in addition to design and code inspection, the IBM Houston software development process also contains the phase of formal requirements analysis and inspection. The requirements, which are specified in precise terms and formulas, are much like the low-level design documents in commercial software. The rationale for the heavy focus on the front end of the process, of course, is to remove defects as early as possible in the software life cycle. Indeed, one of the four metrics they use to manage quality is the early detection percentage, which is actually inspection defect removal effectiveness. From Ryan (1987) and Kolkhorst and Macina (1988):

$$\text{Early detection percentage} = \frac{\text{Number of major inspection errors}}{\text{Total number of errors}} \times 100\%$$

where total number of errors is the sum of major inspection errors and valid discrepancy reports (discrepancy report is the mechanism for tracking test defects).

According to IBM Houston's definitions, a major inspection error is any error found in a design or code inspection that would have resulted in a valid discrepancy report (DR) if the error had been incorporated into the software. Philosophical differences, errors in comments or documentation, and software maintenance issues are some inspection errors that may be classified as minor and do not enter into this count. Valid DRs document that the code fails to meet the letter, intent, or operational need of the requirements. These DRs require a code fix, documented waiver, or user note to the customer.

From the preceding formula it appears that the denominator does not include defects from the field, when the software is being used by customers. In this case, however, it is more of a conceptual difference rather than a practical one because the number of field defects for the shuttle software systems is so small.

IBM Houston's data also substantiated a strong correlation between inspection defect removal effectiveness and product quality (Kolkhorst and Macina, 1988). For software releases from November 1982 to December 1986, the early detection percentages increased from about 50% to more than 85%. Correspondingly, the product defect rates decreased monotonically from 1984 to 1986 by about 70%. Figures 6.1 and 6.2 show the details.

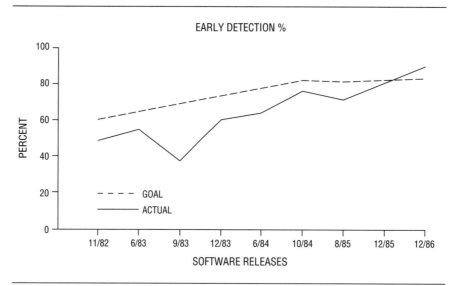

FIGURE 6.1
Early Detection of Software Errors

(*Source:* Kolkhorst, B. G., and A. J. Macina, "Developing Error-Free Software,"*IEEE AES Magazine,* November 1988, pp. 25–31, Fig. 4. Copyright © 1988 IEEE, with permission to reprint.)

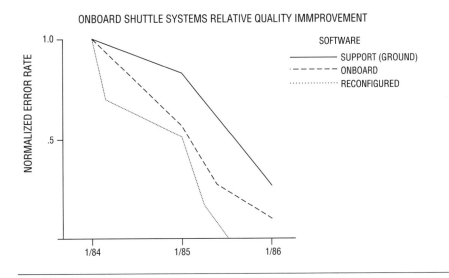

ONBOARD SHUTTLE SYSTEMS RELATIVE QUALITY IMMPROVEMENT

FIGURE 6.2
Relative Improvement of Software Types

(*Source:* Kolkhorst, B. G., and A. J. Macina, "Developing Error-Free Software," *IEEE AES Magazine,* November 1988, pp. 25–31, Fig. 5. Copyright © 1988 IEEE, with permission to reprint.)

The effectiveness measure by Dunn (1987) differs little from Fagan's and Jones' second definition. Specifically,

$$E = \frac{N}{N+S} \times 100\%$$

where

$E$ = effectiveness of activity (development phase)

$N$ = number of faults (defects) found by activity (phase)

$S$ = number of faults (defects) found by subsequent activities (phases).

According to Dunn (1987), this metric can be tuned by selecting only those defects present at the time of the activity and susceptible to detection by the activity.

More recently, Daskalantonakis (1992) described the metrics used at Motorola for software development. In Chapter 4 we gave a brief summary of those metrics. Two of the metrics are in fact for defect removal effectiveness: total defect containment effectiveness (TDCE) and phase containment effectiveness ($PCE_i$). For immediate reference, we restate the two metrics:

$$TDCE = \frac{\text{Number of prerelease defects}}{\text{Number of prerelease defects} + \text{Number of postrelease defects}}$$

$$PCE_i = \frac{\text{Number of phase } i \text{ errors}}{\text{Number of phase } i \text{ errors} + \text{Number of phase } i \text{ defects}}$$

where phase $i$ errors are problems found during that development phase in which they were introduced, and phase $i$ defects are problems found later than the development phase in which they were introduced.

The definitions and metrics of defect removal effectiveness just discussed differ little from one to another. However, there are some subtle differences that may cause confusion. Such differences are negligible if the calculation is for the overall effectiveness of the development process, or there is only one phase of inspection. However, if there are separate phases of activities and inspections before code integration and testing, which is usually the case in large-scale development, the differences could be quite significant. The reason is that when the inspection of an early phase (for example, high-level design inspection) took place, the defects from later phases of activities (for example, coding defects) could not have been injected into the product yet. Therefore, "defects present at removal operation" may be very different (less than) from "defects found plus defect found later or "$N + S$." In this regard Dunn's (1987) view on the fine tuning of the metric is to the point. Also, Motorola's $PCE_i$ could be quite different from others. In the next section we take a closer look at this metric.

## 6.2  A Closer Look at Defect Removal Effectiveness

To define defect removal effectiveness clearly, we must first understand the activities in the development process that are related to defect injections and to removals. Defects are injected into the product or intermediate deliverables of the product (for example, design document) at various phases. It is wrong to assume that all defects of software are injected at the beginning of development. Table 6.1 shows an example of the activities in which defects can be injected or removed for a development process.

| Development Phase | Defect Injection | Defect Removal |
|---|---|---|
| Requirements | Requirements gathering process and the development of programming functional specifications | Requirement analysis and review |
| High-level design | Design work | High-level design inspections |
| Low-level design | Design work | Low-level design inspections |
| Code implementation | Coding | Code inspections |
| Integration/build | Integration and build process | Build verification test |
| Unit test | Bad fixes | Testing itself |
| Component test | Bad fixes | Testing itself |
| System test | Bad fixes | Testing itself |

TABLE 6.1
Activities Associated with Defect Injection and Removal

For the development phases before testing, the development activities themselves are subject to defect injection, and the reviews or inspections at the end of the phase activities are the key vehicle for defect removal. For the testing phases, the testing itself is for defect removal. When the problems found by testing are fixed incorrectly, there is also a chance of defect injection. In fact, even for the inspection steps, there are chances for bad fixes. Figure 6.3 describes the detailed mechanics of defect injection and removal at each step of the development process. From the figure, defect removal effectiveness for each development step, therefore, can be defined as

$$\frac{\text{Defects removed (at the step)}}{\text{Defects existing on step entry} + \text{Defects injected during development (of the step)}} \times 100\%$$

This is the conceptual definition. Note that defects removed is equal to defects detected minus incorrect repairs. If an ideal data tracking system existed, all elements in Figure 6.3 could be tracked and analyzed. However, in reality, it is extremely difficult to reliably track incorrect repairs. Assuming the percentages of incorrect repair or bad fixes are not high (based on our experience), defects removed can be approximated by defects detected. From our experience with the AS/400, about 2% are bad fixes during testing so this assumption seems reasonable. If the bad-fix percentage is high, one may want to adjust the effectiveness metric accordingly, if an estimate is available.

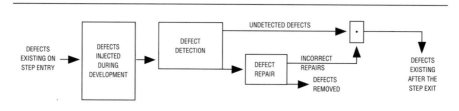

FIGURE 6.3
Defect Injection and Removal of a Process Step

To derive an operational definition, we propose a matrix approach by cross-classifying defect data in terms of the development phase in which the defects are found (and removed) and the phases in which the defects are injected. This requires that for each defect found, its origin (the phase where it was introduced) be decided by the inspection group (for inspection defects) or by agreement between the tester and the developer (for testing defects). Let us look at the example in Figure 6.4.

Once the defect matrix is established, calculations of various effectiveness measures are straightforward. The matrix is triangular because the origin of a defect is always at or prior to the current phase. In this example, there were no formal requirements inspections so we are not able to assess the effectiveness of the requirements phase. But in the requirements phase, defects can be injected that can be found later in the development cycle. Therefore, the requirements phase also appears in the matrix as one of the defect origins. The diagonal values for the testing phases represent the number of bad fixes. In this example all bad fixes are detected and fixed, again correctly, within the same phase. There are cases, however, where bad fixes may go undetected until subsequent phases.

| WHERE FOUND | DEFECT ORIGIN | | | | | | | | |
| --- | --- | --- | --- | --- | --- | --- | --- | --- | --- |
| | REQUIREMENTS | HIGH-LEVEL DESIGN | LOW-LEVEL DESIGN | CODE | UNIT TEST | COMPONENT TEST | SYSTEM TEST | FIELD | TOTAL |
| RQ | — | | | | | | | | — |
| I0 | 49 | 681 | | | | | | | 730 |
| I1 | 6 | 42 | 681 | | | | | | 729 |
| I2 | 12 | 28 | 114 | 941 | | | | | 1095 |
| UT | 21 | 43 | 43 | 223 | 2 | | | | 332 |
| CT | 20 | 41 | 61 | 261 | — | 4 | | | 387 |
| ST | 6 | 8 | 24 | 72 | — | — | 1 | | 111 |
| FIELD | 8 | 16 | 16 | 40 | — | — | — | 1 | 81 |
| TOTAL | 122 | 859 | 939 | 1537 | 2 | 4 | 1 | 1 | 3465 |

**FIGURE 6.4**
Defect Data Cross-Tabulated by Where Found (phase on which defect was found) and Defect Origin

Based on the conceptual definition given earlier, we calculate the various effectiveness metrics in the following.

*High-Level Design Inspection Effectiveness; IE (I0):*

Defects removed at I0: 730

Defects existing on step entry (escapes from requirements phase): 122

Defects injected in current phase: 859

$$\text{IE (I0)} = \frac{730}{122 + 859} \times 100\% = 74\%$$

*Low-Level Design Inspection Effectiveness; IE (I1):*

Defects removed at I1: 729

Defects existing on step entry (escapes from requirements phase and I0):
$122 + 859 - 730 = 251$

Defects injected in current phase: 939

$$IE\ (I1) = \frac{729}{251 + 939} \times 100\% = 61\%$$

*Code Inspection Effectiveness; IE (I2):*

Defects removed at I1: 1095

Defects existing on step entry (escapes from requirements phase, I0 and
I1): $122 + 859 + 939 - 730 - 729 = 461$

Defects injected in current phase: 1537

$$IE\ (I2) = \frac{1095}{461 + 1537} \times 100\% = 55\%$$

*Unit Test Effectiveness; TE (UT):*

Defects removed at I1: 332

Defects existing on step entry (escapes from all previous
phases): $122 + 859 + 939 + 1537 - 730 - 729 - 1095 = 903$

Defects injected in current phase (bad fixes): 2

$$TE\ (UT) = \frac{332}{903 + 2} \times 100\% = \frac{332}{905} \times 100\% = 37\%$$

For the testing phases, the defect injection (bad fixes) is usually a small number.
In such cases, effectiveness can be calculated by an alternate method (Dunn's formula or Jones' second formula as discussed earlier). In cases where the bad fixes rate
is high, the original method should be used.

Effectiveness =

$$\frac{\text{Defects removed at current phase}}{\text{Defects removed at current phase} + \text{Defects removed at subsequent phases}} \times 100\%$$

$$\text{TE (UT)} = \frac{332}{332 + 387 + 111 + 81} \times 100\% = \frac{332}{911} \times 100\% = 36\%$$

*Component Test Effectiveness; TE (CT):*

$$\text{TE (CT)} = \frac{387}{387 + 111 + 81} \times 100\% = 67\%$$

*System Test Effectiveness; TE (ST):*

$$\text{TE (ST)} = \frac{111}{111 + 81} \times 100\% = 58\%$$

*Overall Inspection Effectiveness; IE:*

$$\text{IE} = \frac{730 + 729 + 1095}{122 + 859 + 939 + 1537} \times 100\% = \frac{2554}{3457} \times 100\% = 74\%$$

or

$$\text{IE} = \frac{\text{Defects removed by inspections}}{\text{All defects}} \times 100\% = \frac{730 + 729 + 1095}{3465} \times 100\% = 74\%$$

*Overall Test Effectiveness; TE:*

$$\text{TE} = \frac{332 + 387 + 111}{332 + 387 + 111 + 81} \times 100\% = 91\%$$

*Overall Defect Removal Effectiveness of the Process; DRE:*

$$\text{DRE} = \left(1 - \frac{81}{3465}\right) \times 100\% = 97.7\%$$

From the matrix of Figure 6.4 it is easy to understand that the $PCE_i$ used by Motorola is somewhat different from phase defect removal effectiveness. $PCE_i$ refers to the ability of the phase inspection to remove defects that were introduced during a particular phase, whereas phase defect removal effectiveness as discussed here references the overall ability of the phase inspection to remove defects that were present at that time. The latter includes the defects that were introduced at that particular phase as well as defects that escaped from previous phases. Let us look at the $PCE_i$ values of our example.

        I0:     681/859 = 79%

        I1:     681/939 = 73%

        I2:     941/1537 = 61%

        UT:   2/2 = 100%

        CT:   4/4 = 100%

        ST:   1/1 = 100%

Assume further that the data in Figure 6.4 are the defect data for a new project with 100,000 lines of source code (100 KLOC). Then we can calculate a few more interesting metrics such as the product defect rate, the phase defect removal rates, phase defect injection rates, the percent distribution of defect injection by phase, and phase-to-phase defect escapes. For instance, the product defect rate is 81/100 KLOC = 0.81 defects per KLOC in the field (for four years of customer usage). The phase defect removal and injection rates are shown in Table 6.2

Having gone through the numerical example, we can now formally define the operational definition of defect removal effectiveness. The definition requires information of all defect data (including field defects) in terms of both defect origin and at which stage the defect is found and removed. The definition is based on the defect origin/where found matrix.

        Let $j = 1, 2, \ldots, k$ denote the phases of software life cycle.

        Let $i = 1, 2, \ldots, k$ denote the inspection or testing types associated with the life-cycle phases including the maintenance phase (phase $k$).

| Phase | Defects/KLOC (removal) | Defect Injection per KLOC | Total Defect Injection (%) |
|---|---|---|---|
| Requirements | — | 1.2 | 3.5 |
| High-level design | 7.3 | 8.6 | 24.9 |
| Low-level design | 7.3 | 9.4 | 27.2 |
| Code | 11.0 | 15.4 | 44.5 |
| Unit test | 3.3 | — | |
| Component test | 3.9 | — | |
| System test | 1.1 | — | |
| Total | 33.9 | 34.6 | 100.1 |

TABLE 6.2
Phase Defect Removal and Injection Rates from Figure 6.3.

Then matrix M (Figure 6.5) is the defect origin/where found matrix. In the matrix, only cells $N_{ij}$, where $i \geq j$ (cells at the lower left-hand triangle), contain data. Cells on the diagonal ($N_{ij}$ where $i = j$) contain the numbers of defects that were injected and detected at the same phase; cells below the diagonal ($N_{ij}$ where $i > j$) contain the numbers of defects that originate in earlier development phases and were detected later. Cells above the diagonal are empty because it is not possible for an earlier development phase to detect defects that are originated in a later phase. The row marginals ($N_{i.}$) of the matrix are defects by removal activity, whereas the column marginals ($N_{.j}$) are defects by origin.

*Phase defect removal effectiveness ($PDRE_i$) can be phase inspection effectiveness [IE(i)] or phase test effectiveness [TE(i)]:*

$$PDE_i = \frac{N_{i.}}{\sum_{m=1}^{i} N_{.m} - \sum_{m=1}^{i-1} N_{m.}}$$

*Phase defect containment effectiveness ($PDCE_i$):*

$$PDCE_i = \frac{N_{ii}}{N_{.i}}$$

DEFECT ORIGIN

| | | $j=1$ | $j=2$ | $j=3$ | $\ast$ | $\ast$ | $\ast$ | $\ast$ | $j=k$ | |
|---|---|---|---|---|---|---|---|---|---|---|
| | $i=1$ | $N_{11}$ | | | | | | | | $N_{1.}$ |
| | $i=2$ | $\ast$ | $N_{22}$ | | | | | | | $N_{2.}$ |
| | $i=3$ | $\ast$ | $\ast$ | $N_{33}$ | | | | | | $N_{3.}$ |
| WHERE FOUND | $\ast$ | $\ast$ | $\ast$ | $\ast$ | $\ast$ | | | | | . |
| | $\ast$ | $N_{ij}$ $(i>=j)$ | $\ast$ | $\ast$ | $\ast$ | $\ast$ | | | | $N_{i.}$ |
| | $\ast$ | $\ast$ | $\ast$ | $\ast$ | $\ast$ | $\ast$ | $N_{ij}$ $(i=j)$ | | | . |
| | $\ast$ | $\ast$ | $\ast$ | $\ast$ | $\ast$ | $\ast$ | $\ast$ | $\ast$ | | . |
| | $i=k$ | $\ast$ | $\ast$ | $\ast$ | $\ast$ | $\ast$ | $\ast$ | $\ast$ | $N_{kk}$ | $N_{K.}$ |
| | | $N\ast 1$ | $N\ast 2$ | $N\ast 3$ | $\ast$ | $\ast$ | $N\ast j$ | $\ast$ | $N\ast k$ | N-GRAND TOTAL |

FIGURE 6.5
Defect Origin/Where Found Matrix

*Overall inspection effectiveness (IE):*

$$IE = \frac{\sum_{i=1}^{I} N_{i.}}{\sum_{i=1}^{k} N_{i.} = N}$$

where I is the number of inspection phases.

*Overall test effectiveness (TE):*

$$TE = \frac{\sum_{i=I+1}^{k-1} N_{i.}}{\sum_{i=I+1}^{k} N_{i.}}$$

where $I+1, I+2, \ldots, k-1$ are the testing phases.

*Overall defect removal effectiveness (DRE) of the development process:*

$$\text{DRE} = \frac{\sum_{i=1}^{k-1} N_{i.}}{N}$$

## 6.3 Defect Removal Effectiveness and Quality Planning

Phase defect removal effectiveness and other related metrics associated with effectiveness analyses (such as defect removal and defect injection rates) are useful for quality planning and quality management. These measurements give a clear indication regarding which phase of the development process we should focus on for improvement (for example, unit test in our example in Figure 6.4). Effectiveness analyses can be done for the entire project as well as for local areas, such as at the component level or for specific departments within an organization, and the control chart technique can be used to enforce consistent improvement across the board (for example, Figure 5.14 in Chapter 5). Longitudinal release-to-release monitoring of these metrics can give a good feel for the process capability of the development organization. In addition, experiences from previous releases provide the basis for phase-specific target setting and for quality planning.

### 6.3.1 Phase-Based Defect Removal Model (DRM)

The phase-based defect removal model summarizes the interrelations among three metrics—defect injection, defect removal, and effectiveness. It takes a set of error-injection rates and a set of phase-effectiveness rates as input, then models the defect removal pattern step by step. It takes a simplified view of Figure 6.3 and works like this:

> Defects at the exit of a development setup
> = Defects escaped from previous setup
> + Defects injected in current setup
> − Defects removed in current setup

| Phase | (A) Defect Escaped From Previous Phase (per KLOC) | (B) Defect Injection (per KLOC) | Subtotal (A+B) | Removal Effective- ness | Defect Removal (per KLOC) | Defects at Exit of Phase (per KLOC) |
|---|---|---|---|---|---|---|
| Require- ments | — | 1.2 | 1.2 | — | — | 1.2 |
| High-level design | 1.2 | 8.6 | 9.8 × | 74% = | 7.3 | 2.5 |
| Low-level design | 2.5 | 9.4 | 11.9 × | 61% = | 7.3 | 4.6 |
| Code | 4.6 | 15.4 | 20.0 × | 55% = | 11.0 | 9.0 |
| Unit test | 9.0 | — | 9.0 × | 36% = | 3.2 | 5.8 |
| Component test | 5.8 | — | 5.8 × | 67% = | 3.9 | 1.9 |
| System test | 1.9 | — | 1.9 × | 58% = | 1.1 | 0.8 |
| Field | 0.8 | | | | | |

TABLE 6.3

Example of Phase-Based Defect Removal Model

For example, the metrics derived from data in Figure 6.4 can be modeled step by step as shown in Table 6.3.

Now if we are planning for the quality of a new release, we can modify the values of the parameters based on the set of improvement actions that we are going to take. If we plan to improve the effectiveness of I2 and unit test by 5%, how much can we expect to gain in the final product quality? What are the new targets for defect rates for each phase (before the development team exits the phase)? If we invest in a defect prevention process and in an intensive program of technical education and plan to reduce the error injection rate by 10%, how much could we gain? Approximate answers to questions like these could be obtained through the DRM, given that the DRM is developed from pre- vious experience of the organization with similar development processes.

Be aware that the DRM is a quality management tool, not a device for software reliability estimation. Unlike the other parametric models that we will discuss in later chapters, the DRM cannot reliably estimate the product quality level. It cannot do so because the error injection rates may vary from case to case even for the same development team. The rationale behind this model is that if one can ensure that the defect-removal pattern by phase is similar to one's experience, one can reasonably expect that the quality of the current project should be similar.

### 6.3.2  Some Characteristics of a Special Case Two-Phase Model

Remus and Zilles (1979) elaborated the mathematical relationships among defect removal effectiveness, the number of defects found during the front end of the development process (before the code is integrated), the number found during testing, and the number remaining when the product is ready to ship to customers. They derived some interesting characteristics of the defect removal model in a special case:

1.  There are only two phases of defect removal.
2.  The defect removal effectiveness for the two phases is the same.

In the Remus and Zilles model, the percentage of bad fixes is also included as one of the parameters; the derivation involves twenty-some formulas. Here we take a simplified approach without taking bad fixes into account. Interestingly, despite taking a different approach, we arrived at the same conclusion as Remus and Zilles'.

Assume there are two broad phases of defect removal activities:

1.  Those activities handled directly by the development team (design reviews, code inspections, unit test)—for large software projects, such activities take place before the code is integrated into the system library.
2.  The formal machine tests after code integration.

Further assume that the defect removal effectiveness for the two broad phases is the same. Define:

MP = Major problems found during reviews/inspections and unit test (from phase 1); these are the problems that if not fixed, will result in testing defects or defects in the field.

PTR = Problem tracking report after code integration: errors found during formal machine tests.

$\mu$   = MP/PTR, $\mu > 1$ (*Note:* The higher the value of $\mu$, the more effective the front end.)

$Q$   = Number of defects in the released software, i.e., defects found in the field (customer usage).

TD  = Total defects for the entire life of the software = MP + PTR + $Q$.

By definition of effectiveness:

$$\text{Phase 1 effectiveness E1} = \frac{MP}{TD}$$
$$\text{therefore} : MP = E1 \times TD \quad (6.1)$$

$$\text{Phase 2 effectiveness E2} = \frac{PTR}{TD - MP}$$
$$\text{therefore: } PTR = E2 \times (TD - MP) \quad (6.2)$$

By the assumption that the two phases have the same effectiveness:

$$E1 = E2$$
$$\frac{MP}{TD} = \frac{PTR}{TD - MP}$$

Thus,

$$PTR = \frac{(TD - MP) \times MP}{TD} \quad (6.3)$$

Then,

$$Q = TD\,(1 - E1)\,(1 - E2)$$
$$TD\,(1 - E1)^2$$

$$= TD\left(1 - \frac{MP}{TD}\right)^2$$

$$= \frac{TD^2 - 2\,TD\,MP + MP^2}{TD}$$

$$= (TD - MP)\frac{(TD - MP)}{TD}$$

$$= (TD - MP)\frac{(TD - MP) \times MP}{TD} \times \frac{1}{MP}$$

$$= (TD - MP) \times PTR \times \frac{1}{MP} \quad \left[\text{from Eq. } (6.3)\right]$$

$$= \frac{1}{\mu} \times (TD - MP)$$

$$= \frac{1}{\mu} \times (Q + MP + PTR - MP)$$

$$= \frac{1}{\mu} \times (Q + PTR)$$

Therefore,

$$Q = \frac{PTR}{\mu - 1} \quad (6.4)$$

By the same token, it can be shown that:

$$Q = \frac{MP}{\mu(\mu - 1)} \quad (6.5)$$

Furthermore, from the definition of $\mu$:

$$\mu = \frac{MP}{PTR}$$

$$= \frac{E1 \times TD}{E2 \times (TD - MP)}$$

$$= \frac{TD}{TD - MP} \quad [E1 = E2]$$

$$= \frac{TD}{PTR + Q} \begin{bmatrix} TD = MP + PTR + Q \\ TD - MP = PTR + Q \end{bmatrix}$$

$$\mu(PTR + Q) = TD$$

$$\mu(Q\mu - Q + Q) = TD \quad [\text{from Eq. (6.4), } PTR = Qu - Q]$$

Therefore,

$$Q = TD/\mu^2 \quad (6.6)$$

Equations (6.4) to (6.6) can be quite useful for quality planning. The equations can be applied to absolute numbers as well as normalized rates (e.g., defects per KLOC). Given the number of MP and $\mu$, or PTR and $\mu$, one can estimate the number of defects remained in the product by Eqs. (6.4) and (6.5). Also, assuming we use the lifetime defect rate (TD) of a predecessor product to approximate that of the current product being developed, given a target product quality level to shoot for, Eq.(6.6) can determine the value of $\mu$ that we need to achieve in order to reach the target. Choosing a specific value of $\mu$ determines how much focus a project should have on front-end defect removal. Once the $\mu$ target is set, the team can determine what specific defect removal techniques to use (for example, formal inspection, function verification by owner, team verifications, rigorous unit testing, etc.). For example, if we use the data from the example of Figure 6.4 (TD = 34.6 defects/KLOC, $Q$ = 0.81 defects/KLOC for life of customer use), then the value of $\mu$ should be:

$$0.81 = 34.6/\mu^2$$
$$\mu^2 = 34.6/0.81 = 42.7$$
$$\mu = 6.5$$

This means that if the effectiveness is the same for the two phases, then the number of defects to be removed by the first phase must be at least 6.5 times of the number to be removed by testing in order to achieve the quality target.

Note that the equations described in this section are only valid under the assumptions stated. They cannot be generalized. Although Eqs. (6.4) and (6.5) can be used to estimate product quality, this special case DRM is still not a projection model. The equal effectiveness assumption cannot be verified until the product defect rate $Q$ is known or estimated via an independent method. If this assumption is violated, the results will not be valid.

## 6.4  Cost Effectiveness of Phase Defect Removal

In addition to the defect removal effectiveness by phase *per se,* the cost aspect of defect removal must be considered for efficient quality planning. Defect removal at earlier development phases is generally less expensive. The closer the defects are found relative to where and when they are injected, the less the removal and rework effort. Fagan (1976) contended that rework done at the I0, I1, and I2 inspection levels can be 10 to 100 times less expensive than if it is done in the last half of the process (formal testing phases after code integration). According to Freedman and Weinberg (1982, 1984), in large systems, reviews can reduce the number of errors reaching the testing phases by a factor of 10, and such reductions cut testing costs by 50% to 80% including review costs. Remus (1983) studied the cost of defect removal during the three major life-cycle phases of design and code inspection, testing, and customer use (maintenance phase) based on data from IBM's Santa Teresa (California) Laboratory. He found the cost ratio for the three phases to be 1 to 20 to 82. In 1989, based on sample data from IBM Rochester, we found the defect removal ratio for the three phases for the AS/400 similar to Remus', at 1 to 13 to 92. *Caution:* These numbers may not be interpreted straightforwardly because defects that escaped to the formal testing phases and to the field are more difficult to find. When we invest and improve the front-end process to catch (or better yet to prevent) these more difficult defects, the ratio may decrease. Nonetheless, as long as the marginal costs of additional front-end defect removal remains less than testing and field maintenance, additional investment in the front end is warranted.

Our sample study also revealed interesting but understandable findings. The cost of defect removal is slightly higher for I0 inspection than for I1 and I2 (Figure 6.6). The main reason for this is that external interfaces are being impacted and more personnel are involved in the I0 inspection meetings. The cost for creating and answering a problem trouble report during test (i.e., problem determination cost) is correlated with the testing phase, defect origin, and defect severity (1 being the most severe and 4 the least) (Figure 6.7).

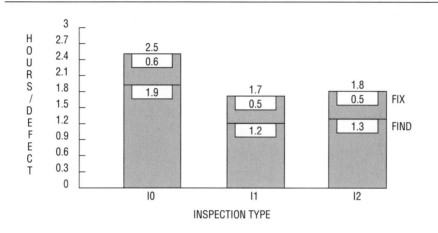

FIGURE 6.6
Cost of Defect Removal by Inspection Phase

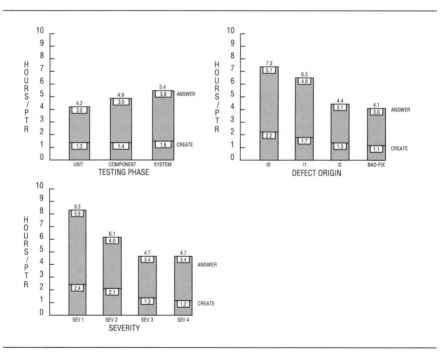

FIGURE 6.7
Cost of Creating and Answering a Problem Trouble Report by Several Variables

Although front-end defect removal activities in the form of reviews, walk-throughs, and inspections are less expensive than testing, in general practice, these methods are not rigorous enough. Fagan's inspection method is a combination of a formal review, an inspection, and a walkthrough. It consists of five steps: overview (for communications and education), preparation (for education), inspection (to find errors and to walk through every line of code), rework (to fix errors), and follow-up (to ensure all fixes are applied correctly). Such a combination has made Fagan's method somewhat more formal and therefore more effective than previous methods. The Active Design Reviews method, introduced by Parnas and Weiss (1985), represents an important advance. The approach involves conducting several different, brief reviews rather than one large review, thereby avoiding many of the difficulties of conventional reviews. More recently, Knight and Myers (1991) proposed the phased inspection method to improve the rigor of the process. It consists of a series of coordinated partial inspections called phases (therefore, the term is used differently). Each phase is designed to achieve a desirable property in the product (for example, portability, reusability, or maintainability), and the responsibilities of each inspector are specified and tracked. Knight and Myers defined two different types of phases. The first type, referred to as a single-inspector phase, is a rigidly formatted process driven by a list of unambiguous checks, for examples, internal documentation, source code layout, source code readability, programming practices, and local semantics. The second type of phase, designed to check for those properties of the software that cannot be captured in a precise yes or no statement (such as functionality and freedom from defects), is called the *multi-inspector* phase. Multiple personnel conduct independent examinations and then compare findings to reach reconciliation. To facilitate and enforce the process, the phased inspection method also involves the use of an on-line computer tool. The tool contains navigation facilities for displaying the work product, documentation display facilities, facilities for the inspector to record his/her comments, and facilities to enforce the inspection process.

Improvements such as the preceding offer organizations much promise for improving the front-end defect removal effectiveness. Beyond reviews and inspections, one can even adopt formal methods such as the Cleanroom functional verification (as discussed in Chapter 2).

---

## 6.5 Summary

Effective defect removal during the development process is central to the success of a software project. Despite the fact that variations exist in terms of terminology and operational definition (error detection efficiency, removal efficiency, early detection percentage, phase defect removal effectiveness, phase defect containment effectiveness, etc.), the importance of the concept of defect removal effectiveness and its measurement is well recognized. Literature and industry examples substantiate the hypothesis that effective front-end defect removal leads to improved quality of the end product. The relative cost of front-end defect removal is much lower compared to formal testing at the back end and the maintenance phase when the product is in the field.

To measure phase defect removal effectiveness, it is best to use the matrix approach in which the defect data are cross-tabulated in terms of defect origin and the phase in which the defects are found. Such an approach permits the estimation of phase defect injection and phase defect removal. In general, the shorter the time between defect origin and when the defect is found, the more effective and the less expensive the development process will become. The special case of the two-phase defect removal model even provides a linkage between the relative effectiveness of front-end defect removal and the estimated outcome of the quality of the product.

In quality planning it is important that, in addition to the final quality goals, factors such as the defect model, the phase defect removal targets, the process and specific methods used, the possible effectiveness of the methods, and so forth be examined. Inclusion of these factors in early planning enhances achievement of the software's quality goals.

It should be cautioned that defect removal effectiveness and defect removal models are useful quality planning and management tools. However, they are not equipped for quality or reliability projections; they are not predictive models. In the next several chapters, we discuss the parametric models that were developed to perform such tasks.

## References

1. Daskalanatonakis, M.K., "A Practical View of Software Measurement and Implementation Experiences within Motorola," *IEEE Transactions on Software Engineering,* Vol SE-18, 1992, pp. 998–1010.

2. Dunn, R. H., "The Quest for Software Reliability," *Handbook of Software Quality Assurance,* G. G. Schulmeyer and J. I. McManus, Eds., New York: Van Nostrand Reinhold, 1987, pp. 342–384.

3. Fagan, M. E., "Design and Code Inspections to Reduce Errors in Program Development," *IBM Systems Journal,* Vol. 15, No. 3, 1976, pp. 182–211.

4. Freedman, D. P., and G. M. Weinberg, *Handbook of Walkthroughs, Inspections, and Technical Reviews,* Boston, Mass.: Little, Brown and Company, 1982.

5. Freedman, D. P., and G. M. Weinberg, "Reviews, Walkthroughs, and Inspections," *IEEE Transactions on Software Engineering,* Vol. SE-10, No. 1, January 1984, pp. 68–72.

6. Jones, C., *Programming Productivity,* New York: McGraw-Hill, 1986.

7. Knight, K. C., and E. A. Myers, "Phased Inspections and Their Implementation," *ACM SIGSOFT Software Engineering Notes,* Vol. 16, No. 3, July 1991, pp. 29–35.

8. Kolkhorst, B. G., and A. J. Macina, "Developing Error-Free Software," *IEEE AES Magazine,* November 1988, pp. 25–31.

9. Parnas, D. W., and D. M. Weiss, "Active Design Reviews: Principles and Practices," *Proceedings of Eighth International Conference on Software Engineering,* London, England, IEEE Computer Society, August 1985.

10. Remus, H., "Integrated Software Validation in the View of Inspections/Review," *Proceedings of the Symposium on Software Validation,* Darmstadt, Germany, Amsterdam: North Holland, 1983, pp. 57–64.

11. Remus, H., and S. Zilles, "Prediction and Management of Program Quality," *Proceedings of the Fourth International Conference on Software Engineering,* Munich, IEEE Computer Society, 1979, pp. 341–350.

12. Ryan, J., "This Company Hates Surprises: The IBM Federal Systems Division Leaves No Stone Unturned in Its Quest to Produce Error-Free Software for NASA's Space Shuttle," *Quality Progress,* September 1987, pp. 12–16.

# 7

## The Rayleigh Model

Following on our discussions on defect removal effectiveness and the phase-based defect removal model, this chapter discusses a formal model of software reliability: the Rayleigh model. The Rayleigh model is a formal parametric model in the sense that it is based on a specific statistical distribution. When the parameters of the statistical distribution are estimated based on the data from a software project, projections about the defect rate of the project can be made based on the model.

### 7.1 Reliability Models

Software reliability models are used to estimate the reliability or the number of latent defects of the software product when it is available to the customers. Such an estimate is important for two reasons: (1) as an objective statement of the quality of the product and (2) for resource planning for the software maintenance phase. The criteria variable under study is the number of defects (or defect rate normalized to lines of code) in specified time intervals (weeks, months, etc.), or the *time between failures*. Reliability models can be broadly classified into two categories: static models and dynamic models (Conte *et al.,* 1986). A static model uses other attributes of the

project or program modules to estimate the number of defects in the software. A
dynamic model, usually based on statistical distributions, uses the current development defect patterns to estimate end-product reliability. A static model of software
quality estimation has the following general form:

$$y = f(x_1, x_2, \ldots, x_k) + e$$

where the dependent variable $y$ is the defect rate or the number of defects, and the independent variables $x_i$ are the attributes of the product, the project, or the process through
which the product is developed. They could be size (lines of code), complexity, skill
level, count of decisions, and other meaningful measurements. The error term is $e$
(because models don't completely explain the behavior of the dependent variable).

Coefficients of the independent variables in the formula are estimated based on
data from previous products. For the current product or project, the values of the
independent variables are measured, then plugged into the formula to derive estimates of the dependent variable—the product defect rate or number of defects.

Static models are static in the sense that the coefficients of their parameters
are estimated based on a number of previous projects. The product or project of
interest is treated as an additional observation in the same population of previous
projects. In contrast, the parameters of the dynamic models are estimated based
on multiple data points gathered to date from the product of interest; therefore,
the resulting model is specific to the product for which the projection of reliability is attempted.

From our observation and experience, static models are generally less superior
than dynamic models when the unit of analysis is at the product level and the purpose is to estimate product-level reliability. Such modeling is better for hypothesis
testing (to show that certain project attributes are related to better quality or reliability) than for estimation of reliability. When the unit of analysis is much more granular, such as at the program module level, the static models can be powerful—not for
product-level reliability estimates, but for providing clues to software engineers on
how to improve the quality of their design and implementation. The complexity metrics and models are good examples of this type of modeling, and in Chapter 10 we
discuss this topic in more detail.

Dynamic software reliability models, in turn, can be classified into two categories: those that model the entire development process and those that model the
back-end formal testing phase. The former is represented by the Rayleigh model.
The latter is represented by the exponential model and other reliability growth models, which are the subject of Chapter 8. A common denominator of dynamic models

is that they are all expressed as a function of time in development or its logical equivalent (such as development phase).

---

## 7.2  The Rayleigh Model

The Rayleigh model is a member of the family of the Weibull distribution. The Weibull distribution has been used for decades for reliability analysis in various fields of engineering, ranging from the fatigue life of deep-groove ball bearings to electron tube failures and the overflow incidence of rivers. It is one of the three known extreme-value distributions (Tobias, 1986). One of its marked characteristics is that the tail of its probability density function approaches zero asymptotically, but never reaches it. Its cumulative distribution function (CDF) and probability density function (PDF) are:

$$\text{CDF}: \ F(t) = 1 - e^{-(t/c)^m}$$

$$\text{PDF}: \ f(t) = \frac{m}{t}\left(\frac{t}{c}\right)^m e^{-(t/c)^m}$$

where $m$ is the shape parameter, $c$ is the scale parameter, and $t$ is time. When applied to software, the PDF often means the defect density (rate) over time or the defect arrival pattern (valid defects) and the CDF means the cumulative defect arrival pattern.

Figure 7.1 shows several Weibull probability density curves with varying values for the shape parameter $m$. For reliability applications in an engineering field, the choice of a specific model is not arbitrary. The underlying assumptions must be considered and the model must be supported by empirical data. Of the Weibull family, the two models that have seen applications in software reliability are the models with the shape parameter value $m = 2$ and $m = 1$.

The Rayleigh model is a special case of the Weibull distribution when $m = 2$. Its CDF and PDF are:

$$\text{CDF}: \ F(t) = 1 - e^{-(t/c)^2}$$

$$\text{PDF}: \ f(t) = \frac{2}{t}\left(\frac{t}{c}\right)^2 e^{-(t/c)^2}$$

The Rayleigh PDF first increases to a peak and then decreases at a decelerating rate. The $c$ parameter is a function of $t_m$, the time at which the curve reaches its peak. By taking the derivative of $f(t)$ with respect to $t$, setting it to zero and solving the equation, $t_m$ can be obtained.

$$t_m = \frac{c}{\sqrt{2}}$$

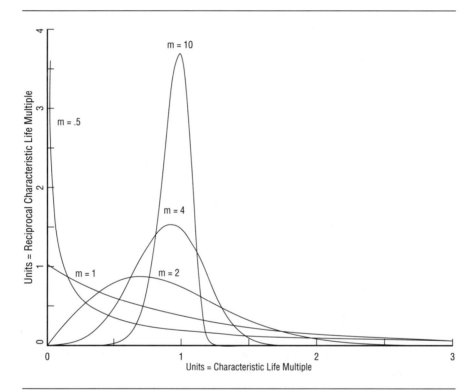

FIGURE 7.1
Weibull Probability Density

After $t_m$ is estimated, the shape of the entire curve can be determined. The area below the curve up to $t_m$ is 39.35% of the total area.

    The preceding formulas represent a standard distribution; specifically the total area under the PDF curve is 1. In actual applications, a constant $K$ is multiplied to the formulas ($K$ is the total number of defects or the total cumulative defect rate). If we also substitute

$$c = t_m \sqrt{2}$$

in the formulas, we get the following. To specify a model from a set of data points, $K$ and $t_m$ are the parameters that need to be estimated.

$$F(t) = K\left[1 - e^{-(1/2t^2_m)t^2}\right]$$

$$f(t) = K\left[\left(\frac{1}{t_m}\right)^2 t\, e^{-(1/2t^2_m)t^2}\right]$$

It has been empirically well established that software projects follow a life-cycle pattern described by the Rayleigh density curve (Norden, 1963; Putnam, 1978). Early applications of the model in software were mainly for staffing estimation over time for the life cycle of software projects. More recent work demonstrated that the defect removal pattern of software projects also follows the Rayleigh pattern. In 1982 Trachtenberg (1982) examined the month-by-month error histories of software projects and found that the composite error pattern of those projects resembled a Rayleigh-like curve. In 1984 Gaffney of the IBM Federal Systems Division reported the development of a model based on defect counts at six phases of the development process commonly used in IBM: high-level design inspections, low-level design inspections, code inspections, unit test, integration test, and system test. Gaffney observed that the defect pattern of his data by the six-phase development process followed a Rayleigh curve. Following the system test phase is the phase of field use (customer use). The number of latent defects in the field is the target for estimation. By developing a Rayleigh model to fit his data, Gaffney was able to project the expected latent defects in the field. In Putnam's recent work, the application of the Rayleigh model in estimating the number of software defects is included—in addition to his well-known work on software size and resource estimation (Putnam and Myers, 1992). By validating the model with systems for which defect data are available (including the Space Shuttle development and radar development projects), Putnam and Myers (1992) found that the total actual defects were within 5% to 10% of the defects predicted from the model. Data fits of a few other systems, for which the validity of the data is doubtful, however, were not as good. As in Trachtenberg's study, the time unit for the Rayleigh model in Putnam and Myers' application is expressed in terms of months from the project start.

Figure 7.2 shows an example of a Rayleigh curve that models the defect removal pattern of an IBM AS/400 product in relation to a six-step development process, which is very similar to that used used by Gaffney. Given the defect removal pattern up through ST, the purpose is to estimate the defect rate when the product is shipped: the post general-availability phase (GA) in the figure. In this example the

*X*-axis is the development phase, which can be regarded as one form of logical equivalent of time.

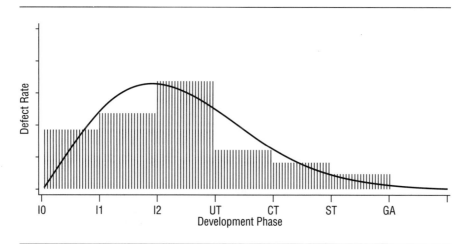

FIGURE 7.2
Rayleigh Model

## 7.3  Basic Assumptions

Using the Rayleigh curve to model software development quality involves two basic assumptions. The first assumption is that the defect rate observed during the development process is positively correlated with the defect rate in the field, as illustrated in Figure 7.3. In other words, the higher the curve (more area under it), the higher the field defect rate (the GA phase in the figure), and vice versa. This is related to the concept of error injection. Assuming the defect removal effectiveness remains relatively unchanged, the higher defect rates observed during the development process are indicative of higher error injection; therefore, it is likely that the field defect rate will also be higher.

The second assumption is that given the same error injection rate, if more defects are discovered and removed earlier, fewer will remain in later stages. As a result, the field quality will be better. This relationship is illustrated in Figure 7.4, in which the areas under the curves are the same but the curves peak at varying points. Curves that peak earlier have smaller areas at the tail, the GA phase.

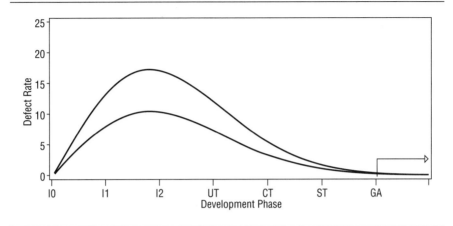

FIGURE 7.3
Rayleigh Model Illustration I

Both assumptions just stated are closely related to the "Do it right the first time" principle. This principle means that if each step of the development process is executed properly with minimum errors being injected, the end-product quality will be good. It also implies that if errors are injected, they should be removed as early as possible—preferably before the formal testing phases when the costs of finding and fixing the defects are much higher than that at the front end.

To formally examine the assumptions, we conducted a hypothesis-testing study based on component data for an AS/400 product. A *component* is a group of modules that perform specific functions such as spooling, printing, message handling, file handling, and so forth. The product we used had 65 components, so we had a good-sized sample. Defect data at high-level design inspection (I0), low-level design inspection (I1), code inspection (I2), component test (CT), system test (ST), and operation (customer usage) were available. For the first assumption, we expect significant positive correlations between the in-process defect rates and the field defect rate. Because software data sets are rarely normally distributed, robust statistics need to be used. In our case, because the component defect rates fluctuated widely, we decided to use Spearman's rank-order correlation. We could not use the Pearson correlation because correlation analysis based on interval data, and regression analysis for that matter, is very sensitive to extreme values, which may lead to misleading results.

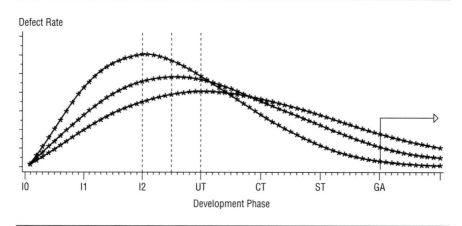

FIGURE 7.4
Rayleigh Model Illustration II

Table 7.1 shows the Spearman rank-order correlation coefficients between the defect rates of the development phases and the field defect rate. Significant correlations are observed for I2, CT, ST, and all phases combined (I0, I1, I2, CT, and ST). For I0 and I1 the correlations are not significant. This finding is not surprising because (1) I0 and I1 are the earliest development phases and (2) in terms of the defect removal pattern, the Rayleigh curve peaks after I1.

| Phase | Rank-Order Correlation | $n$ | Significance Level |
|---|---|---|---|
| I0 | .11 | 65 | not significant |
| I1 | .01 | 65 | not significant |
| I2 | .28 | 65 | .02 |
| CT | .48 | 65 | .0001 |
| ST | .49 | 65 | .0001 |
| All (I0, I1, I2, CT, ST) | .31 | 65 | .01 |

TABLE 7.1
Spearman Rank Order Correlations

Overall, the findings shown in Table 7.1 strongly substantiate the first assumption of the Rayleigh model. The significance of these findings should be emphasized because they are based on component-level data. For any type of analysis, the more granular the unit of analysis, the less chance it will obtain statistical significance. At the product or system level, our experience with the AS/400 strongly supports this assumption. As another case in point, the Space Shuttle software system developed by IBM Houston has achieved a minimal defect rate (it is even defect free for the onboard software). The defect rate observed during the IBM Houston development process (about 12 to 18 defects per KLOC), not coincidentally, is much lower than the industry average (about 40 to 60 defects per KLOC).

To test the hypothesis with regard to the second assumption of the Rayleigh model, we have to control for the effects of variations in error injection. Because error injection varies among components, cross-sectional data are not suitable for the task. Longitudinal data are better but what is needed is a good control experiment. Our experience indicates that even developing different functions by the same team in different releases may be subject to different degrees of error-proneness. This is especially the case if one release is for a major-function development and the other release is for small enhancements.

In a control-experiment situation, a pool of developers with similar skills and experiences must be selected and then randomly assigned to two groups, the experiment group and the control group. The two groups develop the same functions at time 1 separately using the same development process and method. At time 2, the two groups develop another set of functions, again separately and again with the same functions for both groups. However at time 2, the experiment group intentionally does much more front-end defect removal and the control group uses the same method as at time 1. Moreover, the functions at time 1 and time 2 are similar in terms of complexity and difficulty. If the testing defect rate and field defect rate of the project by the experiment group at time 2 are clearly lower than that at time 1 after taking into account the effect of time (which is reflected by the defect rates of the control groups at the two times), then the second assumption of the Rayleigh model is substantiated.

Without control-experiment data, we can look at the second assumption from a somewhat relaxed standard. In this regard, IBM Houston's data again lend strong support for this assumption. As discussed in Chapter 6, for software releases by IBM Houston for the Space Shuttle software system from November 1982 to December 1986, the early detection percentages increased from about 50% to more than 85%. Correspondingly, the product defect rates decreased monotonically by about 70% (see Figures 6.1 and 6.2 in Chapter 6). Although the error injection rates also decreased moderately, the effect of early defect removal is evident.

---

## 7.4 Implementation

Implementation of the Rayleigh model is not difficult. If the defect data (defect counts or defect rates) are reliable, the model parameters can be derived from the data by computer programs that use statistical functions available in many statistical software packages. After the model is defined, estimation of end-product reliability can be achieved by substitution of data values into the model.

Figure 7.5 shows a simple example of implementation of the Rayleigh model in SAS, which uses the nonlinear regression procedure. From the several methods in nonlinear regression, we chose the DUD method for its simplicity and efficiency (Ralston and Jennrich, 1978). DUD is a derivative-free algorithm for nonlinear least squares. It competes favorably with even the best derivative-based algorithms when evaluated on a number of standard test problems.

The SAS program estimates model parameters, produces a graph of fitted model versus actual data points on a GDDM79 graphic terminal screen (as shown in Figure 7.2), performs chi square goodness-of-fit tests, and derives estimates for the latent-error rate. The probability ($p$ value) of the chi square test is also provided. If the test results indicate that the fitted model does not adequately describe the observed data ($p > .05$), a warning statement is issued in the output. If proper graphic support is available, the colored graph on the terminal screen can be saved as a file and plotted via graphic plotting devices.

In the program of Figure 7.5, $r$ represents $t_m$ as discussed earlier. The program implements the model on a six-phase development process. Because the Rayleigh model is a function of time (as are other reliability models), input data have to be in terms of defect data by time. The following time equivalent values for the development phases are used in the program:

$$I0 — 0.5$$

$$I1 — 1.5$$

$$I2 — 2.5$$

$$UT — 3.5$$

$$CT — 4.5$$

$$ST — 5.5$$

```
/****************************************************************/
/*                                                            */
/*  SAS program for estimating software latent-error rate based  */
/*      on the Rayleigh model using defect removal data during   */
/*      development                                           */
/*                                                            */
/*  ----------------------------------------------------------  */
/*                                                            */
/*  Assumes: A 6-phase development process: High-level design(I0)*/
/*          Low-level design (I1), coding(I2), Unit test (UT),  */
/*          Component test (CT), and System test (ST).        */
/*                                                            */
/*  Program does:                                             */
/*      1) estimate Rayleigh model parameters                 */
/*      2) plot graph of Rayleigh curve versus actual defect rate */
/*          on a GDDM79 terminal screen (e.g., 3279G)          */
/*      3) perform chi-square goodness-of-fit test, indicate   */
/*          whether the model is adequate or not              */
/*      4) derive latent error estimate                       */
/*                                                            */
/*  User input required:                                      */
/*      A: input defect rates and time equivalents of         */
/*          the six development phases                        */
/*      B: initial values for iteration                       */
/*      C: defect rates                                       */
/*      D: adjustment factor specific to product/development   */
/*          site                                              */
/*                                                            */
/****************************************************************/
TITLE1 'RAYLEIGH MODEL - DEFECT REMOVAL PATTERN';
OPTIONS label center missing=0 number linesize=95;

/****************************************************************/
/*                                                            */
/*  Set label value for graph                                 */
/*                                                            */
/****************************************************************/
proc format;
     value jx 0='I0'
              1='I1'
              2='I2'
              3='UT'
              4='CT'
              5='ST'
              6='GA'
              7=' '
              ;


/****************************************************************/
/*                                                            */
/*  Now we get input data                                     */
/*                                                            */
/****************************************************************/
```

FIGURE 7.5 (Page 1 of 4)
An SAS Program for the Rayleigh Model

```
data temp;
/*------------------------------------------------------------*/
/*  INPUT A:                                                  */
/*  In the INPUT statement below, Y is the defect removal rate */
/*  per KLOC, T is the time equivalent for the development    */
/*  phases: 0.5 for I0, 1.5 for I1, 2.5 for I2, 3.5 for UT,   */
/*  4.5 for CT, and 5.5 for ST.                               */
/*  Input data follows the CARDS statement.                   */
/*------------------------------------------------------------*/
        INPUT Y T;
CARDS;
9.2   0.5
11.9  1.5
16.7  2.5
5.1   3.5
4.2   4.5
2.4   5.5
;
/***************************************************************/
/*                                                           */
/* Now we estimate the parameters of the Rayleigh distribution */
/*                                                           */
/***************************************************************/
proc NLIN method=dud outest=out1;
/*------------------------------------------------------------*/
/* INPUT B:                                                   */
/* The non-linear regression procedure requires initial input */
/* for the K and R parameters in the PARMS statement.  K is  */
/* the defect rate/KLOC for the entire development process, R is */
/* the peak of the Rayleigh curve.  NLIN takes these initial  */
/* values and the input data above, goes through an iteration */
/* procedure, and comes up with the final estimates of K and R. */
/* Once K and R are determined, we can specify the entire     */
/* Rayleigh curve, and subsequently estimate the latent-error */
/* rate.                                                      */
/*------------------------------------------------------------*/
     PARMS K=49.50 to 52 by 0.1
           R=1.75 to 2.00 by 0.01;
     *bounds K<=50.50,r>=1.75;
 model y=(1/R**2)*t*K*exp((-1/(2*r**2))*t**2);

data out1; set out1;
     if _TYPE_ = 'FINAL';
proc print data=out1;




/***************************************************************/
/*                                                           */
/* Now we prepare to plot the graph                          */
/*                                                           */
/***************************************************************/
/*------------------------------------------------------------*/
/* Specify the entire Rayleigh curve based on the estimated   */
```

FIGURE 7.5 (Page 2 of 4)

An SAS Program for the Rayleigh Model

```
/* parameters                                                        */
/*---------------------------------------------------------------*/
data out2; set out1;
    B=1/(2*R**2);
    do I=1 to 140;
       J=I/20;
       RAY=exp(-B*(J-0.05)**2) - exp(-B*J**2);
       DEF=ray*K*20;
       output ;
    end;
label DEF='DEFECT RATE';
/*---------------------------------------------------------------*/
/* INPUT C:                                                      */
/* Prepare for the histograms in the graph, values on the right  */
/* hand side of the assignment statements are the actual         */
/* defect removal rates--same as those for the INPUT statement   */
/*---------------------------------------------------------------*/
data out2 ; set out2;
if 0<=J<1 then DEF1=9.2 ;
if 1<=J<2 then DEF1=11.9 ;
if 2<=J<3 then DEF1=16.7 ;
if 3<=J<4 then DEF1=5.1 ;
if 4<=J<5 then DEF1=4.2 ;
if 5<=J<=6 then DEF1=2.4 ;
label J='DEVELOPMENT PHASES';
;


/******************************************************************/
/*                                                              */
/* Now we plot the graph on a GDDM79 terminal screen(e.g., 3279G)*/
/* The graph can be saved and plotted out through graphics       */
/* interface such as APGS                                        */
/*                                                              */
/******************************************************************/
    goptions device=GDDM79;
  * GOPTIONS DEVICE=GDDMfam4 GDDMNICK=p3820 GDDMTOKEN=img240x
          HSIZE=8 VSIZE=11;
  * OPTIONS DEVADDR=(.,.,GRAPHPTR);

proc gplot data=out2;
 plot DEF*J  DEF1*J/overlay vaxis=0 to 25 by 5 vminor=0 fr
                      hminor=0;
    symbol1 i=joint v=none c=red;
    symbol2 i=needle v=none   c=green;
    format j jx.;

/******************************************************************/
/*  Now we compute the chi-square goodness-of-fit test          */
/*     Note that the CDF should be used instead of              */
/*     the PDF.  The degree of freedom is                       */
/*     n-1-#parameters, in this case, n-1-2                     */
/*                                                              */
/******************************************************************/
data out1; set out1;
    DO i=1 to 6;
    OUTPUT;
    END;
    keep K R;
```

FIGURE 7.5 (Page 3 of 4)
An SAS Program for the Rayleigh Model

```
data temp2; merge out1 temp;
    T=T + 0.5;
    T_1 = T-1;
    b=1/(R*R*2);
    E_rate = K*(exp(-b*T_1*T_1) - exp(-b*T*T));
    CHI_sq = ( y  - E_rate)**2 / E_rate;
proc sort data=temp2; by T;
data temp2; set temp2; by T;
    if T=1 then T_chisq = 0;
    T_chisq + CHI_sq;


proc sort data=temp2; by K T;
data temp3; set temp2; by K T;
    if LAST.K;
    df = T-1-2;
    p= 1- PROBCHI(T_chisq, df);
    IF p>0.05 then
        RESULT='Chi-square test indicates that model is adequate.   ';
    ELSE
        RESULT='Chi-square test indicates that model is inadequate. ' ;

    keep T_chisq df p RESULT;
proc print data=temp3;


/****************************************************************/
/*  INPUT D - the value of ADJUST                             */
/*  Now we estimate the latent-error rate.  The Rayleigh model */
/*  is known to under-estimate.                               */
/*  To have good predictive validity, it                      */
/*  is important to use an adjustment factor based on the     */
/*  prior experience of your product.                         */
/****************************************************************/
data temp4; set temp2; by K T;
    if LAST.K;

    ADJUST = 0.15;

    E_rate = K*exp(-b*T*T);
    Latent= E_rate + ADJUST;
    label Latent = 'Latent Error Rate per KCSI';
    keep Latent;
proc print data=temp4 label;



 RUN;
CMS FILEDEF * CLEAR ;
ENDSAS;
```

FIGURE 7.5 (Page 4 of 4)

## An SAS Program for the Rayleigh Model

Existing implementations are available in industry. One such example is the Software LIfe-cycle Model tool (SLIM) developed by Quantitative Software Management, Inc., of McLean, Virginia. SLIM is a software product designed to help software managers estimate the time, effort, and cost required to build medium and large software systems. It embodies the software life-cycle model developed by Putnam (Putnam and Myers, 1992), using validated data from many projects in the industry. Although the main purpose of the tool is for life-cycle project management, estimating the number of software defects is one of the important elements. Central to the SLIM tool are two important management indicators. The first is the productivity index (PI), a "big picture" measure of the total development capability of the organization. The second is the manpower buildup index (MBI), a measure of staff buildup rate. It is influenced by schedule pressure, task concurrency, and resource constraints. The inputs to SLIM include software size (lines of source code, function points, modules, or uncertainty), process productivity (methods, skills, complexity, and tools), and management constraints (maximum people, maximum budget, maximum schedule, and required reliability). The outputs from SLIM include the staffing curve, the cumulative cost curve over time, probability of project success over time, reliability curve and the number of defects in the product, along with other metrics. In SLIM the $X$-axis for the Rayleigh model is in terms of months from the start of the project.

Consequent to Gaffney's work (1984), in 1985 the IBM Federal Systems Division at Gaithersburg, Maryland, developed a PC program called the Software Error Estimation Reporter (STEER). The STEER program implements a discrete version of the Rayleigh model by matching the input data with a set of 11 stored Rayleigh patterns and a number of user patterns. The stored Rayleigh patterns are expressed in terms of percent distribution of defects for the six development phases mentioned earlier. The matching algorithm involves taking logarithmic transformation of the input data and the stored Rayleigh patterns, calculating the separation index between the input data and each of the stored patterns, and choosing the stored pattern with the lowest separation index as the best-fit pattern.

Several questions arise about the STEER approach. First, the matching algorithm is somewhat different from statistical estimation methodologies, which derive estimates of model parameters directly from the input data points based on theoretically proven procedures. Second, it always produces a best-match pattern even when none of the stored patterns is statistically adequate in describing the input data. There is no mention of how little of the separation index indicates a good fit. Third, the stored Rayleigh patterns are far apart; specifically, they range from 1.00 to 3.00 in terms of $t_m$, with a huge increment of 0.25. Therefore, they are not sensitive enough for estimating the latent-error rate, which is usually a very small number.

There are, however, circumventions to the last two problems. First, use the separation index conservatively; be skeptical of the results if the index exceeds 1. Second, use the program iteratively: After selecting the best-match pattern (for instance, the one with $t_m = 1.75$), calculate a series of slightly different Rayleigh patterns that center at the best-match pattern (for instance, patterns ranging from $t_m = 1.50$ to $t_m = 2.00$, with an increment of 0.05 or 0.01), and use them as user patterns to match with the input data again. The outcome will surely be a better "best match."

When used properly, the first two potential weak points of STEER can become its strong points. In other words, STEER plays down the role of formal parameter estimation and relies heavily on matching with existing patterns. If the feature of self-entered user patterns is well utilized (for instance, use defect patterns of projects from the same development organizations that have characteristics similar to those of the project for which estimation of defects is sought), then empirical validity is established. From our experience in software reliability projection, the most important factor in achieving predictive validity, regardless of the model being used, is to establish empirical validity with historical data.

Table 7.2 shows the defect removal patterns of a number of projects, the defect rates observed during the first year in the field, the life-of-product (four years) projection based on the first-year data, and the projected total latent defect rate (life-of-product) from STEER. The data show that the STEER projections are very close to the LOP projections based on one year of actual data. One can also observe that the defect removal patterns and the resulting field defects lend support to the basic assumptions of the Rayleigh model as discussed earlier. Specifically, more front-loaded defect patterns lead to lower field defect rates and vice versa.

| | | | | | | | | | | **Defects Per KLOC** | |
| Project | LOC | Language | High-Level Design | Low-Level Design | Code | Unit Test | Integra-tion Test | System Test | First-Year Field Defect | LOP Field Defect | STEER Estimate |
|---------|------|----------|-------|-------|------|------|------|------|------|------|------|
| A | 680K | Jovial | 4 | — | 13 | 5 | 4 | 2 | 0.3 | 0.6 | 0.6 |
| B | 30K | PL/1 | 2 | 7 | 14 | 9 | 7 | — | 3.0 | 6.0 | 6.0 |
| C | 70K | BAL | 6 | 25 | 6 | 3 | 2 | 0.5 | 0.2 | 0.4 | 0.3 |
| D | 1700K | Jovial | 4 | 10 | 15 | 4 | 3 | 3 | 0.4 | 0.8 | 0.9 |
| E | 290K | ADA | 4 | 8 | 13 | — | 8 | 0.1 | 0.3 | 0.6 | 0.7 |
| F | 70K | — | 1 | 2 | 4 | 6 | 5 | 0.9 | 1.1 | 2.2 | 2.1 |
| G | 540K | ADA | 2 | 5 | 12 | 12 | 4 | 1.8 | 0.6 | 1.2 | 1.1 |
| H | 700K | ADA | 6 | 7 | 14 | 3 | 1 | 0.4 | 0.2 | 0.4 | 0.4 |

TABLE 7.2

Defect Removal Patterns and STEER Projections

## 7.5  Reliability and Predictive Validity

In Chapter 3 we examined issues associated with reliability and validity. In the context of modeling, reliability refers to the degree of change in the model output due to chance fluctuations in the input data. In specific statistical terms, reliability relates closely to the confidence interval of the estimate: the narrower the confidence interval, the more reliable the estimate, and vice versa. Confidence interval, in turn, is related to the sample size: larger samples yield narrower confidence intervals. Therefore, for the Rayleigh model, which is implemented on a six-phase development process, the chance of having a satisfactory confidence interval is very slim. Our recommendation is to use as many models as appropriate and rely on intermodel reliability to establish the reliability of the final estimates. For example, in addition to the Rayleigh model, one can attempt the exponential model or other reliability growth models (see Chapter 8). Although the confidence interval for each model estimate may not be satisfactory, if the estimates by different models are close to each other, our confidence about the estimates is strengthened. In contrast, if the estimates from different models are not consistent, we will not have much confidence in our estimates even if the confidence interval for each single estimate is small. In such cases more investigation is needed to understand and to reconcile the differences across models before a final estimate is decided.

Predictive validity refers simply to the accuracy of model estimates. The foremost thing to achieve predictive validity is to make sure that the input data are accurate and reliable. As discussed in an earlier chapter, there is much room for improvement in data quality in the software industry in general, including defect tracking in software development. Within the development process, usually the tracking system and the data quality are better at the back end (testing) than at the front end (requirements analysis, design reviews, and code inspections). Without accurate data it is impossible to obtain accurate estimates.

Second, and not less important, to establish predictive validity, model estimates and actual outcomes must be compared and empirical validity must be established. Such empirical validity is of utmost importance because the validity of software reliability models, according to the state of the art, is context specific. A model may work well in a certain development organization for a group of products using certain development processes, but not in dissimilar environments. No universally good software reliability model exists. By establishing empirical validity, we ensure that the model works in the context intended. For instance, when applying the Rayleigh to the AS/400 data, we verified the model based on many releases of the System/38 and System/36 data. We found that the Rayleigh model consistently underestimated the software field defect rate. To improve its predictive validity, we calibrated the model output with an adjustment factor, which is the mean difference between the Rayleigh estimates and the actual defect rates reported. The calibration is logical, given the similar structural parameters in the development process among the three computer systems, including organization, management, and work force.

Interestingly, Wiener-Ehrlich and associates also found that the Rayleigh model underestimated the manloading scores of a software project at the tail (Wiener-Ehrlich *et al.,* 1984). It may be that the model is really too optimistic for software applications. A Weibull distribution with an *m* of less than 2 (for example, 1.8) might work better for software. This is a worthwhile research topic if reliable and complete data (including process as well as field defect data) for a large number of projects are available. It should be cautioned that when one models the data with the Weibull distribution to determine the value of the *m* parameter, one should ensure that the complete data set is used. If incomplete data are used (for example, in-process data for the current project), the *m* value thus obtained will be artificially high, which will lead to underestimates of the software defects. This is because *m* is the shape parameter of the Weibull distribution; it will fit the shape of the current available data points during the estimation process. Therefore, for in-process data, a fixed *m* value should be used when modeling with the Weibull distribution. We have seen examples of misuse of the Weibull distribution with in-process data, resulting in invalid estimates of software defects.

## 7.6 Summary

The Rayleigh model is a special case of the Weibull distribution family, which has been widely used for reliability studies in various fields. Supported by a large body of empirical data, software projects were found to follow a life-cycle pattern described by the Rayleigh curve, for both resource and staffing demand and defect discovery/removal patterns. The Rayleigh model is implemented in several software products for quality assessment, which are available in the industry. It can also be implemented easily via statistical software packages, such as the example provided in this chapter.

Compared to the phase-based defect removal model, the Rayleigh model is a formal parametric model that can be used for projecting the latent software defects when the development work is complete and when the product is ready to ship to customers. The rationale behind the model fits well with the rationale for effective software development. Specifically, while the defect removal effectiveness approach focuses on defect removal, the Rayleigh encompasses both defect prevention (reduction in defect rates) and early defect removal.

In addition to quality projection, another strength of the Rayleigh model is that it provides an excellent framework for quality management. After we discuss the reliability growth models in the next chapter, in Chapter 9 we will revisit the Rayleigh model in its capacity as a quality management model.

# References

1. Conte, S. D., H. E. Dunsmore, and V. Y. Shen, *Software Engineering Metrics and Models,* Menlo Park, Calif.: The Benjamin/Cummings Publishing Company, 1986.
2. Gaffney, Jr., J. E., "On Predicting Software Related Performance of Large-Scale Systems," *CMG XV,* San Francisco, December 1984.
3. Norden, P. V., "Useful Tools for Project Management," *Operations Research in Research and Development,* B. V. Dean, Ed., New York: John Wiley & Sons, 1963.
4. Putnam, L. H., "A General Empirical Solution to the Macro Software Sizing and Estimating Problem," *IEEE Transactions on Software Engineering,* Vol. SE-4, 1978, pp. 345–361.
5. Putnam, L. H., and W. Myers, *Measures for Excellence: Reliable Software on Time, Within Budget,* Englewood Cliffs, N.J.: Yourdon Press, 1992.
6. Ralston, M. L., and R. I. Jennrich, "DUD, a Derivative-Free Algorithm for Nonlinear Least Squares," *Technometrics,* Vol. 20, 1978, pp. 7–14.
7. Tobias, P. A., and D. C. Trindade, *Applied Reliability,* New York: Van Nostrand Reinhold Company, 1986.
8. Trachtenberg, M., "Discovering How to Ensure Software Reliability," *RCA Engineer,* Jan./Feb. 1982, pp. 53–57.
9. Wiener-Ehrlich, W. K., J. R. Hamrick, and V. F. Rupolo, "Modeling Software Behavior in Terms of a Formal Life Cycle Curve: Implications for Software Maintenance," *IEEE Transactions on Software Engineering,* Vol. SE-10, 1984, pp. 376–383.

# 8

## Exponential Distribution and Reliability Growth Models

Continuing our discussion of software reliability models, in this chapter we cover the class of models called the *reliability growth models*. We first discuss the exponential model; then we concisely describe several notable reliability growth models in the literature; and in later sections we discuss several issues such as model assumptions, criteria for model evaluation, the modeling process, and the test compression factor.

In contrast to Rayleigh, which models the defect pattern of the entire development process, reliability growth models are usually based on data from the formal testing phases. Indeed it makes more sense to apply these models during the final testing phase when development is virtually complete, especially when the testing is customer oriented. The rationale is that defect arrival or failure patterns during such testing is a good indicator of the reliability of the product when used by customers. During such postdevelopment testing, when failures occur and defects are identified and fixed, the software becomes more stable, and reliability grows over time. Therefore models that address such a process are called reliability growth models.

## 8.1 The Exponential Model

The exponential model is yet another special case of the Weibull family, with the shape parameter $m$ equal to 1. It is best used for statistical processes that decline monotonically to an asymptote. Its cumulative distribution function (CDF) and probability density function (PDF) are:

$$\text{CDF}: F(t) = 1 - e^{-(t/c)}$$
$$= 1 - e^{-\lambda t}$$

$$\text{PDF}: f(t) = \frac{1}{c} e^{-(t/c)}$$
$$= \lambda e^{-\lambda t}$$

where $c$ is the scale parameter, $t$ is time, and $\lambda = 1/c$. When applied to software reliability, $\lambda$ is referred to as the *error detection rate* or *instantaneous failure rate*. In statistical terms it is also called the *hazard rate*.

Again the preceding formulas represent a standard distribution—the total area under the PDF curve is 1. In actual application, the total number of defects or the total cumulative defect rate $K$ needs to be multiplied to the formulas. $K$ and lambda ($\lambda$) are the two parameters for estimation when deriving a specific model from a data set.

The exponential distribution is the simplest and most important distribution in reliability and survival studies. The failure data of much equipment and many processes are well described by the exponential distribution: bank statement and ledger errors, payroll check errors, light bulb failure, automatic calculating machine failure, radar set component failure, and so forth. The exponential distribution plays a role in reliability studies analogous to that of normal distribution in other areas of statistics.

In software reliability the exponential distribution is one of the better known models and is often the basis of many other software reliability growth models. For instance, Misra (1983) used the exponential model to estimate the defect-arrival rates for the Shuttle Ground System software of the National Aeronautics and Space Administration (NASA). The software provided the flight controllers at the Johnson Space Center with processing support to exercise command and control over flight operations. Actual data from a 200-hour flight mission indicated that the model worked very well. Furthermore, the mean value function (CDF) of the Goel-Okumoto (1979) nonhomogeneous Poisson process model (NPPM) is in fact the exponential model.

Figures 8.1 and 8.2 show an example of the exponential model applied to the data of one of the AS/400 software products. We have modeled the weekly defect-arrival data since the start of system test, when the development work was virtually complete. The system-testing stage uses customer interfaces, tests external requirements, and simulates end-user application environments. The pattern of defect arrivals during this stage, therefore, should be indicative of the latent-defect rate when the system is shipped.

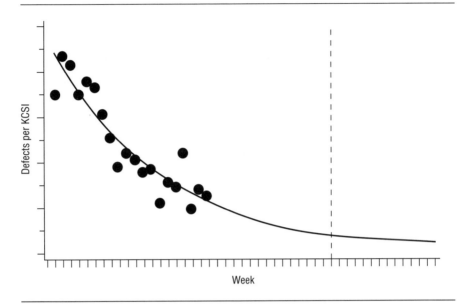

FIGURE 8.1
Exponential Model—Density Distribution

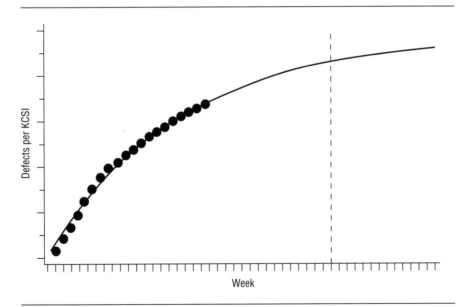

FIGURE 8.2
Exponential Model—Cumulative Distribution

Like the Rayleigh model, simple and quick implementation of the exponential model is not difficult when powerful statistical software is available. For example, it can be implemented via SAS programs similar to the one shown in Figure 7.5 of the previous chapter. Of course, if a high degree of usability and various scenarios are desired, more elaborate software is needed.

Besides programming, the following should be taken into consideration when applying the exponential distribution for reliability projection or estimating the number of software defects. First, as with all types of modeling and estimation, the more accurate and precise the input data, the better the outcome. Data tracking for software reliability estimation is done either in terms of precise CPU execution time or on a calendar-time basis. Normally execution-time tracking is for small projects or special reliability studies; calendar-time tracking is common for large-scale commercial development. When calendar-time data are used, a basic assumption for the exponential model is that the testing effort is homogeneous throughout the testing phase. Ohba (1984) noted that the model does not work well for calendar-time data with a nonhomogeneous time distribution of testing effort. Therefore, this assumption must be examined when using the model. For instance, in the example shown in Figures 8.1 and 8.2 the testing effort remained consistently high and homogeneous throughout the system test phase; a separate team of testers worked intensively based on a predetermined test plan. The product was also large in size (>100 KLOC) and therefore the trend of the defect arrival rates tended to be quite stable even though no execution-time data were available.

To verify the assumption, indicators of the testing effort, such as the person-hours in testing for each time unit (for example, day or week), test cases run, or the number of variations executed, are needed. In the case where the testing effort is clearly not homogeneous, some sort of normalization has to be made. Otherwise models other than the exponential distribution should be considered.

As an example of normalization, let us assume the unit of the calendar time is a week and it is clear that the weekly testing effort is not homogeneous. Further assume that weekly data on the number of person-hours in testing are known. Simple adjustments such as the following can reduce artificial fluctuations in the data and can make the model work better:

1. Accumulate the total person-hours in testing for the entire testing phase and calculate the average number of person-hours in testing per week, $n$.

2. Starting from the beginning of testing, calculate the defect rates (or defect count) for each $n$ person-hour units. Allocate the defect rates to the calendar week in sequence. Specifically, allocate the defect rate observed for the first $n$ person-hours of testing to the first week; allocate the defect rate observed for the second $n$ person-hours of testing to the second week, and so forth.

3. Use the allocated data as weekly input data for the model.

Second, the more data points available, the better the model will perform—assuming there is an adequate fit between the model and the data. The question is, when the test is in progress how many data are needed for the model to yield reasonably adequate output? Ehrlich and associates (1990) investigated this question using data from AT&T software that was a transmission-measurement system for remote testing of special service circuits. They assessed the predictive validity of the exponential model with data at 25%, 50%, 60%, 70%, and 80% into test, and at test completion. They found that at 25% into test the model results were way off. At 50% the results improved considerably but were still not satisfactory. At 60% into test, the exponential model had satisfactory predictive validity. Although it is not clear whether these findings can be generalized, they provide a good reference point for real-time modeling.

## 8.2 Reliability Growth Models

The exponential model can be regarded as the basic form of the software reliability growth models. For the past two decades, software reliability modeling has been one of the most active areas in software engineering. More than a hundred models have been proposed in professional journals and at software conferences, each having its own assumptions, applicability, and limitations. Unfortunately, there are not many models that have been tested in practical environments with real data, and even fewer models are in use. From the practical software development point of view, for some models the cost of gathering data is too expensive; some models are not understandable; and some simply do not work when examined. For instance, Elbert and associates (1992) examined seven reliability models with data from a large and complex software system containing millions of lines of source code. They found that while some models gave reasonable results, others provided unrealistic estimates. Despite a good fit between the model and the data, some models predicted the probability of error detection as a negative value. The range of the estimates of the defects of the system from these models is incredibly wide—from 5 to 6 defects up to 50,000.

Software reliability growth models can be classified into two major classes, depending on the criteria variable (dependent variable) of the model. For the *time between failures models,* the variable under study is the time between failures. This is the earliest class of models proposed for software reliability assessment. It is expected that the successive failure times will get longer as defects are removed from the software product. A common approach of this class of model is to assume that the time between, say, the $(i-1)$'st and the $i$'th failures follows a distribution whose parameters are related to the number of latent defects remaining in the product after the $(i-1)$'st failure. The distribution used is supposed to reflect the improvement in reliability as defects are detected and removed from the product. The parameters of the distribution are to be estimated from the observed values of times between failures. Mean time to next failure is usually the parameter to be estimated for the model.

For the *fault count models* the criteria variable is the number of faults or failures (or normalized rate) in a specified time interval. The time can be CPU execution time or calendar time such as hour, week, or month. The time interval is fixed *a priori* and the number of defects or failures observed during the interval is treated as a random variable. As defects are detected and removed from the software, it is expected that the observed number of failures per unit time will decrease. The number of remaining defects or failures is the key parameter to be estimated from this class of models.

In the following we concisely describe several models in each of the two classes. The models are selected based on our experience and may or may not be a good representation of the many models available in the literature. We first summarize three time between failures models, followed by three fault count models.

## 8.2.1 Jelinski-Moranda (J-M) Model

The J-M model is one of the earliest models in software reliability research (Jelinski and Moranda, 1972). It is a time between failures model. It assumes there are $N$ software faults at the start of testing, that failures occur purely at random, and that all faults contribute equally to cause a failure during testing. It also assumes the fix time is negligible and that the fix is perfect for each failure that occurs. Therefore, the software product's failure rate improves by the same amount at each fix. The hazard function (the instantaneous failure rate function) at time $t_i$, the time between the $(i-1)$'st and $i$'th failures, is given by:

$$Z(t_i) = \phi[N - (i-1)]$$

where $N$ is the number of software defects at the beginning of testing and $\phi$ is a proportionality constant. Note that the hazard function is constant between failures but decreases in steps of $\phi$ following the removal of each fault. Therefore as each additional fault is removed, the time between failures is expected to be longer.

.

## 8.2.2  Littlewood (LW) Models

The LW model (Littlewood, 1981) is similar to the J-M model, except it assumes that different faults have different sizes, thereby contributing unequally to failures. Larger sized faults tend to be detected and fixed earlier. As the number of errors is driven down with the progress in test, so is the average error size, causing a law of diminishing return in debugging. The introduction of the error size concept makes the model assumption more realistic. In real-life software operation, the assumption of equal failure rate by all faults can hardly be met, if at all. Latent defects that reside in code paths that rarely get executed by customers' operational profiles may not be manifested for years.

Littlewood also developed several other models such as the Littlewood nonhomogeneous Poisson process (LNHPP) model (Miller, 1986). The LNHPP model is similar to the LW model except that it assumes a continuous change in instantaneous failure rate rather than discrete drops when fixes take place.

## 8.2.3  Goel-Okumoto (G-O) Imperfect Debugging Model

The J-M model assumes that the fix time is negligible and that the fix is perfect for each failure. In other words, it assumes perfect debugging. However, in practice this is not always the case. In the process of fixing a defect, new defects may be injected. Indeed, defect fix activities are known to be error-prone. During the testing stages, the percentage of defective fixes in large commercial software development organizations may range from 1% or 2% to more than 10%. Goel and Okumoto (1978) proposed an imperfect debugging model to overcome the limitation of the assumption. In this model the hazard function during the interval between the $(i-1)$'st and the $i$'th failures is given by

$$Z(t_i) = [N - p(i-1)]\lambda$$

where $N$ is the number of faults at the start of testing, $p$ is the probability of imperfect debugging, and $\lambda$ is the failure rate per fault.

## 8.2.4  Goel-Okumoto Nonhomogeneous Poisson Process Model (NHPP)

The NHPP model (Goel and Okumoto, 1979) is concerned with modeling the number of failures observed in given testing intervals. Goel and Okumoto proposed that the cumulative number of failures observed at time $t$, $N(t)$, can be modeled as a nonhomogeneous Poisson process—as a Poisson process with a time-dependent failure rate. They proposed that the time-dependent failure rate follows an exponential distribution. The model is given by

$$P\{N(t) = y\} = \frac{[m(t)]^y}{y!} e^{-m(t)}, \quad y = 0, 1, 2, \ldots$$

where

$$m(t) = a(1 - e^{-bt})$$

$$\lambda(t) \equiv m'(t) = abc^{-bt}$$

In the model, $m(t)$ is the expected number of failures observed by time $t$; $\lambda(t)$ is the failure density; $a$ is the expected number of failures to be observed eventually; and $b$ is the fault detection rate per fault. As seen, $m(t)$ and $\lambda(t)$ are the cumulative distribution function $[F(t)]$ and the probability density function $[f(t)]$, respectively, of the exponential function discussed in the last section. The parameters $a$ and $b$ correspond to $K$ and $\lambda$. Therefore the NHPP model is a straight application of the exponential model. The reason it is called NHPP is perhaps because of the emphasis on the probability distribution of the estimate of the cumulative number of failures at a specific time $t$, as represented by the first equation. For fitting the model curve from actual data and for projecting the number of faults remaining in the system, it is mainly by means of the mean value function (CDF).

Note that in this model the number of faults to be detected, $a$, is treated as a random variable whose observed value depends on the test and other environmental factors. This is fundamentally different from the other models that treat the number of faults to be a fixed unknown constant.

The exponential distribution assumes a pattern of decreasing defect rates or failures. It has been observed that there are cases in which the failure rate first increases and then decreases. Goel (1982) proposed a generalization of the Goel-Okumoto NHPP model by allowing one more parameter in the mean value function and the failure density function. Such a model is called the Goel generalized nonhomogeneous Poisson process model:

$$m(t) = a(1 - e^{-bt^c})$$
$$\lambda(t) \equiv m'(t) = abc\, e^{-bt^c} t^{c-1}$$

where $a$ is the expected number of faults to be eventually detected, and $b$ and $c$ are constants that reflect the quality of testing. This mean value function and failure density function is actually the Weibull distribution, which we discussed in the last chapter. When the shape parameter $m$ (in the Goel model, it is $c$) equals 1, the Weibull distribution becomes the exponential distribution; when $m$ is 2, it then becomes the Rayleigh model.

## 8.2.5 Musa-Okumoto (M-O) Logarithmic Poisson Execution Time Model

Similar to the NHPP model, in the M-O model the observed number of failures by a certain time, $\tau$, is also assumed to be a nonhomogeneous Poisson process (Musa and Okumoto, 1983). However, its mean value function is different. It attempts to consider that later fixes have a smaller effect on the software's reliability than earlier ones. The logarithmic Poisson process is claimed to be superior for highly nonuniform operational user profiles, where some functions are executed much more frequently than others. Also the process modeled is the number of failures in specified execution time intervals (instead of calendar time). A systematic approach to convert the results to calendar time data (Musa *et al.,* 1987) is also provided. The model, therefore, consists of two components—the execution-time component and the calendar-time component.

The mean value function of this model is given by

$$u(\tau) = \frac{1}{\theta} \ln(\lambda_0 \theta_\tau + 1)$$

where $\lambda$ is the initial failure intensity, and $\theta$ is the rate of reduction in the normalized failure intensity per failure.

## 8.2.6 The Delayed S and Inflection S Models

With regard to the software defect removal process, Yamada *et al.*(1983) argued that a testing process consists of not only a defect detection process, but also a defect isolation process. Because of the time needed for failure analysis, significant delay can occur between the time of the first failure observation and the time of reporting. They offered the delayed S-shaped reliability growth model for such a process, in which the observed growth curve of the cumulative number of detected defects is S-shaped. The model is based on the nonhomogeneous Poisson process but with a different mean value function to reflect the delay in failure reporting:

$$m(t) = k\left[1 - (1 + \lambda t)\, e^{-\lambda t}\right]$$

where $t$ is time, $\lambda$ is the error detection rate, and $K$ is the total number of defects or total cumulative defect rate.

In 1984, Ohba proposed another S-shaped reliability growth model—the inflection S model (Ohba, 1984). The model describes a software failure detection phenomenon with a mutual dependence of detected defects. Specifically, the more failures we detect, the more undetected failures become detectable. This assumption brings a certain realism into software reliability modeling and is a significant improvement over the assumption used by earlier models—the independence of faults in a program. Also based on the nonhomogeneous Poisson process, the model's mean value function is:

$$I(t) = K \frac{1 - e^{-\lambda t}}{1 + i\, e^{-\lambda t}}$$

where $t$ is time, $\lambda$ is the error detection rate, $i$ is the inflection factor, and $K$ is the total number of defects or total cumulative defect rate.

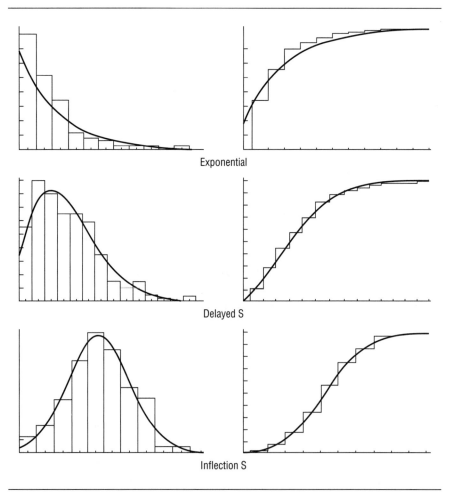

Exponential

Delayed S

Inflection S

FIGURE 8.3
Exponential, Delayed S, and Inflection S Models

The delayed S and inflection S models can be regarded as accounting for the learning period that testers go through as they become familiar with the software at the beginning period of testing. The learning period is associated with the delayed or inflection patterns as described by the mean value functions. The mean value function (CDF) and the failure density function (PDF) curves of the two models, in comparison with the exponential model, are shown in Figure 8.3. The exponential model assumes that the peak of defect arrival is at the beginning of the system test phase, and continues to decline thereafter; the delayed S model assumes a slightly delayed peak; and the inflection S model assumes a later and sharper peak.

## 8.3  Model Assumptions

Reliability modeling is an attempt to summarize the complex reality in precise statistical terms. Because the physical process being modeled (the software failure phenomenon) can hardly be expected to be so precise, unambiguous statements of the underlying assumptions are necessary in the development of a model. In applications, the models perform better when the underlying assumptions are met, and vice versa. In other words, the more reasonable the assumptions, the better a model will be. From the preceding summary of several reliability growth models, we can see that earlier models tend to have more restrictive assumptions. More recent models tend to be able to deal with more realistic assumptions. For instance, the J-M model's five assumptions are:

1.  There are $N$ unknown software faults at the start of testing.
2.  Failures occur randomly—times between failures are independent.
3.  All faults contribute equally to cause a failure.
4.  Fix time is negligible.
5.  Fix is perfect for each failure; there are no new faults introduced during correction.

Altogether these assumptions are difficult to meet in practical development environments. Although assumption 1 does not seem to pose problems, all the others pose limitations to the model. The Littlewood models, with the concept of error size, overcame the restriction imposed by assumption 3. The Goel-Okumoto imperfect debugging model is an attempt to improve assumptions 4 and 5.

Assumption 2 is used in all time between failures models. It requires that successive failure times be independent of each other. This assumption could be met if successive test cases were chosen randomly. However, the test process is not likely to be random; testing, especially functional testing, is not based on independent test cases. If a critical fault is discovered in a code segment, the tester may intensify the testing of associated code paths and look for other potential faults. Such activities may mean a shorter time to next failure. Strict adherence to this assumption therefore is not likely. However, care should be taken to ensure some degree of independence in data points when using the time between failures models.

The previous assumptions pertain to the time between failures models. In general, assumptions of the time between failures models tend to be more restrictive. Furthermore, time between failures data are more costly to gather and require a higher degree of precision.

The basic assumptions of the fault count model are as follows (Goel, 1985):

1. Testing intervals are independent of each other.

2. Testing during intervals is reasonably homogeneous.

3. Numbers of defects detected during nonoverlapping intervals are independent of each other.

As discussed earlier, the assumption of a homogeneous testing effort is the key to the fault count models. If this assumption is not met, some normalization effort or statistical adjustment should be applied. The other two assumptions are quite reasonable, especially if the model is calendar-time based with wide enough intervals (for example, weeks).

For both classes of models the most important underlying assumption is that of effective testing. If the test process is not well planned and test cases are poorly designed, the input data and, hence the model projections, will be overly optimistic. If the models are used for comparisons across product, then additional indicators of the effectiveness or coverage of testing should be included for the interpretation of results.

## 8.4 Criteria for Model Evaluation

For reliability models, in 1984 a group of experts (Iannino *et al.,* 1984) devised a set of criteria for model assessment and comparison. The criteria are listed as follows, by order of importance as determined by the group:

☐ *Predictive validity:* the capability of the model to predict future failure behavior or the number of defects for a specified time period based on the current data in the model.

☐ *Capability:* the ability of the model to estimate with satisfactory accuracy quantities needed by software managers, engineers, and users in planning and managing software development projects or controlling change in operational software systems.

☐ *Quality of assumptions:* the likelihood that the model assumptions can be met, and the assumptions' plausibility from the viewpoint of logical consistency and software engineering experience.

☐ *Applicability:* the model's degree of applicability across different software products (size, structure, functions, etc.).

☐ *Simplicity:* a model should be simple in three aspects: (1) simple and inexpensive to collect data, (2) simple in concept and does not require extensive mathematical background for software development practitioners to comprehend, and (3) readily implemented by computer programs.

From the practitioner's point of view and with recent observations of software reliability models, we contend that the most important criteria are predictive validity, simplicity, and quality of assumptions, in that order of importance. Capability and applicability are less significant. As the state of the art is still maturing and striving to improve its most important objective (predictive accuracy), the extra criteria of demanding more functions (capability) for multiple environments (applicability) seems burdensome. Perhaps the accuracy of software reliability models can best be summarized as follows: Some models sometimes give good results, some are almost universally awful, and none can be trusted to be accurate at all times (Brocklehurst and Littlewood, 1992). A model with good predictive validity but poor capability and narrow applicability is certainly superior to one with good capability and wide applicability but with very poor ability to predict.

In contrast to the order of importance determined by the 1984 group, we think that simplicity is much more important, second only to predictive validity. Experts in software reliability models are usually academicians who are well versed in mathematics and statistics. Many modeling concepts and terminologies are outside the discipline of computer science, let alone easy to comprehend and implement by software developers in the industry. As mentioned earlier, some reliability models have not been tested and used in real-life development projects simply because they are just not understandable. Simplicity, therefore, is a key element in bridging the gap between the state of the art and the state of practice in software reliability modeling.

The quality of the assumptions is also very important. Early models tend to have restrictive and unrealistic assumptions. More recent models tend to have more realistic assumptions. Better assumptions make the model more convincing and more acceptable by software practitioners; they also lead to better predictive validity.

## 8.5  Modeling Process

To model software reliability, the following process or similar procedures should be used.

1. Examine the data. Study the nature of the data (fault counts versus times between failures), the unit of analysis (CPU hour, calendar day, week, month, etc.), the data tracking system and data reliability, and any relevant aspects of the data. Plot the data points against time in the form of a scatter diagram, analyze the data informally, and gain an insight into the nature of the process being modeled. For example, observe the trend, fluctuations, and any peculiar patterns and try to associate the data patterns with what was happening in the testing process. As another example, sometimes if the unit of time is too granular (for example, calendar-time in hours of testing), the noise of the data may become too large relative to the underlying system pattern that we try to model. In such a case a larger time unit such as day or week may yield a better model.

2. Select a model or several models to fit the data based on an understanding of the test process, the data, and the assumptions of the models. The plot in step 1 can provide helpful information for model selection.

3. Estimate the parameters of the model. Different methods may be required depending on the nature of the data. The statistical techniques (such as the maximum likelihood method, the least-squares method, or some other method) and the software tools available for use should be considered.

4. Obtain the fitted model by substituting the estimates of the parameters into the chosen model. At this stage we have a specified model for the data set.

5. Perform goodness-of-fit test and assess the reasonableness of the model. If the model does not fit, a more reasonable model should be selected with regard to model assumptions and the nature of the data. For example, is the lack of fit due to a few data points that were affected by extraneous factors? Is the time unit used too granular so that the noise of the data obscures the underlying trend?

6. Make reliability predictions based on the fitted model. Assess the reasonableness of the predictions based on other available information—actual performance of a similar product or of a previous release of the same product, subjective assessment by the development team and so forth.

To illustrate the modeling process with actual data, we give additional details on the example shown in Figures 8.1 and 8.2. The weekly defect rate data are shown in Table 8.1.

## Step 1:

The data were weekly defect data from the system test, the final phase of the development process. During the test process the software was under formal change control—any defects found are tracked by the electronic problem tracking reports (PTR) and any change to the code must be done through the PTR process, which is enforced by the development support system. Therefore the data were reliable. The density plot and cumulative plot of the data were shown in Figures 8.1 and 8.2 earlier (ignore temporarily the fitted curves).

| Week | Defects/KLOC Arrival | Defects/KLOC Cumulative |
|------|---------------------|--------------------------|
| 1  | .353 | .353  |
| 2  | .436 | .789  |
| 3  | .415 | 1.204 |
| 4  | .351 | 1.555 |
| 5  | .380 | 1.935 |
| 6  | .366 | 2.301 |
| 7  | .308 | 2.609 |
| 8  | .254 | 2.863 |
| 9  | .192 | 3.055 |
| 10 | .219 | 3.274 |
| 11 | .202 | 3.476 |
| 12 | .180 | 3.656 |
| 13 | .182 | 3.838 |
| 14 | .110 | 3.948 |
| 15 | .155 | 4.103 |
| 16 | .145 | 4.248 |
| 17 | .221 | 4.469 |
| 18 | .095 | 4.564 |
| 19 | .140 | 4.704 |
| 20 | .126 | 4.830 |

TABLE 8.1

Weekly Defect Arrival Rates and Cumulative Rates

**Step 2:**

The data indicated an overall decreasing trend (of course, with some noises), there-fore the exponential model was chosen. For other products, we had used the delayed S and inflection S models before. Also, the assumption of the S models, specifically the delayed reporting of failures due to problem determination and the mutual dependence of defects, seems to describe the development process correctly. However, from the trend of the data we did not observe any increase-then-decrease pattern, so we chose the exponential model. We did try the S models for goodness of fit, but they were not as good as the exponential model in this case.

**Step 3:**

We used two methods for model estimation. In the first method we used an SAS pro-gram similar to the one shown in Figure 7.5 in Chapter 7, which used a nonlinear regression approach based on the DUD algorithm (Ralston and Jennrich, 1978). The second method relies on the Software Error Tracking Tool (SETT) software devel-oped by Falcetano and Caruso at IBM Kingston (Falcetano and Caruso, 1988). SETT implemented the exponential model and the two S models via the Marquardt nonlinear least-squares algorithm. Results of the two methods are very close. From the DUD nonlinear regression methods we obtained the following values for the two parameters $K$ and $\lambda$.

$$K = 6.597$$
$$\lambda = 0.0712$$

The asymptotic 95% confidence intervals for the two parameters are:

|     | Lower | Upper |
|-----|-------|-------|
| $K$ | 5.643 | 7.552 |
| $\lambda$ | 0.0553 | 0.0871 |

**Step 4:**

By fitting the estimated parameters from step 3 into the exponential distribution, we obtained the following specified model.

$$f(t) = 6.597 \times 0.0712 \times e^{-0.0712t}$$

$$F(t) = 6.597(1 - e^{-0.0712t})$$

where $t$ is the week number since the start of system test.

**Step 5:**

We conducted the Kolmogorov-Smirnov goodness-of-fit test (Rohatgi, 1976) between the observed number of defects and the expected number of defects from the model in step 4. The Kolmogorov-Smirnov test is recommended for goodness-of-fit testing for software reliability models (Goel, 1985). The test statistic is as follows:

$$D(n) = x \mid F^*(x) - F(x)$$

where $n$ is sample size, $F^*(x)$ is the normalized observed cumulative distribution at each time point (normalized means the total is 1), and $F(x)$ is the expected cumulative distribution at each time point, based on the model. In other words, the statistic compares the normalized cumulative distributions of the observed rates and the expected rates from the model at each point, takes the absolute difference. If the maximum difference, $D(n)$, is less than the established criteria, then the model fits the data adequately.

| Week | Observed Defects/KLOC Cumulative (A) | Model Defects/KLOC Cumulative (B) | $F^*(x)$ | $F(x)$ | $\|F^*(x) - F(x)\|$ |
|---|---|---|---|---|---|
| 1 | .353 | .437 | .07314 | .09050 | .01736 |
| 2 | .789 | .845 | .16339 | .17479 | .01140 |
| 3 | 1.204 | 1.224 | .24936 | .25338 | .00392 |
| 4 | 1.555 | 1.577 | .32207 | .32638 | .00438 |
| 5 | 1.935 | 1.906 | .40076 | .39446 | .00630 |
| 6 | 2.301 | 2.213 | .47647 | .45786 | .01861 |
| 7 | 2.609 | 2.498 | .54020 | .51691 | .02329 |
| 8 | 2.863 | 2.764 | .59281 | .57190 | .02091 |
| 9 | 3.055 | 3.011 | .63259 | .62311 | .00948 |
| 10 | 3.274 | 3.242 | .67793 | .67080 | .00713 |
| 11 | 3.476 | 3.456 | .71984 | .71522 | .00462 |
| 12 | 3.656 | 3.656 | .75706 | .75658 | .00048 |
| 13 | 3.838 | 3.842 | .79470 | .79510 | .00040 |
| 14 | 3.948 | 4.016 | .81737 | .83098 | .01361 |
| 15 | 4.103 | 4.177 | .84944 | .86438 | .01494 |
| 16 | 4.248 | 4.327 | .87938 | .89550 | .01612 |
| 17 | 4.469 | 4.467 | .92515 | .92448 | .00067 |
| 18 | 4.564 | 4.598 | .94482 | .95146 | .00664 |
| 19 | 4.704 | 4.719 | .97391 | .97659 | .00268 |
| 20 | 4.830 | 4.832 | 1.00000 | 1.00000 | .00000 |

$D(n) = .02329$

TABLE 8.2

Weekly Defect Arrival Rates and Cumulative Rates

Table 8.2 shows the calculation of the test. Column (A) is the third column in Table 8.1. Column (B) is the cumulative defect rate from the model. The $F^*(x)$ and $F(x)$ columns are the normalization of columns (A) and (B), respectively. The maximum of the last column, $|F^*(x) - F(x)|$, is .02329. The Kolmogorov-Smirnov test statistic for $n = 20$, and $p$ value = .05 is .294 (Rohatgi, 1976, p. 661, Table 7). Because the $D(n)$ value for our model is .02329, which is less than .294, the test indicates that the model is adequate.

**Step 6:**

We calculated the projected number of defects for the next four years after completion of system test. The projection from this model was very close to the estimate from the Rayleigh model and to the actual field defect data.

At IBM Rochester we have been using the reliability modeling techniques for estimating the defect level of software products for some years. The Rayleigh model, the exponential model, and the two S-type models are the ones we found to have good applicability to AS/400's process and data. We also rely on cross-model reliability to assess the reasonableness of the estimates. Furthermore, historical data are used for model calibration and for adjustment of the estimates. Actual field defect data confirmed the predictive validity of this approach; the differences between actual numbers and estimates are small.

## 8.6  Test Compression Factor

As the example and other cases in the literature illustrate (for example, Misra, 1983; Putnam and Myers, 1992), a fair degree of accuracy to project the remaining number of defects can be achieved by software reliability models, based on testing data. This is especially the case if the project is large, where defect arrivals tend not to fluctuate too much; if the system is not for safety-critical missions; and if environment-specific factors are taken into account when choosing a model. For safety-critical systems, the requirements for reliability and, hence, for reliability models, are much more stringent.

Even though the projection of the total number of defects (or defect rates) may be reasonably accurate, it does not mean that one can extend the model density curve from the testing phase to the maintenance phase (customer usage) directly. The defect arrival patterns of the two phases may be quite different, especially for commercial projects. During testing the sole purpose is to find and remove defects; test cases are maximized for defect detection, therefore, defect arrival during test is usually higher. In contrast, in customers' applications it takes time to encounter defects—when the applications hit usual scenarios. Therefore, defect arrivals may tend to spread. Such a difference between testing-defect density and field-defect density is called the *compression factor*. The value of the compression factor varies, depending on the testing environments and the customer usage profiles. It is expected to be larger when the test strategy is based on partition and limit testing and smaller for random testing or customer-environment testing. In the assessment by Elbert and associates (1992) on three large-scale commercial projects, the compression factor was 5 for two projects and for the third, 30. For projects that have extensive customer beta tests, models based on the beta test data may be able to extrapolate to the field use phase.

Figure 8.4 shows a real-life example of compression of defect density between testing and initial data from the field. For the upper panel, the upper curve represents the extrapolated cumulative defect rate based on testing data. The lower curve is the actual cumulative field defect rate. Although the end points of the two curves at four-year life of product are close, the upper curve has a much faster buildup rate. The difference is even more drastically shown in the lower panel, in which the two defect density curves are contrasted. The extrapolated curve based on testing data is very front loaded and declines much faster. In vivid contrast, the actual field defect arrival is much more spread out. It even follows a different density pattern (a delayed S or a Rayleigh-like pattern).

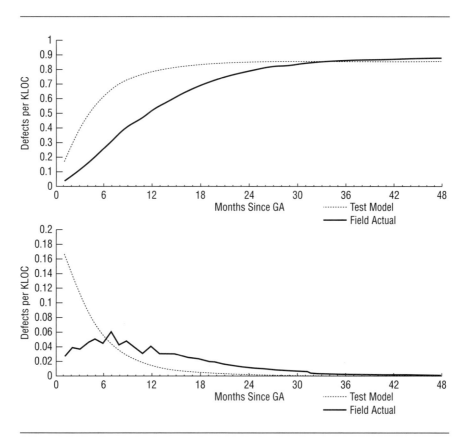

FIGURE 8.4
Compression Illustration—Cumulative and Density Curves

Therefore, for software maintenance planning, we should (1) use the reliability models to estimate the total number of defects or defect rate only and (2) spread the total defect rate into arrival pattern over time based on historical patterns of field defect arrivals.

The field defect arrival patterns, in turn, can be modeled by the same process. Our experience with several midrange operating systems indicates that the arrival curves follow the exponential or the S models. Figure 8.5 shows the field defect arrival patterns of a major release of both the System/38 and the AS/400 operating systems.

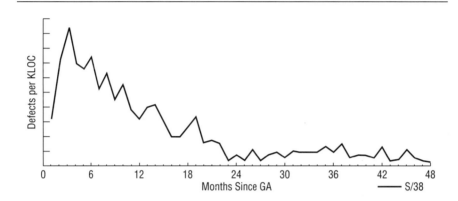

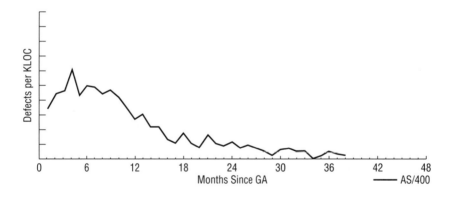

FIGURE 8.5
Field Defect Arrival Pattern—System/38 and AS/400 Operating Systems

## 8.7 Summary

The exponential distribution, another special case of the Weibull distribution family, is the simplest and perhaps most widely used distribution in reliability and survival studies. In software, it is best used for modeling the defect arrival pattern at the back end of the development process—for example, the final formal test phase. When calendar-time data are used (versus execution-time data), a key assumption for the exponential model is that the testing effort is homogeneous throughout the testing phase. If this assumption is not met, normalization of the data with respect to test effort is needed for the model to work well.

In addition to the exponential model, numerous software reliability growth models have been proposed, each having its own assumptions, applicability, and limitations. However, not many have been verified in practical environments with industry data, and even fewer are in use. Based on the criteria variable they use, software reliability growth models can be classified into two major classes: *time between failures models* and *fault count models*. In this chapter we summarized several more well-known models in each class and illustrated the modeling process using a real-life example. From the practitioner's vantage point, the most important criteria for evaluating and choosing software reliability growth models are predictive validity, simplicity, and quality of assumptions.

Software reliability models are most often used for reliability projection before the software is shipped to customers and when development work is complete. They can also be used to model the failure pattern or the defect arrival pattern in the field and, hence, provide valuable input to maintenance planning.

## References

1. Brocklehurst, S., and B. Littlewood, "New Ways to Get Accurate Reliability Measurements," *IEEE Software,* July 1992, pp. 34–42.
2. Ehrlich, W. K., S. K. Lee, and R. H. Molisani, "Applying Reliability Measurement: A Case Study," *IEEE Software,* March 1990, pp. 46–54.
3. Elbert, M. A., R. C. Howe, and T. F. Weyant, "Software Reliability Modeling," *ASQC Quality Congress Transactions,* Nashville, Tenn., 1992, pp. 933–940.
4. Falcetano, M. J., and J. M. Caruso, IBM Kingston, New York, Private Communication, 1988.
5. Goel, A. L., "Software Reliability Modeling and Estimation Techniques," Report RADC-TR-82-263, Rome Air Development Center, October 1982.
6. Goel, A. L., "Software Reliability Models: Assumptions, Limitations, and Applicability," *IEEE Transactions on Software Engineering,* Vol. SE-11, 1985, pp. 1411–1423.
7. Goel, A. L., and K. Okumoto, "An Analysis of Recurrent Software Failures in a Real-Time Control System," *Proceedings ACM Annual Technology Conference,* ACM, Washington, D.C., 1978, pp. 496–500.
8. Goel, A. L., and K. Okumoto, "A Time-Dependent Error-Detection Rate Model for Software Reliability and Other Performance Measures," *IEEE Transactions on Reliability,* Vol. R-28, 1979, pp. 206–211.
9. Iannino, A., J. D. Musa, K. Okumoto, and B. Littlewood, "Criteria for Software Reliability Model Comparisons," *IEEE Transactions on Software Engineering,* Vol. SE-10, 1984, pp. 687–691.

10. Jelinski, Z., and P. Moranda, "Software Reliability Research," *Statistical Computer Performance Evaluation,* W. Freiberger, Ed., New York: Academic Press, 1972, pp. 465–484.

11. Littlewood, B., "Stochastic Reliability Growth: A Model for Fault Removal in Computer Programs and Hardware Designs," *IEEE Transactions on Reliability,* Vol. R-30, 1981, pp. 313–320.

12. Lyu, M. R., and A. Nikora, "Applying Reliability Models More Effectively," *IEEE Software,* July 1992, pp. 43–52.

13. Miller, D. R., "Exponential Order Statistic Models of Software Reliability Growth," *IEEE Transactions on Software Engineering,* Vol. SE-12, 1986, pp. 12–24.

14. Misra, P. N., "Software Reliability Analysis," *IBM Systems Journal,* Vol. 22, 1983, pp. 262–270.

15. Musa, J. D., A. Iannino, and K. Okumoto, *Software Reliability: Measurement, Prediction, Application,* New York: McGraw-Hill, 1987.

16. Musa, J. D., and K. Okumoto, "A Logarithmic Poisson Execution Time Model for Software Reliability Measurement," *Proceedings Seventh International Conference on Software Engineering,* Orlando, IEEE Computer Society Press, Los Alamitos, Calif., 1983, pp. 230–238.

17. Ohba, M., "Software Reliability Analysis Models," *IBM Journal of Research and Development,* Vol 28, 1984, pp. 428–443.

18. Putnam, L.H., and W. Myers, *Measures for Excellence: Reliable Software on Time, Within Budget,* Englewood Cliffs, N.J.: Yourdon Press, 1992.

19. Ralston, M. L., and R. I. Jennrich, "DUD, a Derivative-Free Algorithm for Nonlinear Least Squares," *Technometrics,* Vol. 20, 1978, pp. 7–14.

20. Rohatgi, V. K., *An Introduction to Probability Theory and Mathematical Statistics,* New York: John Wiley & Sons, 1976.

21. Wiener-Ehrlich, W. K., J. R. Hamrick, and V. F. Rupolo, "Modeling Software Behavior in Terms of a Formal Life Cycle Curve: Implications for Software Maintenance," *IEEE Transactions on Software Engineering,* Vol. SE-10, 1984, pp. 376–383.

22. Yamada, S., M. Ohba, and S. Osaki, "S-Shaped Reliability Growth Modeling for Software Error Detection," *IEEE Transactions on Reliability,* Vol. R-32, 1983, pp. 475–478.

# 9

## Quality Management Models

The models discussed in Chapters 7 and 8 are for reliability estimations. In this chapter we discuss models that can be used for quality management. We also give examples of in-process quality reports that support the models and discuss the recently proposed method of in-process defect type analysis—the orthogonal defect classification.

It is important to assess the quality of a software product, project the number of defects, or estimate the mean time to next failure when development work is complete. It is more important to monitor and manage the quality of the software when it is under development. Such a task is the purpose of the software quality management models. Although some models can be used for both reliability estimations and quality management, as we will see in later sections, how the models are used for quality management is different from that for reliability estimations. On the one hand, quality management models must be able to provide early signs of warning or of improvement so that timely actions can be planned and implemented. On the other hand, they can be less precise and less mathematical when compared to predictive models.

For a development organization, the quality management model(s) to be used must cover the early development phases if it is to be helpful. Models based on data collected at the end of the development process allow little time for action, if needed.

The reliability growth models, which are based on system-test data when development work is virtually complete, therefore, may not be as useful for in-process quality management as for reliability assessment. Nonetheless, the reliability growth models are useful for quality management in terms of tracking current status and determining when to end system testing for a specific predetermined quality goal.

Unlike the reliability models, which are numerous and include constantly emerging new ones, there are few models for in-process quality management in the literature. In the following sections we describe those models we know about and use.

## 9.1 The Rayleigh Model Framework

Perhaps the most important principle in software engineering is "do it right the first time." The principle speaks to the importance of managing quality throughout the entire development process. Our interpretation of the principle, in the context of software quality management, is threefold:

☐ The best scenario is to prevent errors from being injected into the development process.

☐ When errors are introduced, improve the front end of the development process to remove as many of them as early as possible. Specifically, in the context of the waterfall development process, rigorous design reviews and code inspections are needed. In the Cleanroom methodology, function verification by the team is used.

☐ If the project is beyond the design and code phases, unit tests and any additional tests by the developers serve as the gatekeeper for defects that escaped the front-end process before the code is integrated into the configuration management system (the system library). In other words, the phase of unit test or preintegration test (the development phase prior to system integration) is the last chance to do it right the first time.

The Rayleigh model is a good overall model for quality management. It articulates the points on defect prevention and early defect removal related to the preceding items. Based on the model, if the error injection rate is reduced, the entire area under the Rayleigh curve becomes smaller, leading to a smaller projected field defect rate. Also, more defect removal at the front end of the development process will lead to a lower defect rate at later testing phases and during maintenance. Both scenarios aim to lower the defects in the last testing phases, which in turn lead to fewer defects in the field. The relationship between formal machine-testing defects and field defects, as described by the model, is congruent with the famous counterintuitive principle in software testing by Myers (1979), which basically states that the more defects found during formal testing, the more that remained to be found later. The reason for that is because at the late stage of formal testing, error injection of the development process (mainly during design and code implementation) is basically determined (except for bad fixes during testing). High testing defect rates indicate that the error injection is high; hence, if no extra effort is exerted, more defects will escape to the field.

If we use the iceberg analogy to describe the relationship between testing and field defect rates, the tip of the iceberg is the testing defect rate and the submerged part the field defect rate. The size of the iceberg is equivalent to the amount of error injection. By the time formal testing starts, the iceberg is already formed and its size determined. The larger its tip, the larger the entire iceberg. To reduce the submerged part, extra effort must be applied to make the iceberg more exposed above the water. Figure 9.1 shows a schematic representation of the iceberg analogy.

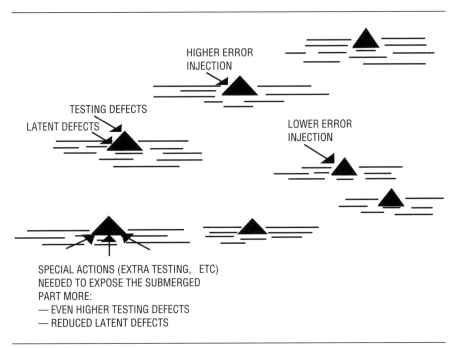

FIGURE 9.1
Error Injection, Testing Defects, and Latent Defects

A Rayleigh model derived from a previous release or from historical data can be used to track the pattern of defect removal of the project under development. If the current pattern is more front loaded than the model would predict, it is a positive sign, and vice versa. If the tracking is via calendar time such as month or week (versus by development phase) and when enough data points are available, early estimation of model parameters can be performed. Quality projections based on early data would not be reliable compared to the final estimate at the end of the development cycle. Nonetheless, for in-process quality management, the data points can indicate the direction of the quality in the current release so that timely actions can be taken.

Perhaps more important than for quality projections, the Rayleigh framework can serve as the basis for quality improvement strategy—especially the two principles associated with defect prevention and early defect removal. At IBM Rochester the two principles are in fact the major directions for our improvement strategy in development quality. For each direction, actions are formulated and implemented. For instance, to facilitate early defect removal, actions implemented include focus on the design review/code inspection (DR/CI) process; deployment of moderator training (for review and inspection meeting); use of an inspection checklist; use of in-process escape measurements to track the effectiveness of reviews and inspections; use of mini builds to flush out defects by developers before the system library build takes place; and many others. Plans and actions to reduce error injection include the laboratory-wide implementation of the defect prevention process; the use of powerful workstations and associated CASE tools for development; focus on communications among teams to prevent interface defects; and others. The bidirectional quality improvement strategy is illustrated in Figure 9.2 by the Rayleigh model. In summary, the goal is to shift the peak of the Rayleigh curve to the left while lowering it as much as possible. The ultimate target of IBM Rochester's strategy is to achieve the defect injection/removal pattern represented by the lowest curve, one with an error injection rate similar to the IBM Houston's Space Shuttle software projects.

This type of strategy can be implemented whether the defect removal pattern of an organization follows a Rayleigh curve or not. If not, the discrete phase-based defect model can be used. What is essential is that the phase-based defect removal targets be set to reflect an earlier defect removal pattern compared to the baseline. Then action plans should be implemented to achieve the targets.

One major problem with the defect removal model is related to the assumption of the error injection rate. When setting defect removal targets for a project, error injection rates can be estimated based on previous experience. However, one has no way of knowing how accurate such estimates are when applied to the current release. When tracking the defect removal rates against the model, lower actual defect removal could be the result of lower error injection or poor reviews and inspections. In contrast, higher actual defect removal could be the result of higher error injection or better reviews and inspections. From the in-process defect removal data of the project under development, how do we know which scenario (better defect removal, higher error injection, lower error injection, or poorer defect removal) the project belongs to? To solve this problem, additional indicators must be incorporated into the context of the model for better interpretation of the data.

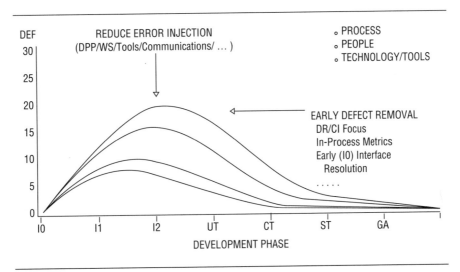

FIGURE 9.2
Rayleigh Model—Directions for Development Quality Improvement

One such additional indicator is the quality of the process execution. For instance, at IBM Rochester the metric of inspection effort (operationalized as the number of hours the team spent on design and code inspections normalized per thousand lines of source code inspected) is used as a proxy indicator for how rigorous the inspection process is executed. This metric, in combination with the inspection defect rate, can provide useful interpretation of the defect model. Specifically, a 2 × 2 matrix such as that shown in Figure 9.3 can be used. The high-low comparisons are between actual data and the model, or between the current and previous releases of a product.

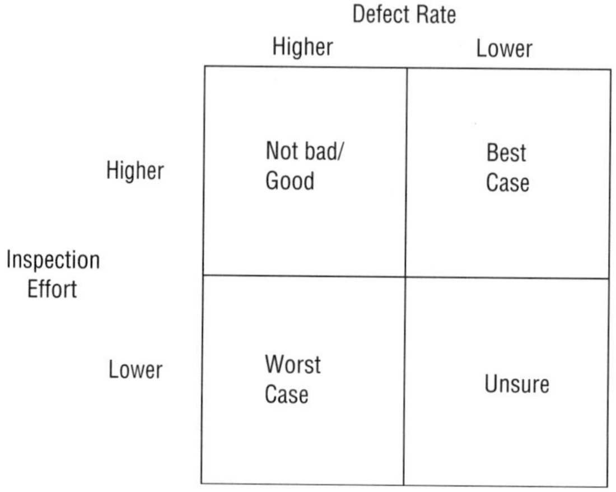

Defect Rate

|  | Higher | Lower |
|---|---|---|
| Higher | Not bad/ Good | Best Case |
| Lower | Worst Case | Unsure |

Inspection Effort

FIGURE 9.3

Inspection Effort/Defect Rate Scenarios When Comparing Actuals to Model

☐ *Best case scenario—high effort/low defect rate:* an indication that the design/code was cleaner before inspections, and yet the team spent enough effort in DR/CI (design review/code inspection) that better quality was ensured.

☐ *Good/not bad scenario—high effort/high defect rate:* an indication that error injection may be high, but higher effort spent is a positive sign and that may be why more defects were removed. If effort is significantly higher than the model target, this situation may be a good scenario.

☐ *Unsure scenario—low effort/low defect rate:* not sure whether the design and code were better, therefore less time in inspection was needed or inspections were hastily done, hence finding fewer defects. In this scenario we need to rely on the team's subjective assessment and other information for a better determination.

☐ *Worst case scenario—low effort/high defect rate:* an indication of high error injection but inspections were not rigorous enough. Chances are more defects remained in the design or code at the exit of the inspection process.

Figures 9.4 and 9.5 show a real-life example of the high effort/high defect rate scenario from two software products. Compared to a predecessor product, the inspection effort of the current product increased by more than 60%, and as a result the defect removal during the design and code inspection process was much higher than the predecessor product. As a result of the front-end effort, the test defect rate was significantly lower, and better field quality was observed. When development work was almost complete and lower test defect rates were observed, it was quite clear that the product would have better quality. However, during the front-end development it would have been difficult to interpret the defect removal pattern without the effort/defect matrix as part of the defect model.

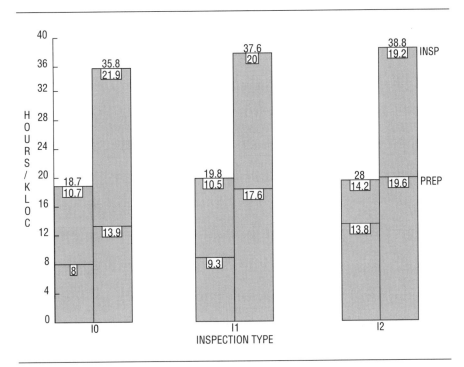

FIGURE 9.4

Inspection Effort Comparison by Phase Between Two Products

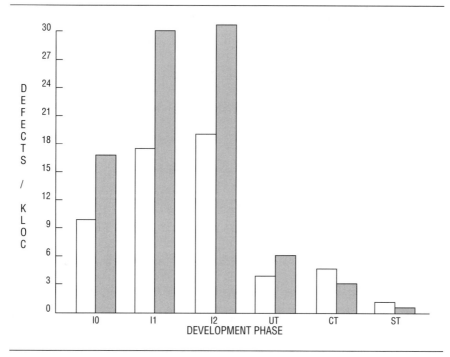

FIGURE 9.5
Defect Removal Patterns of Two Products

## 9.2 The PTR Submodel

Although the Rayleigh model, which covers all phases of the development process, can be used as the overall defect model, we need more specific models for better tracking of development quality. For example, the testing phases may span a number of months. For the waterfall process we used in previous examples, formal testing phases include component test, component regression test, and system test. For in-process quality management, one must also ensure that the chronological pattern of testing defect removal is also on track. To derive a testing defect model, once again the Rayleigh model or other parametric models can be used if such models adequately describe the testing defect arrival patterns.

   If the existing parametric models do not fit the defect patterns, special models for assessing in-process quality have to be developed. Furthermore, in large-scale software development, there is a common practice that the existing reliability models cannot address: the practice of continuous integration. Sequential chunks of code are integrated when ready and this integration occurs throughout the development cycle until system test starts. To address this situation we developed a simple nonparametric PTR submodel for testing defect tracking. It is called a PTR model because in many development organizations testing defects are tracked via some kind of problem tracking report (PTR), which is a part of the change control process during testing. Valid PTRs are, therefore, valid code defects. It is a submodel because it is part of the overall defect removal model. Simply put, the PTR submodel spreads over time the number of defects that are expected to be removed during the machine-testing phases so that more precise tracking is possible. It is a function of three variables:

1. Planned or actual lines of code integrated over time
2. Expected overall PTR rate (per thousand lines of code)
3. PTR-surfacing pattern after the code is integrated.

The expected overall PTR rate can be estimated from historical data. Lines-of-code (LOC) integration over time is usually available in the current implementation plan. The PTR-surfacing pattern after code integration depends on both testing activities and the driver-build schedule. For instance, if a new driver is built every week, the PTR discovery/fix/integration cycle will be faster than that for biweekly or monthly drivers. Assuming similar testing efforts, if the driver-build schedule differs from the previous release, adjustment to the previous release pattern is needed. If the current release is the first release, it is more difficult to establish a base pattern. Once a base pattern is established, subsequent refinements are relatively easy. For the AS/400 system, the base pattern was estimated from the earlier developed System/38 data and refined several times during the development process. The pattern of the initial release of AS/400 involved a seven-month spread of PTRs after code was integrated:

> 1st month:  17%
>
> 2nd month:  22%
>
> 3rd month:  20%
>
> 4th month:  16%
>
> 5th month:  12%
>
> 6th month:  9%
>
> 7th month:  4%

In other words, it was estimated that after each chunk of code was integrated, it took about seven months to virtually test out the defects.

To derive the PTR model curve, the following steps can be used:

1. Determine the code integration plan; plot the lines of code to be integrated over time (for example, Figure 9.6).

2. For each code integration, multiply the expected PTR rate with the KLOC for each planned integration to get the expected number of PTRs for each integration.

3. Spread over time the number of PTRs for each integration based on the PTR spread pattern and sum the number of PTRs for each time point to get the model curve.

4. Update the model when the integration plan (e.g., KLOC to be integrated over time) changes or actual integration data become available.

5. Plot the curve and track the current project in terms of months from the general availability (GA) date.

A calculator or a simple spreadsheet program is sufficient for the calculations involved in the model.

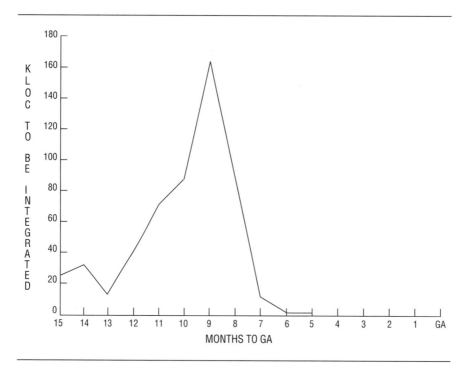

FIGURE 9.6

Planned KLOC Integration Over Time of a Software Project

Figure 9.7 shows an example of the PTR submodel with actual data. The code integration changes over time during development, so the model is updated periodically. In addition to quality tracking, the model also serves as a powerful quality impact statement for any slip in code integration or testing schedule. Specifically, any delay in development and testing will skew the model to the right, and the intersection of the model line and the vertical line of the GA date will become higher.

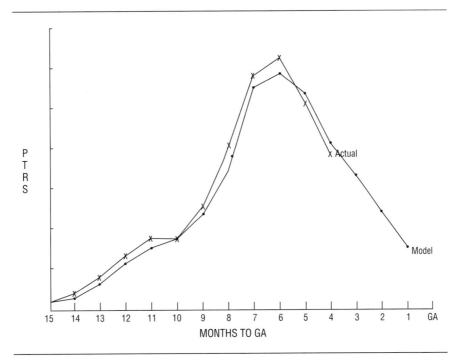

FIGURE 9.7
PTR Submodel

(*Source:* Kan, S. H., "Modeling and Software Development Quality," *IBM Systems Journal,* Vol. 30, No. 3, 1991, pp. 351–362. Copyright © 1991 International Business Machines Corporation. Reprinted with permission from *IBM Systems Journal.*)

Note that the PTR model is a nonparametric model and is not meant for projection. Its purpose is to enable the comparison of the actual testing defect arrival versus a desired/expected curve for in-process quality management. Compared to the model curve, if the actual defect arrivals increase and peak earlier and decline faster relative to the GA date, that is positive, and vice versa. When data from the previous release of the same product are available, and the code integration over time is similar for the two releases, the simplest way to gauge the testing-defect arrival pattern is to use the curve of the previous release as the model. Figure 9.8 shows such a comparison. Given that the test coverage and effectiveness of the releases are comparable, the PTR arrival patterns suggest that the current release will have a substantially lower defect rate. The data points are plotted in terms of number of weeks before GA. The mesa points in the early and later segments of the curves represent Christmas week and July 4th week, respectively.

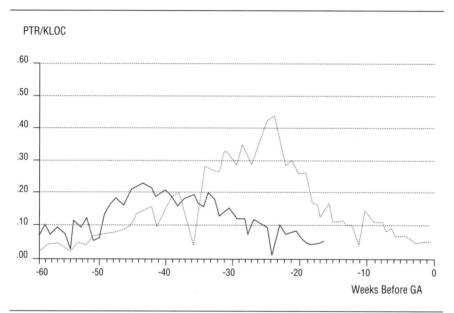

FIGURE 9.8
Testing Defect Arrival Patterns of Two Releases of a Product

## 9.3 The PTR Arrival/Backlog Projection Model

Near the end of the development cycle, a key question to ask is whether the scheduled code-freeze date can be met without sacrificing quality. Will the PTR arrival and backlog decrease to the predetermined desirable levels by the code-freeze date? The PTR submodel discussed earlier is clearly not able to accomplish this task because it is a tracking tool, not a projection tool. In contrast, the exponential model and other reliability growth models based on system-test data, while being sufficient for the task, requires data points well into the system test. Moreover, the analytic models may or may not be adequate depending on the goodness of fit. For cases like this, other types of modeling approaches may be needed. Here we present an example that we call the PTR arrival/backlog projection model. Its purpose is to project the PTR arrivals and backlog at the end of the development process. Analytical models aside, our approach was to derive empirical models based on available data from the current project. If we were able to capture key explanatory variables in the models, we should be able to tap the correct message of the data with a certain degree of confidence. In this regard the general linear model approach is readily available. From experience, we know that polynomial time terms combined with other relevant variables usually form good projection models.

This model is different from the exponential model in several aspects. First, the time frame covers all machine testing (all PTRs) after the code is integrated (part of unit test, component test, component regression test, and system test). The exponential model applies only to defect arrivals during system test. Second, the data for this model are PTR arrivals and backlog while the exponential model includes only valid PTRs (defects).

In our model building, the following sets of predictor variables were tested and their relationship with PTR arrival and backlog were specified:

- □ *Chronological time:* The rationale is to capture the chronological pattern of the development process. It is well known that software development follows life-cycle–like systematic processes. The specific time trend, however, varies between systems. It may be linear or polynomial patterns of second degree or higher, a Fourier series, or some other forms.

- □ *Time lag variables:* This set of variables is relevant because the data are of a time series nature and we need to assess the length of memory of these time series processes. Is this week's PTR number affected by the PTR occurrence of the preceding five weeks? four weeks? or the preceding fourth and third weeks but not the immediate two weeks? Does this process have memory at all? Testing this set of variables can give answers to questions like these.

- □ *Cumulative thousand lines of code (KLOC) integrated:* This variable is important because code was not integrated just at one point in time. Throughout the development cycle, pieces of code were integrated into the system library for testing. The number of PTRs is strongly related to the size of the code being tested.

- □ *Significant activities such as the onset of component test, system test, and other events:* This set of variables is dichotomous with 1 denoting the presence of the event and 0 denoting absence.

Prior to statistical testing of significance, scatterplots were used to examine the patterns of bivariate relationships and to detect potential outliers (Figures 9.9 and 9.10). For PTR arrival, a few obvious outliers were found, namely, the weeks of Thanksgiving, Christmas, and New Year's Day. The conspicuously low PTR arrivals for these weeks were apparently attributed to fewer working days as well as fewer programmers, which were artifacts of our calendar-time data. The values for these weeks, therefore, were replaced by the medians of the five consecutive data points centering at the weeks of interest. Values for the weeks of Memorial Day, Independence Day, and Labor Day were likewise substituted although they were not particularly low. For the backlog data, no adjustment is necessary because the data are of a cumulative nature.

PTR

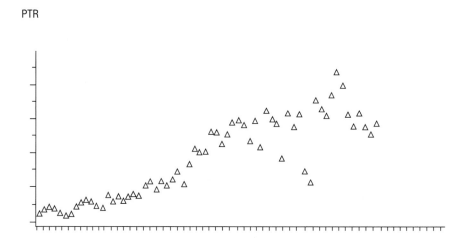

WEEK

FIGURE 9.9
PTR Arrival by Week

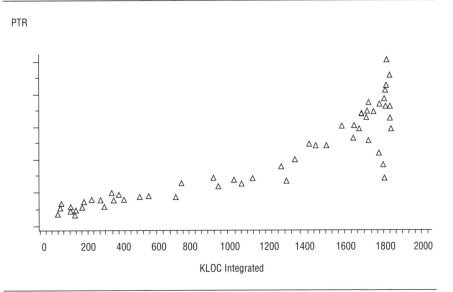

FIGURE 9.10
PTR Arrival by KLOC Integrated

When the patterns of bivariate relationships were specified and separate significance tests performed, the independent variables were put together in a model and their net effects were estimated simultaneously by the method of least squares. For both the arrival and backlog data, several models were attempted and the final model was chosen based on the highest $R^2$ value.

The number of PTR weekly arrivals was found to be a linear combination of a cubic pattern of time, a quadratic pattern of KLOC, the number of arrivals in the preceding week, and the presence or absence of the system test:

$$PTR\ arrival = Constant + f(Week,\ Week^2,\ Week^3,\ KLOC,\ KLOC^2,$$
$$\#\ Arrivals\ in\ preceding\ week,\ System\ test) + e$$

The equation of the model is as follows:

$$PTR\ arrival =$$
$$107.28764 - 3.22800 \times Week + 0.78017 \times Week^2$$
$$- 0.01048 \times Week^3$$
$$- 0.29980 \times KLOC + 0.00015 \times KLOC^2$$
$$+ 0.18030 \times \#\ Arrivals\ in\ preceding\ week$$
$$+ 140.50424 \times System\ test$$

The model was highly significant ($F = 169.6$, $df_1 = 7$, $df_2 = 55$, $p = 0.0001$) as were its component terms. All independent variables together accounted for 95.6% of the total variation of the arrival data. This $R^2$ translates to a multiple correlation of 0.978 between the model and the actual data.

Figure 9.11 compares the PTR arrival projection model with actual data points for the projection period. The model produces a projection that is accurate within a week in terms of when the PTR arrivals would decrease to the predetermined desirable level prior to code-freeze.

A PTR backlog model was likewise established and the projection was borne out very well.

This analysis showed that the PTR arrival and backlog processes at the end of the development cycle are predictable with fairly good accuracy. Both our models are sufficiently strong, explaining about 95% of the total variation of the dependent variables. Both series of projections were borne out amazingly well, and were within one week in estimating the time of meeting the criteria levels.

The approach can be used in similar situations where projections for future dates are needed. It is especially useful when analytical models are not applicable. However, it requires a fairly large number of data points and the data collected must pass the last inflection point of the process for the projections to be accurate. Another key is to capture significant variables in the model in order to obtain the highest $R^2$ possible. After the initial model is derived, updates should be done periodically when new data points become available. It is advisable to attempt different projection scenarios based on differing assumptions, hence giving a broader perspective for the assessment.

At the beginning of a process when few data points are available, analytical models or models based on past experiences can be derived for management purposes. When sufficient data are available, the best model can be determined based on goodness-of-fit tests. Combined with graphic techniques, the modeling approach is a very useful tool for software project management.

Unlike other models discussed, the PTR arrival/backlog projection model is really a modeling approach rather than a specific model. Statistical expertise, modeling experience, and a thorough understanding of the data are necessary in order to deal with issues pertaining to model assumptions, variables specification, and final model selection. A desirable outcome often depends on the model's $R^2$ and on the validity of the assumptions.

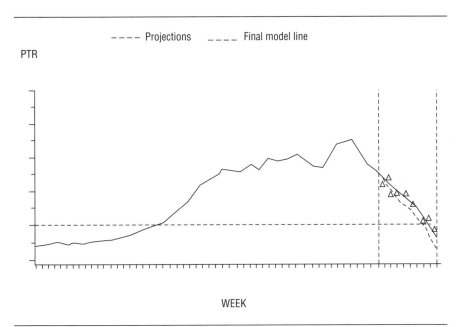

**FIGURE 9.11**
**PTR Arrival Projection Model**

(*Source:* Kan, S. H., "Modeling and Software Development Quality," *IBM Systems Journal*, Vol. 30, No. 3, 1991, pp. 351–362. Copyright © 1991 International Business Machines Corporation. Reprinted with permission from *IBM Systems Journal.*)

## 9.4  Reliability Growth Models

Although reliability growth models are meant for reliability assessment, they are also useful for quality management at the back end of the development process. Models developed from a previous product or a previous release of the same product can be used to track the testing defects of the current product. To experience significant improvement, the defect arrival rate (or failure density) of the current project must fall below the model curve. Figure 9.12 shows an example from a product of the AS/400 system. Each data point represents a weekly defect arrival rate during the system test phase. The defect arrival patterns as denoted by the triangles and circles represent two later releases of the same product. Compared to the baseline model curve, both new releases have witnessed a significant reduction in defect rate during system test.

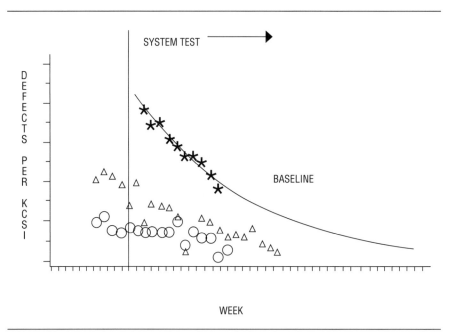

**FIGURE 9.12**
Reliability Growth Model for Quality Management

As a second example, several years ago when another product was just about at the start of system test, the PTR arrival rates were found to be unusually high compared to the model. It was clear that if proceeding in a business-as-usual manner, the quality of the product would not meet its quality goal. A special quality improvement program (QIP) was then proposed, evaluated, approved, and swiftly implemented. The program involved five extra activities:

1. *Blitz testing:* "artistic" testing in stressful environments
2. *Customer evaluation:* invited customers to the development laboratory to conduct customer testing

3.  *Code inspections:* additional inspections of error-prone modules, espe-
    cially those routines that are difficult to test such as the error
    recovery/exception handling routines

4.  *Design reviews:* rereview of designs of suspect components and modules

5.  *Extension of system test:* improved test suites and lengthened test schedules
    to allow thorough final test execution.

Because of the special QIP activities, the product ship date was delayed one month.
As a result, more than 250 would-be field defects were found and removed. The field
quality of the product, as evidenced by field defect arrivals for the past several years,
improved significantly.

Figure 9.13 shows the defect arrival pattern of the product during system test.
The data points represent the weekly defect rate (per thousand new and changed
code—KCSI). The asterisks represent the defect arrival from the originally planned
system test. The circles represent the total defect rates including the defect discovered and removed via the QIP activities. Since the QIP activities and defects were
specially marked in the defect tracking system, we were able to assess the additional
defect removal by the program.

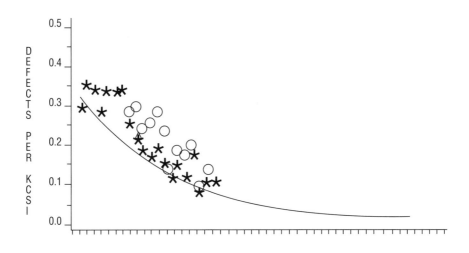

FIGURE 9.13
High Defect Arrival During System Test Compared to Model

When using the reliability growth models as a quality management tool, one of the advantages is that comparisons can be made when the first data points become available. If unfavorable signs are detected (for instance, defect arrivals are much too high), timely actions can be taken. In contrast, for reliability assessment and projection, a substantial amount of data has to be available for the models to be reliable. For models with an inflection point (such as the delayed S and inflection S models), data must be available beyond the inflection point if the models are to work. As discussed in the last chapter, studies showed that the exponential process model needs to have data of about 60% into system test in order to provide reasonably adequate fit and projection. Therefore, the reliability models can be used more liberally for quality management than for reliability projection.

The typical use of reliability models for quality management, as described in the software reliability literature, is to determine the end date of testing given a reliability goal or a specific defect level to be achieved. If the model derived from the current data indicates less-than-desirable quality, then more testing will be done until the reliability reaches the desired goal. This strategy assumes that there is an abundance of extra test cases available or the generation of extra test cases is relatively easy. For large commercial development projects, such an assumption may be difficult to meet. Test plans and test cases are developed over time along with design and code development; adding effective extra test cases is not a task that can be accomplished in a short time. Therefore, actions other than simply prolonging the testing (such as customer beta test, special stress testing, etc.) should also be considered.

Managing development quality based on reliability models at the back end should be used as the last step within the broader context of a series of quality management models. It should not be used as the sole model. A software development quality management system should put as much focus as possible at the front end, and actions should be triggered as early as possible if negative indicators are observed. Actions taken at design, code, unit test, integration time, and even at early formal machine testing time, are apt to be more cost effective and have a smaller chance of affecting the delivery date. Unfortunately, in the software reliability literature, one often gets the impression that the main way to achieve quality is to keep on testing until the defect-arrival rate or the mean-time-to-failure rate reaches the desirable level. Such a testing strategy to achieve quality improvement is not a good one. It is more applicable to research projects than to large-scale commercial developments, which often do not have the luxury to react at the back end and to delay delivery. The QIP example given earlier was the last major improvement action of that product, not the only one.

Finally, when interpreting the defect arrival data against a predetermined model, the variable of testing effort or coverage must be taken into consideration. For instance, if the defect arrivals are substantially below the model curve (as is the case in Figure 9.12), questions such as "are the lower defects due to less effective testing or really due to better quality?" must be asked. In this regard, the effort/defect matrix in Figure 9.3 also applies to the testing phases.

## 9.5  Criteria for Model Evaluation

As discussed in the previous chapter we contended that the most important criteria for evaluating reliability models are predictive validity, simplicity, and quality of assumptions, in that order of importance. With regard to quality management models, we propose that timeliness of quality indications, scope of coverage of the development process, and capability be the major criteria for evaluation.

The earlier a model can detect signs of quality problems or improvements, the more time is available for proactive planning. Furthermore, corrections made in the early phases of the development process are much less expensive than those made at the back end. In Chapter 6 we have elaborated the cost effectiveness of defect removal by development phase.

Model coverage of all phases of the entire development process is important. To have a good quality end product, quality in the intermediate deliverables at each phase, as defined by the phase entry and exit criteria, is a prerequisite. Each development phase must be managed and appropriate quality actions implemented. In case a single model cannot perform the tasks adequately, the use of multiple models is recommended.

While we contended that capability (other than predictability) is not an important criterion for software reliability models at the current state of the art, to the contrary, it is very important for management models. If capability refers to the model's ability to provide information for planning and managing software development projects, that is the purpose of quality management models. For instance, given the current in-process defect injection and removal pattern, will the project be likely to achieve its quality goal? If the effectiveness of the design review process improves by certain points, what is the possible impact on end-product quality? While quality management models may never reach the degree of accuracy and precision that reliability models have (or aim for), it is their capability to provide hints and findings for various in-process management questions that distinguish them as a separate category of software quality engineering models.

## 9.6  In-Process Metrics and Reports

We have thus far discussed an overall framework and the models associated with the framework for quality management during the development process. To facilitate the implementation of these models, we need a defect tracking and reporting system and a set of related in-process metrics. This is especially true for large development projects for which many teams are involved. In-process measurements and feedback, therefore, need to be available at various levels, ranging from the component team (several members) level to the entire product and system, which may involve more than one organization. In this section we present some examples of in-process metrics and reports.

```
                         DEFECT    RATE
              Significant HIGHER <----------------> Significant LOWER
           +--------------------------------+----------------------------+
           |          ***  H H  ***         |         ***  H L  ***      |
    I      |                                |                            |
    N Sign |    SCENARIO 2: GOOD/NOT BAD     |   SCENARIO 1: BEST CASE    |
    S HIG- |                                |                            |
    P HER  | * MAY NEED EMPHASIS ON DEFECT  | * ASK IF INSPECTION        |
    E      |     PREVENTION                 |     EFFECTIVE?             |
    C      |                                |                            |
    T      | * KEEP UP THE GOOD INSPECTION  | * IF YES, INDICATION OF GOOD |
    I      |     EFFORT                      |     QUALITY                 |
    O      |                                |                            |
    N      |--------------------------------|----------------------------|
           |          ***  L H  ***         |         ***  L L  ***      |
    E Sign |                                |                            |
    F LOW- |    SCENARIO 4: WORST CASE       |   SCENARIO 3: UNSURE       |
    F ER   |                                |                            |
    O      | * INDICATION OF LOW QUALITY     | * LOOK FOR OTHER INDICATORS |
    R      |                                |     SUCH AS REWORK TIME     |
    T      | * CONSIDER REINSPECTION         | * INCREASE INSPECTION EFFORT |
           | * MAY NEED EMPHASIS ON          |                            |
           |     PREVENTION                 |                            |
           | * NEED TO INCREASE EFFORT AND   |                            |
           |     IMPROVE INSPECTION RIGOR    |                            |
           |                                |                            |
           +--------------------------------+----------------------------+
```

In addition to the matrix above, also ask these questions:

- Have all mandatory reviewers attended?
- Were the inspectors well prepared?
- Were all materials covered?
- Was the meeting time adequate for the amount and complexity of materials?

FIGURE 9.14

Example of an Inspection Report—Effort/Defect Matrix

Figures 9.14 and 9.15 show examples of reports that can support the implementation of the front end of the Rayleigh model—the design and code inspection phases. Figure 9.14 is the implementation version of the effort/defect matrix in Figure 9.3. It is the first part of the inspection report and provides guidelines for interpretation and for actions with regard to the data in Figure 9.15.

In Figure 9.15 the number of inspections completed so far by stage (I0, I1, and I2) is shown. Information on actual lines of code inspected (Insp LOCs), total lines of code in the current plan for the department (DCR LOC), number of defects found, inspection effort in terms of preparation hours and actual inspection hours, rework hours, and the number of participants at the inspections (#Ats) are shown in the first part of the upper panel. Shown in the second part of the first panel (defined by double dashed lines) are the normalized metrics such as percent inspection coverage (%Insp CVG), defects per thousand lines of code (Defs/Kloc), preparation hours per KLOC (PrepHr/Kloc), actual inspection hours per KLOC (InspHr/Kloc), total hours on inspection (the sum of preparation time and actual inspection time) per KLOC (TotHrs/Kloc), rework hours per KLOC (RwrkHr/Kloc) to complete the design or coding phase, and the average number of participants per inspection. The system model in terms of inspection defect rates (Sys Model) and inspection effort (Sys Stddr) are also presented for comparison.

In the second panel the same information for the previous release of the same team or department is shown. In the bottom panel comparisons are made according to the scenarios of the effort/defect matrix. For each phase of inspection, two comparisons are made: current release compared to the previous release, and current release compared to the system model. Specifically, the first comparison involves comparing "Defs/Kloc" and "TotHrs/Kloc" in the first panel with the corresponding numbers in the second panel. The second comparison involves comparing "Defs/Kloc" with "Sys Model" and "TotHrs/Kloc" with "Sys Stddr" within the first panel (current release). The report also automatically flags the total inspection effort (TotHrs/Kloc) if its value is lower than the system standard (Sys Stddr). As discussed in Chapter 6 on defect removal effectiveness, inspection defect removal is much more cost effective compared to testing. Therefore, if a team's inspection effort is below the system standard, the minimum the team should do is to examine if there is enough rigor in their inspections, and if not, take actions accordingly.

```
                      Summary Inspection Report        Date:
                    Defect Rate and Inspection Effort   Time:
===============================================================================
*** Dept/Comp    A                                   Release  N
---- ------ -------- -------- ------ ------ ------- ------- ------ ------
Insp    #      Insp    DCR            Prep   Insp    Total  Rwrk     #
Type  Insps   Locs    Locs    Defs  Hours  Hours   Hours  Hours   Ats
---- ------ -------- -------- ------ ------ ------- ------- ------ ------
I0      64    23604    38077    298  502.1  464.1   966.2  164.2   556
I1      19     9620    38077    203  151.6  158.6   310.2  122.7    86
I2     136    30886    38077   1059  760.6  671.8  1432.4  574.4   529

*** Dept/Comp    A                                   Release  N
---- ------ -------- -------- ------ ------ ------- ------- ------ ------
Insp  %Insp   Defs    Sys    PrepHr InspHr TotHrs   Sys   RwrkHr  #At
Type   CVG   /Kloc   Model   /Kloc  /Kloc  /Kloc   Stddr  /Kloc  /Insp
---- ------ -------- -------- ------ ------ ------- ------- ------ ------
I0    62.0    12.6     7.0    21.3   19.7   40.9    19.6    7.0    8.7
I1    25.3    21.1    15.0    15.8   16.5   32.2    22.8   12.8    4.5
I2    81.1    34.3    13.0    24.6   21.8   46.4    26.0   18.6    3.9

===============================================================================
*** Dept/Comp    A                                   Release  N-1
---- ------ -------- -------- ------ ------ ------- ------- ------ ------
Insp    #      Insp    DCR            Prep   Insp    Total  Rwrk     #
Type  Insps   Locs    Locs    Defs  Hours  Hours   Hours  Hours   Ats
---- ------ -------- -------- ------ ------ ------- ------- ------ ------
I0      58    42917    51652    679  540.0  413.4   953.4  371.5   627
I1      43    28924    51652    499  264.7  262.2   526.9  210.5   330
I2     107    44904    51652   1168  869.1  734.0  1603.1  620.8   488

*** Dept/Comp    A                                   Release  N-1
---- ------ -------- -------- ------ ------ ------- ------- ------ ------
Insp  %Insp   Defs    Sys    PrepHr InspHr TotHrs   Sys   RwrkHr  #At
Type   CVG   /Kloc   Model   /Kloc  /Kloc  /Kloc   Stddr  /Kloc  /Insp
---- ------ -------- -------- ------ ------ ------- ------- ------ ------
I0    83.1    15.8     7.0    12.6    9.6   22.2    19.6    8.7   10.8
I1    56.0    17.3    15.0     9.2    9.1   18.2    22.8    7.3    7.7
I2    86.9    26.0    13.0    19.4   16.3   35.7    26.0   13.8    4.6
===============================================================================
I0 : Compared to previous release          you are at  HL  +------+------+
   : Compared to system standard & model  you are at  HH  | HH   | HL   |
I1 : Compared to previous release          you are at  HH  |      |      |
   : Compared to system standard & model  you are at  HH  |------|------|
I2 : Compared to previous release          you are at  HH  |      |      |
   : Compared to system standard & model  you are at  HH  | LH   | LL   |
                                                          +------+------+

===============================================================================
```

FIGURE 9.15

Example of an Inspection Report—Inspection Effort and Defect Rate

Note that for the effort/design matrix, the inspection effort matrix is a proxy variable to measure how well and how rigorously the inspection process was executed. It is one operational definition to measure process quality, but not the only one. An alternative could be the inspection team's assessment and the inspection scoring approach. Specifically, instead of (or in addition to) the tracking of inspection effort, the inspection team assesses the effectiveness of the inspection and the quality of the design (or code) at the end of an inspection. Simple questionnaires such the one shown in Table 9.1 can be used.

| | Response | | | | | | | | | |
| --- | --- | --- | --- | --- | --- | --- | --- | --- | --- | --- |
| | **Poor** | | | **Acceptable** | | | | | **Excellent** | |
| Design | 1 | 2 | 3 | 4 | 5 | 6 | 7 | 8 | 9 | 10 |
|   Work meets requirements | 1 | 2 | 3 | 4 | 5 | 6 | 7 | 8 | 9 | 10 |
|   Understandability of design | 1 | 2 | 3 | 4 | 5 | 6 | 7 | 8 | 9 | 10 |
|   Extendibility of design | 1 | 2 | 3 | 4 | 5 | 6 | 7 | 8 | 9 | 10 |
|   Documentation of design | 1 | 2 | 3 | 4 | 5 | 6 | 7 | 8 | 9 | 10 |
|   Effectiveness of this inspection | 1 | 2 | 3 | 4 | 5 | 6 | 7 | 8 | 9 | 10 |
| Does another inspection need to be held? | | | | | \_\_\_\_\_Yes | | | | \_\_\_\_\_No | |

| | Response | | | | | | | | | |
| --- | --- | --- | --- | --- | --- | --- | --- | --- | --- | --- |
| | **Poor** | | | **Acceptable** | | | | | **Excellent** | |
| Code Implementation | 1 | 2 | 3 | 4 | 5 | 6 | 7 | 8 | 9 | 10 |
|   Work meets design | 1 | 2 | 3 | 4 | 5 | 6 | 7 | 8 | 9 | 10 |
|   Performance considerations | 1 | 2 | 3 | 4 | 5 | 6 | 7 | 8 | 9 | 10 |
|   Understandability of implementation | 1 | 2 | 3 | 4 | 5 | 6 | 7 | 8 | 9 | 10 |
|   Maintainability of implementation | 1 | 2 | 3 | 4 | 5 | 6 | 7 | 8 | 9 | 10 |
|   Documentation | 1 | 2 | 3 | 4 | 5 | 6 | 7 | 8 | 9 | 10 |
|   Effectiveness of this inspection | 1 | 2 | 3 | 4 | 5 | 6 | 7 | 8 | 9 | 10 |
| Does another inspection need to be held? | | | | | \_\_\_\_\_Yes | | | | \_\_\_\_\_No | |

TABLE 9.1

Example of an Inspection Scoring Questionnaire

It is preferable to conduct two assessments for each inspection, one before and one after (when rework is complete). Such pre- and postinspection evaluations provide information on the effect of the inspection process. For the preinspection assessment, the question on whether another inspection is needed may not apply.

The inspection scores can then be used as indicators of the process quality as well as the interim product (design and code) quality. When data on multiple inspections are available, the technique of control charting can be used for in-process quality control. For instance, the team may establish a requirement for mandatory rework or reinspection if the score of a design or an implementation is below the lower control limit.

When using the inspection scoring approach, factors related to small team dynamics should be considered. Data from this approach may not be unobtrusive and therefore should be interpreted carefully, and within the context of the development organization and the process used. For instance, there may be a tendency among the inspection team to avoid giving low scores even though the design or implementation is poor. A score of 5 (acceptable) may actually be a 2 or a 3. Therefore, it is important to use a wider response scale (such as the 10-point scale) instead of a narrow one (such as a 3-point scale). A wider response scale provides enough room to express (and observe) variations and, once enough data are available, valid interpretations can be developed.

Figure 9.16 shows another example of inspection defect reports. The defects are classified in terms of defect origin (RQ—requirements, SD—system design, I0—high-level design, I1—low-level design, I2—code development) and defect type (LO—logic, IF—interface, DO—documentation). The major purpose of the report is to show two metrics—in-process escape rate and percent of interface defects. The concept of in-process escape rate is related to the concept of defect removal effectiveness that was examined in Chapter 6. The effectiveness metric is a powerful metric but not an in-process metric. It cannot be calculated until all defect data for the entire development process become available. The in-process escape metric asks the question in a different way. The effectiveness metric asks "what is the percentage of total defects found and removed by this phase of inspection?", whereas the in-process escape metric asks "among the defects found by this phase of inspection, what is the percentage that should have been found by previous phases?" The lower the in-process escape rate, the more likely that the effectiveness of the previous phases was better. The in-process escape metric also supports the earlier defect removal approach. For example, if among the defects found by I2 there is a high percentage that should have been found by I1, that means I1 was not done well enough and remedial actions should be implemented.

```
                        Summary Inspection Report        Date:
                        By Defect Origin and Defect Type  Time:
=================================================================
*** Dept/Comp          A                            Release  N
---- ----      --------------------      ----------------------------------
Insp           <-- Defect  Origin -->    <------ % DISTRIBUTIION ------->
Type Defs      RQ  CAI  I0   I1   I2      RQ   SD   I0     I1     I2 TOT
---- ----      --------------------      ----------------------------------
I0    298      26   15  257   0    0     8.7  5.0  86.2   ---    --- 100%
I1    203       0    0   10  193   0     0.0  0.0   4.9  95.1    --- 100%
I2   1059      11    0   41   97  910    1.0  0.0   3.9   9.2   85.9 100%


---- ---- ------- ----          ------------------      ------------------------
Insp   #   Insp                 <- Defect Type ->        <-- Defect   Type  -->
Type Insp  Locs Defs              LO   IF   DO           %LO   %IF    %DO    Tot
---- ---- ------- ----          ------------------      ------------------------
I0    64  23604  298              56   79  163          18.8  26.5   54.7  100%
I1    19   9620  203             138    9   56          68.0   4.4   27.6  100%
I2   136  30886 1059             684   65  310          64.6   6.1   29.3  100%
=================================================================
*** Dept/Comp          A                            Release  N-1
---- ----      --------------------      ----------------------------------
Insp           <-- Defect  Origin -->    <------ % DISTRIBUTIION ------->
Type Defs      RQ  CAI  I0   I1   I2      RQ   SD   I0     I1     I2 TOT
---- ----      --------------------      ----------------------------------
I0    679      22    2  655   0    0     3.2  0.3  96.5   ---    --- 100%
I1    499       5    0   50  444   0     1.0  0.0  10.0*  89.0   --- 100%
I2   1168       4    1   19  125 1019    0.3  0.1   1.6  10.7   87.2 100%
---- ---- ------- ----          ------------------      ------------------------
Insp   #   Insp                 <- Defect Type ->        <-- Defect   Type  -->
Type Insp  Locs Defs              LO   IF   DO           %LO   %IF    %DO    Tot
---- ---- ------- ----          ------------------      ------------------------
I0    58  42917  679              95  143  441          14.0  21.1   64.9  100%
I1    43  28924  499             254   35  210          50.9   7.0   42.1  100%
I2   107  44904 1168             668   78  422          57.2   6.7   36.1  100%
=================================================================
*** IN-PROCESS ESCAPE RATE SYSTEM TARGET
I1 defects : <= 5% are escapes from HLD
I2  -"-    : <= 2% are escapes from HLD
I2  -"-    : <= 6% are escapes from LLD


*** INTERFACE DEFECT REDUCTION
I0        : Interface issues finalized at I0 exit
I1 & I2   : Goal is to reduce interface defects to
            <= 5% of total defects


(*)       : EXCEEDS system target significantly (2x+)
            Consider RE-INSPECTION AND OTHER ACTIONS.
(@)       : EXCEEDS system target significantly (2x+).
            Consider RE-INSPECTION AND OTHER ACTIONS. MAKE
            SURE INTERFACE ISSUES ARE FINALIZED AT I0 EXIT.
=================================================================
NOTE: When interpreting * and @, be careful with small numbers.
```

FIGURE 9.16

Example of an Inspection Report—Defect Origin and Defect Type

The rationale of the metric of percentage of interface defects is that a large percentage of defects throughout the development life cycle (from design defects to field defects) is due to interface issues. Furthermore, interface problems are to a large extent related to human communications and, therefore, preventable. Reducing interface defects should be an objective in in-process quality management. One of the objectives of high-level design is to finalize interface issues at the exit of I0. Therefore, it is logical to see high percentages of interface defects at I0. However, at subsequent phases, if the percent of interface defects remains high, it implies that the goal of resolving interface issues at I0 has not been achieved. In this example, the predetermined targets for in-process escape rates and for interface defect reduction were also shown in the report, and exceptions were flagged.

---

```
              Unit Test Coverage and Defect Report              Date:
                                                                Time:
              Status = Approved, Integrated, Completed, Closed
              PRODUCT = XX  COMPONENT=ALL  DEPT= B  RELEASE= N
```

| | | | | | | | | | | TOTAL |
| | | | | | DEFS | UT | TOTAL | DEFS/ | PTR/ | DEFS/ |
| PROD | CPID | DCRLOC | UTLOC | %CVG | (DCR) | PTRS | DEFS | UT-KLOC | DCR KLOC | DCR KLOC |
|------|------|--------|-------|------|-------|------|-------|---------|----------|-----------|
| XX | CP1 | 20 | 30 | 100.0 | 4 | 1 | 5 | 133.3 | 50.0 | 250.0 |
| XX | CP2 | 4084 | 4315 | 100.0 | 67 | 9 | 76 | 15.5 | 2.2 | 18.6 |
| XX | CP3 | 175 | 175 | 100.0 | 1 | 0 | 1 | 5.7 | 0.0 | 5.7 |
| XX | CP4 | 3983 | 3959 | 99.4 | 16 | 1 | 17 | 4.0 | 0.3 | 4.3 |
| XX | CP5 | 7406 | 7389 | 99.8 | 134 | 39 | 173 | 18.1 | 5.3 | 23.4 |
| XX | CP6 | 2589 | 1289 | 49.8 | 6 | 0 | 6 | 4.7 | 0.0 | 2.3 |
| XX | CP7 | 2947 | 2845 | 96.5 | 50 | 2 | 52 | 17.6 | 0.7 | 17.6 |
| XX | CP8 | 735 | 700 | 95.2 | 8 | 3 | 11 | 11.4 | 4.1 | 15.0 |
| XX | CP9 | 2570 | 1292 | 50.3 | 16 | 20 | 36 | 12.4 | 7.8 | 14.0 |
| XX | CP10 | 6888 | 1300 | 18.9 | 19 | 4 | 23 | 14.6 | 0.6 | 3.3 |
| XX | CP11 | 441 | 304 | 68.9 | 8 | 4 | 12 | 26.3 | 9.1 | 27.2 |
| XX | CP12 | 2 | 2 | 100.0 | 0 | 1 | 1 | 0.0 | 500.0 | 500.0 |
| XX | TOTAL | 31840 | 23600 | 74.1 | 329 | 84 | 413 | 13.9 | 2.9 | 13.3 |

---

FIGURE 9.17

Example of a Unit Test Coverage and Defect Report

Figure 9.17 shows a report on unit test coverage and defects. Ideally unit tests are conducted before code integration. Due to various reasons (dependency, schedule pressures, etc.), it is not uncommon that some unit tests are done after code integration. The in-process metrics and reports, therefore, should reflect the state of practice and encourage defect removal before integration. In Figure 9.17 the columns include the product ID (PROD), the ID of the components (CPID) that the organization owns, the lines of code by components for the current release (DCRLOC), the lines of code that have been unit tested so far (UTLOC), the unit test coverage so far (%CVG = UTLOC × 100/DCRLOC), the number of unit test defects found before integration [DEFS (DCR)], the number of unit test defects found after integration and expressed in the form of problem-tracking reports (UT PTRs), and the normalized rates. The key interests of the report are the ratio of preintegration defect removal [DEFS (DCR)] to postintegration defects (UT PTRS) and the overall unit test defect rate (TOTAL DEFS/DCR KLOC). The interpretation is that the higher the ratio and the higher defect removal before integration, the better. Components with high unit test defects found after code integration should be examined closely. Comparisons can also be made for the same components between two consecutive releases to reveal if improvements are being made toward an earlier defect removal pattern.

Figure 9.18 shows the test defect rate by phase. In addition to postintegration unit test defects (UT), defects found during the build and integration process (BI), component test (CT), component regression test (CRT), system test (ST), and early customer programs (customer field test, customer early burn-in program, etc.) are also shown. The column DCR LOC again shows the lines of new and changed code for the current release. The DEFS/KLOC column shows the defect rate per KLOC. The three components that have 0 in the DCR LOC column are the components that did not have new and changed code for that particular release but took part in the testing effort to remove defects in the existing code.

Data from Figure 9.18, together with data for unit test and the front-end inspections, provide sufficient information for the overall defect removal patterns for the entire development process. These in-process metrics and reports cannot be used in a piecemeal fashion. They should be used together within the context of the quality management models.

```
                    PTR BY TEST ACTIVITY
         DEPT: C      PROD: YY    CPID: ALL      Date:
                    Release:    N               Time:
```

| PROD | CPID | UT | BI | CT | CRT | ST | ECP | TOTAL | DCR LOC | DEFS/ KLOC |
|------|------|-----|-----|-----|-----|-----|-----|-------|---------|------------|
| YY | COMP1 | 2 | 0 | 3 | 0 | 0 | 0 | 5 | 1150 | 4.3 |
| YY | COMP2 | 2 | 0 | 16 | 6 | 5 | 0 | 29 | 940 | 30.9 |
| YY | COMP3 | 0 | 0 | 2 | 0 | 1 | 0 | 3 | 0 | -- |
| YY | COMP4 | 1 | 0 | 3 | 2 | 1 | 0 | 7 | 50 | 140.0 |
| YY | COMP5 | 0 | 0 | 1 | 0 | 2 | 0 | 3 | 1050 | 2.9 |
| YY | COMP6 | 1 | 0 | 2 | 3 | 4 | 1 | 11 | 0 | -- |
| YY | COMP7 | 0 | 2 | 4 | 0 | 1 | 0 | 7 | 605 | 11.6 |
| YY | COMP8 | 1 | 0 | 7 | 0 | 0 | 0 | 8 | 51 | 156.9 |
| YY | COMP9 | 1 | 1 | 3 | 1 | 1 | 0 | 7 | 172 | 40.7 |
| YY | COMP10 | 0 | 0 | 1 | 0 | 0 | 0 | 1 | 0 | -- |
| YY | COMP11 | 3 | 0 | 13 | 3 | 8 | 0 | 27 | 1775 | 15.2 |
| YY | COMP12 | 0 | 1 | 1 | 0 | 0 | 0 | 2 | 293 | 6.8 |
| YY | COMP13 | 0 | 0 | 8 | 4 | 5 | 0 | 17 | 800 | 21.3 |
| YY | COMP14 | 0 | 0 | 1 | 0 | 0 | 0 | 1 | 200 | 5.0 |
| YY | COMP15 | 1 | 0 | 0 | 0 | 0 | 0 | 1 | 25 | 40.0 |
| YY | TOTAL | 12 | 4 | 65 | 19 | 28 | 1 | 129 | 7111 | 18.1 |

-- Not applicable

FIGURE 9.18
Example of a Defects by Test Phase Report

In addition to the basic metrics and reports, there are many more that are useful for in-process quality management. The first of such is perhaps the test defect origin report. Similar to the inspection defect origin report, this reports classifies defects for each test phase by where they should have been found. For instance, when a defect is reported during a system test, its test origin (UT, CT, or ST) will be determined by involved parties. Usually it is easier to delineate if a certain defect is a system test type defect or not, than to distinguish the difference between a unit test defect and a component test defect.

Other reports such as severity distribution of test defects, defect cause by test phase, and changes during the test phases due to performance reasons also provide important indicators with regard to the quality of the product. Testing defect rates have a strong correlation with field defect rates; the severity of test defects is also a good indicator of the severity distribution of field defects. Severe problems, usually difficult to be circumvented, tend to have a more pervasive impact on customer business. Performance changes, especially the late ones, are error-prone activities. If negative signals are detected from these metrics, proactive actions (for example, special customer evaluation or extended customer burn-in) should be planned before the release of the product.

## 9.7 Orthogonal Defect Classification

Orthogonal defect classification (ODC) is a method for in-process quality management based on defect cause analysis (Chillarege *et al.*, 1992). Defect cause or defect type analysis by phase of development is not new. In many development organizations, metrics associated with defect cause are part of the in-process measurement system. What the ODC authors proposed and claimed is that a set of mutually independent cause categories (orthogonal) can be developed, which can be used across phases of development and across products, and that the distribution of these defect types is associated with process phases. A more or less stable profile of defect-type distribution can be established by phase of development. By examining the distribution of defect types, therefore, one can tell which development phase the current project is at, logically. The authors proposed eight defect types: function, interface, checking, assignment, timing/serialization, build/package/merge, documentation, and algorithm. They contended that functional defects (missing or incorrect functions) are associated with the design phase; interface phase defects are associated with low-level design; checking with low-level design or code implementation; assignment with code, timing/serialization with low-level design; build/package/merge with library tools; documentation defects with publications; and algorithms with low-level design.

The authors showed several examples of the use of ODC. One example illustrated the high percentage of the defect type "function" found at a late stage in the development cycle. Specifically, the defect discovery time was classified into four periods; the last period corresponded approximately to the system test phase. In the last period the number of defects found almost doubled, and the percent of defect type "function" increased to almost 50%. Since the defect type "function" is supposed to be found earlier (during the design phase), the observed distribution indicated a clear departure from the expected process behavior. Given that function defects were the cause of the departure, the analysis also suggested an appropriate design reinspection rather than more intensive testing.

In addition to defect-type analysis, the authors proposed the use of defect triggers for improving testing effectiveness. A defect trigger is a condition that allows a defect to surface. By capturing information on defect triggers during testing and for field defects reported by customers, the test team can improve its test design and test cases based on the information to maximize the defect discovery.

Now being piloted in several IBM development laboratories, the ODC approach is still in the experimental stage and its effect remains to be seen. The focus on defect cause analysis of in-process defect data is a correct approach and the defect trigger concept appears to be useful. However, whether ODC can achieve its claims is an open question. Whether defect cause classification can be truly orthogonal deserves a much closer look. Much like the cause-structure of death of human beings (which has been researched extensively), the interrelations and possible interdependencies of software defect causes merit further research. Moreover, the eight orthogonal defect types proposed by the ODC authors seem to contain a mixture of causes (interface, checking, assignment, etc.) and symptoms (documentation, build/package/merge).

Whether the process associations with defect type can be applied across products uniformly is another open question. Even assuming similar development processes, differences in process details and focus areas may lead to differences in the distribution of defect causes/types. For instance, in the example shown in Figure 9.16, final resolution of interface issues is one of the exit criteria of high-level design inspection (I0). Therefore, higher percentages of interface defects are observed at I0, instead of at low-level design or I1. Another variable is the maturity level of the development process, especially in terms of the error injection rate. A defect-type distribution for a development organization with an error injection rate of 60 defects per KLOC is likely to be different from that with an error injection rate of 20 defects per KLOC. The actions for reducing error injection or defect prevention are likely to have stronger effects on some defect causes than on others.

With regard to using a defect-type distribution for assessing the progress of the project, the ODC method seems to be too indirect. A more direct approach is to use the defect origin (or test origin) or where injected data (such as the example in Figure 9.16). Some may argue that the defect origin data are subjective. However, if the objectives of each development phase are well defined and understood (such as the example in Chapter 2, Section 2.2), and the determination of defect origin is by the inspection team (versus a single developer), then a certain degree of objectivity (or intersubjectivity, for that matter) can be achieved. Note that even for the ODC defect classification, there is also an element of subjectivity involved when entering data. From the process improvement standpoint, perhaps truly objective data is not as important as consistent data on which the team can act. As long as the team's (or the process's) practice in determining defect origin (or test origin) data is consistent, the metric can be used to drive improvement. Of course, the two approaches (defect origin and defect type) are complementary to each other. They should be used together for in-process assessment along with other metrics and models.

Therefore, the use of defect cause analysis in general, or ODC specifically, must be calibrated according to specific development environments, the process used, and the maturity level of the process. It should be an integrated part of the in-process metrics within the context of models. If used alone, its usefulness will be limited.

## 9.8 Summary

Quality management models are valuable for monitoring and managing the quality of the software when it is under development. These models emerged from the practical needs of large-scale software development. Unlike reliability models, which are numerous and with new ones constantly emerging, there are few models for in-process quality management in the literature. Whereas reliability models need to provide precise and predictively valid results, the demand for precision for management models is far less. In contrast, the major criteria for management models are timeliness for quality indications, scope of coverage (of various phases of the development process), and capability (various indicators and attributes of quality). Therefore, when reliability models are used for quality management instead of being a predictive tool, it entails a different focus.

The Rayleigh model (or for that matter the phase-based defect model) provides a nice framework for quality management, covering the entire development process. Within the overall Rayleigh framework, submodels such as the effort/defect matrix, the PTR submodel, the PTR arrival and backlog projection models, and the reliability growth models provide further specifics.

To implement these models, a good tracking and reporting system and a set of related in-process metrics are important. In-process defect-cause analysis, such as the ODC method, can lead to better understanding of the status and quality of the project.

## References

1. Chillarege, R., I. S. Bhandari, J. K. Chaar, M. J. Halliday, D. S. Moebus, B. K. Ray, and M-Y. Wong, "Orthogonal Defect Classification—A Concept for In-Process Measurements," *IEEE Transactions on Software Engineering,* Vol. 18, No. 11, November 1992, pp. 943–956.
2. Kan, S. H., "Modeling and Software Development Quality," *IBM Systems Journal,* Vol. 30, No. 3, 1991, pp. 351–362.
3. Myers, G.J., *The Art of Software Testing,* New York: John Wiley & Sons, 1979.

# 10

# Complexity Metrics and Models

Thus far the reliability and quality management models we discussed are at either the project or the product level. Both types of models tend to treat the software more or less as a black box. In other words, they are based on either the external behavior (e.g., failure data) of the product, or the intermediate process data (e.g., type and magnitude of inspection defects), without looking into the internal dynamics of design and code of the software. In this chapter we describe the relationships between metrics about design and code implementation and software quality. The unit of analysis is more granular, usually at the program-module level. Such metrics and models tend to take an internal view and can provide clues for software engineers to improve quality in their work.

Reliability models are developed and studied by researchers and software reliability practitioners with sophisticated skills in mathematics and statistics; quality management models are developed by software quality professionals and product managers for practical project and quality management. Software complexity research, on the other hand, is usually conducted by computer scientists or experienced software engineers. Like the reliability models, many complexity metrics and models have emerged in the recent past. In this chapter we discuss several key metrics and models, and describe a real-life example of metric analysis and quality improvement.

## 10.1 Lines of Code

The lines-of-code (LOC) count is usually for executable statements. It is actually a count of instruction statements. The interchangeable use of the two terms apparently originated from Assembler programs in which a line of code and an instruction statement are the same thing. Because the LOC count represents the program size and complexity, it is not a surprise that the more lines of code there are in a program, the more defects that are expected. More intriguingly, researchers found that defect density (defects per KLOC) is also significantly related to LOC count. Early studies pointed to a negative relationship: the larger the module size, the smaller the defect rate. For instance, Basili and Perricone (1984) examined FORTRAN modules with fewer than 200 lines of code for the most part and found higher defect density in the smaller modules. Shen and colleagues (1985) studied software written in Pascal, PL/S, and assembly language and found an inverse relationship existed up to about 500 lines. Since larger modules are generally more complex, a lower defect rate is somewhat counterintuitive. Interpretation of this finding rests on the explanation of interface errors: interface errors are more or less constant regardless of module size, and smaller modules are subject to higher error density because of smaller denominators.

More recent studies point to a curvilinear relationship between lines of code and defect rate: Defect density decreases with size and then curves up again at the tail when the modules become very large. For instance, Withrow (1990) studied modules written in Ada for a large project at Unisys and confirmed the concave relationship between defect density (during formal test and integration phases) and module size. Specifically, of a total of 362 modules with a wide range in size (from less than 63 lines to more than 1000), Withrow found the lowest defect density at the size category of about 250 lines. Explanation of the rising tail is readily available. When module size becomes very large, the complexity increases to a level beyond a programmer's immediate span of control and total comprehension. This new finding is also consistent with previous studies in which the defect density of very large modules was not addressed.

Experience from the AS/400 development also lends support to the curvilinear model. Figure 10.1 shows an example. In the example, although the concave pattern is not as significant as that in Withrow's study, the rising tail is still evident.

The curvilinear model between size and defect density sheds new light on software quality engineering. It implies that there may be an optimal program size that can lead to the lowest defect rate. Such an optimum may depend on language, project, product, and environment; apparently many more empirical investigations are needed. Nonetheless, when an empirical optimum is derived by reasonable methods (for example, based on the previous release of the same product, or based on a similar product by the same development group), it can be used as a guideline for new module development.

| Maximum Source Lines of Modules | Average Defect per Thousand Source Lines |
|:---:|:---:|
| 63 | 1.5 |
| 100 | 1.4 |
| 158 | 0.9 |
| 251 | 0.5 |
| 398 | 1.1 |
| 630 | 1.9 |
| 1000 | 1.3 |
| >1000 | 1.4 |

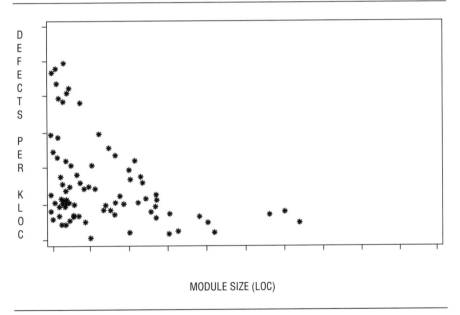

MODULE SIZE (LOC)

FIGURE 10.1
Curvilinear Relationship Between Defect Rate and Module Size

## 10.2  Halstead's Software Science

Halstead (1977) distinguished software science from computer science. The premise of software science is that any programming task consists of selecting and arranging a finite number of program "tokens," which are basic syntactic units distinguishable by a compiler. A computer program, according to software science, is considered a collection of tokens that can be classified as either operators or operands. The primitive measures of Halstead's software science are:

$n_1$ = the number of distinct operators that appear in a program

$n_2$ = the number of distinct operands that appear in a program

$N_1$ = the total number of operator occurrences

$N_2$ = the total number of operand occurrences.

Based on these primitive measures, Halstead developed a system of equations expressing the total vocabulary, the overall program length, potential minimum volume for an algorithm, the actual volume (number of bits required to specify a program), the program level (a measure of software complexity), program difficulty, and other features such as development effort and the projected number of faults in the software. Halstead's major equations include the following:

Vocabulary ($n$)   $n = n_1 + n_2$

Length ($N$)   $N = N_1 + N_2$

$\qquad\qquad = n_1 \log_2(n_1) + n_2 \log_2(n_2)$

Volume ($V$)   $V = N \log_2(n)$

$\qquad\qquad = N \log_2(n_1 + n_2)$

Level ($L$)   $L = V*/V$

$\qquad\qquad = (2/n_1) \times (n_2/N_2)$

Difficulty ($D$)   $D = V/V*$

  (inverse of level)  $= (n_1/2) \times (N_2/n_2)$

Effort ($E$)   $E = V/L$

Faults ($B$)   $B = V/S*$

where $V*$ is the minimum volume represented by a built-in function performing the task of the entire program, and $S*$ is the mean number of mental discriminations (decisions) between errors ($S*$ is 3000 according to Halstead).

Halstead's work has had a great impact on software measurement. His work was instrumental in making metrics studies an issue among computer scientists. However, software science has been controversial since its introduction and has been criticized from many fronts. Areas under criticism include methodology, derivations of equations, human memory models, and others. Empirical studies provided little support to the equations except for the estimation of program length. Even for the estimation of program length, the usefulness of the equation may be subject to dispute. To predict program length, data on $N_1$ and $N_2$ must be available, and by the time $N_1$ and $N_2$ can be determined, the program should be completed or near completion. Therefore, the predictiveness of the equation is limited. As discussed in Chapter 3, both the formula and actual LOC count are functions of $N_1$ and $N_2$; thus they appear to be just two operational definitions of the concept of program length. Therefore correlation exists between them by definition.

In terms of quality, the equation for $B$ appears to be oversimplified for project management, lacks empirical support, and provides no help to software engineers. As $S^*$ is taken as a constant, the equation for faults ($B$) simply states that the number of faults in a program is a function of its volume. This metric is therefore a static metric, ignoring the huge variations in fault rates observed in software products and among modules.

## 10.3 Cyclomatic Complexity

The measurement of cyclomatic complexity by McCabe (1976) was designed to indicate a program's testability and understandability (maintainability). It is the classical graph theory cyclomatic number, indicating the number of regions in a graph. As applied to software, it is the number of linearly independent paths comprising the program. As such it can be used to indicate the effort required to test a program. To determine the paths, the program procedure is represented as a strongly connected graph with a unique entry and exit point. The general formula to compute cyclomatic complexity is:

$$M = V(G) = e - n + 2p$$

where

$V(G)$ = cyclomatic number of $G$

$e$ = number of edges

$n$ = number of nodes

$p$ = number of unconnected parts of the graph.

As an example, Figure 10.2 is a control graph of a simple program that might contain two IF statements. If we count the edges, nodes, and disconnected parts of the graph, we see that $e = 8$, $n = 7$, and $p = 1$, and that $M = 8 - 7 + 2 * 1 = 3$.

Note that $M$ is also equal to the number of binary decisions in a program plus 1. If all decisions are not binary, a three-way decision is counted as two binary decisions and an $n$-way case (select) statement is counted as $n - 1$ binary decisions. The iteration test in a looping statement is counted as one binary decision. In the preceding simple example, since there are two binary decisions, $M = 2 + 1 = 3$.

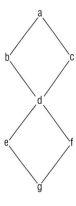

FIGURE 10.2
Simple Control Graph Example

The cyclomatic complexity metric is additive. The complexity of several graphs considered as a group is equal to the sum of the individual graphs' complexities. However, it ignores the complexity of sequential statements. The metric also does not distinguish between different kinds of control flow complexity such as loops versus IF-THEN-ELSE statements or cases versus nested IF-THEN-ELSE statements.

To have good testability and maintainability, McCabe recommended that no program module should exceed a cyclomatic complexity of 10. Because the complexity metric is based on decisions and branches, which is consistent with the logic pattern of design and programming, it appeals to software professionals. Since its inception, cyclomatic complexity has become an active area of research and practical applications. Many experts in software testing recommend use of the cyclomatic representation to ensure adequate test coverage; the use of McCabe's complexity measure has been gaining acceptance by practitioners.

Because of its appeal to programmers and researchers, many studies have been conducted to relate McCabe's complexity measure to defect rate, and moderate to strong correlations were observed. For instance, in a study of software metrics of a large SQL product that consisted of about 1300 modules, Troster (1992) found a relatively strong correlation between McCabe's cyclomatic complexity index and the number of test defects ($r = .48$, $n = 1303$, $p = .0001$). Studies found that the complexity index also correlates strongly with program size—lines of code. Will the correlation between complexity and defect still remain significant after program size is controlled? In other words, is the correlation between complexity and defects a spurious one, because program size affects both complexity and defect level? Many studies have been done with regard to this question and the findings are not always consistent. There are cases where the correlation disappears after the effect of program size is controlled, whereas in other cases the correlation weakens somewhat but remains significant, suggesting a genuine association between complexity and defect level. Our experience belongs to the latter kind.

Sometimes the disappearance of the correlation between complexity and defect level after program size is accounted for may be due to a lack of investigational rigor. It is important that appropriate statistical techniques are used with regard to the nature of the data. For example, in Troster's study he also observed that the LOC count also correlated with the number of test defects quite strongly ($r = 0.49$, $n = 1296$, $p = 0.001$). To partial out the effect of program size, therefore, he calculated the correlation between McCabe's complexity index and testing defect rate (per KLOC). He found that the correlation totally disappeared with $r = 0.002$ ($n = 1296$, $p = 0.9415$). Had Troster stopped there he would have concluded that there is no genuine association between complexity and defect level. Troster, however, realized that he also needed to look at the rank-order correlation. Therefore he also computed the Spearman's rank-order correlation coefficient and found a very respectable association between complexity and defect rate:

Spearman's correlation = 0.27

n = 1296 (number of modules)

p = 0.0001 (highly statistically significant)

These seemingly inconsistent findings, based on our experience and observation of the Troster study, is due to the nature of software data. As discussed before, Pearson's correlation coefficient is very sensitive to extreme data points; it can also be distorted if there is a lot of noise in the data. Defect rate data (normalized to KLOC) tend to fluctuate widely and therefore it is difficult to have significant Pearson correlation coefficients. The rank-order correlation coefficient, which is less precise than the Pearson correlation coefficient but more robust, is more appropriate for such data.

| Inspection Type | Number of Inspections | KLOC | $r$ Lines of Code | $r$ McCabe's Index |
|---|---|---|---|---|
| I0 | 46 | 129.9 | 0.10 | - |
| I1 | 41 | 67.9 | 0.46 | 0.69 |
| I2 | 30 | 35.3 | 0.56 | 0.68 |

TABLE 10.1
Correlation Coefficients Between Inspection Defects and Complexity

As another example, Craddock (1987) reported the use of McCabe's complexity index at low-level design inspections and code inspection (I2). He correlated the number of inspection defects with both complexity and LOC. As shown in Table 10.1, Craddock found that complexity is a better indicator of defects than LOC at the two inspection phases.

Assume that if an organization were able to establish a significant correlation between complexity and defect level, then the McCabe index can be useful in several ways, including the following:

☐ To help identify overly complex parts needing detailed inspections.

☐ To help identify noncomplex parts likely to have a low defect rate and therefore candidates for development without detailed inspections.

☐ To estimate programming and service effort, identify troublesome code, and estimate testing effort.

In a later section in this chapter we describe an example of complexity study in more detail and illustrate how quality improvement can be made via the focus on complexity reduction.

## 10.4  Syntactic Constructs

McCabe's cyclomatic complexity index is a summary index of binary decisions. It does not distinguish different kinds of control flow complexity such as loops versus IF-THEN-ELSES or cases versus IF-THEN-ELSES. Researchers of software metrics also studied the association of individual syntactic constructs with defect level. For instance, Shen and associates (1985) discovered that the number of unique operands ($n_2$) was useful in identifying those modules most likely to contain errors for the three software products they studied. More recently Binder and Poore (1990) have empirically supported the concept of local software quality metrics whose formulation is based on software syntactic attributes. Such local metrics may be specific only to the products under study or the development teams or environments. However, as long as an empirical association with software quality is established, those metrics could provide useful clues for improvement actions. In selecting such metrics for study, whether the metric could be acted on should also be taken into consideration.

In studying the quality and syntactic indicators among a sample of 20 modules of a COBOL compiler product, Lo (1992) found that field defects at the module level can be estimated through the following equations:

$$\text{Field defects} = -2.5 + 0.003\text{LOC} + 0.001\text{Unique operands} \quad (10.1)$$
$$(R^2 = 0.66)$$
$$\text{Field defects} = 0.11\text{IF-THEN} + 0.03\text{Number of calls} \quad (10.2)$$
$$(R^2 = 0.88)$$

While both equations provide satisfactory results, the findings lend nothing for actions. In a second attempt, which included all 66 modules of the entire product, Lo also examined other syntactic constructs and found the following relationship:

$$\text{Field defects} = 0.15 + 0.23\text{DO WHILE} + 0.22\text{SELECT} +$$
$$0.07\text{IF THEN}$$
$$(R^2 = 0.55)$$

In the model all three metrics are statistically significant, with DO WHILE having the most effect. The DO WHILE metric included both DO WHILE . . . END and DO WHILE TO . . . . ? Although the $R^2$ of the model decreased, the findings provide useful clues for improvement. Although it is difficult to avoid the use of IF THEN or to change the number of unique operands, it is feasible to reduce the use of a complex construct such as the DO WHILE or SELECT statement. Upon brainstorming with the development team, Lo found that most developers were having difficulty mastering the DO WHILE construct. As a result, minimizing the use of DO WHILE was one of the actions the team took to reduce defects in the compiler product.

## 10.5  Structure Metrics

Lines of code, Halstead's software science, McCabe's cyclomatic complexity, and other metrics that measure module complexity assume implicitly that each program module is a separate entity. Structure metrics try to take into account the interactions between modules in a product or system and quantify such interactions. Many approaches in structure metrics have been proposed. Some good examples include invocation complexity by McClure (1978), system partitioning measures by Belady and Evangelisti (1981), information flow metrics by Henry and Kafura (1981), and stability measures by Yau and Collofello (1980). Many of these metrics and models, however, are yet to be verified by empirical data from software development projects.

Perhaps the most commonly used design structure metrics are the fan-in and fan-out metrics, which are based on the ideas of coupling proposed by Yourdon and Constantine (1979) and Myers (1978):

   ☐   *Fan-in:* a count of the number of modules that call a given module
   ☐   *Fan-out:* a count of the number of modules that are called by a given module.

In general, modules with a large fan-in are relatively small and simple, and are usually located at the lower layers in the design structure. In contrast, modules that are large and complex are likely to have a small fan-in. Therefore, modules or components that have a large fan-in and large fan-out may indicate a poor design. Such modules have probably not been decomposed correctly and are candidates for redesign. From the complexity and defect point of view, modules with a large fan-in are expected to have negative or insignificant correlation with defect levels, and modules with a large fan-out are expected to have a positive correlation. In the AS/400 experience, we found a positive correlation between fan-out and defect level, and no correlation between fan-in and defects. However, the standard deviations of fan-in and fan-out were quite large in our data. Therefore, our experience was inconclusive.

Henry and Kafura's structure complexity is defined as:

$$C_p = (\text{fan-in} \times \text{fan-out})^2$$

In an attempt to incorporate the module complexity and structure complexity, Henry and Selig's recent work (1990) defined a hybrid form of their information-flow metric as:

$$HC_p = C_{ip} \times (\text{fan-in} \times \text{fan-out})^2$$

where $C_{ip}$ is the internal complexity of procedure $p$, which can be measured by any module complexity metrics such as McCabe's cyclomatic complexity.

Based on various approaches to structure complexity and module complexity measures, Card and Glass (1990) developed a system complexity model:

$$C_t = S_t + D_t$$

where

$C_t$ = system complexity

$S_t$ = structural (intermodule) complexity

$D_t$ = data (intramodule) complexity,

and relative system complexity:

$$C = C_t/n$$

where $n$ is the number of modules in the system.

Structure complexity and data complexity are further defined as:

$$S = \frac{\sum f^2(i)}{n}$$

where

$S$ = structural complexity

$f(i)$ = fan-out of module $i$

$n$ = number of modules in system.

$$D_i = \frac{V(i)}{f(i)+1}$$

where

$D_i$ = data complexity of module $i$

$V(i)$ = I/O variables in module $i$

$f(i)$ = fan-out of module $i$.

$$D = \frac{\sum D(i)}{n}$$

where

$D$   = data (intramodule) complexity

$D(i)$ = data complexity of module $i$

$n$   = number of new modules in system.

Simply put, according to Card and Glass, system complexity is a sum of structural (intermodule) complexity and overall data (intramodule) complexity. Structural complexity is defined as the mean (per module) of squared values of fan-out. This definition is based on the findings in the literature that fan-in is not an important complexity indicator and that complexity increases as the square of connections between programs (fan-out). With regard to data (intramodule) complexity of a module, it is defined as a function that is directly dependent on the number of I/O variables and inversely dependent on the number of fan-outs in the module. The rationale is that the more I/O variables in a module, the more functionality that needs to be accomplished by the module, therefore, the higher internal complexity. On the contrary, more fan-out means that functionality is deferred to modules of lower levels, therefore the internal complexity of a module is reduced. Finally, the overall data complexity is defined as the average of data complexity of all new modules. In Card and Glass' model, only new modules enter into the formula because oftentimes the entire system consists of reused modules, which have been designed, used, aged, and stabilized in terms of reliability and quality.

In Card and Glass' study of eight software projects, they found that the system complexity measure was significantly correlated with subjective quality assessment by a senior development manager and with development error rate. Specifically, the correlation between system complexity and development defect rate was 0.83, with complexity accounting for fully 69% of the variation in error rate. The regression formula thus derived was:

$$\text{Error rate} = -5.2 + 0.4 \times \text{Complexity}$$

In other words, each unit increase in system complexity increases the error rate by 0.4 (errors per thousand lines of code).

Card and Glass' model appears to be quite promising and has an appeal to software development practitioners. They also provided guidelines on achieving a low complexity design. When more validation studies become available the Card and Glass model and related methods may gain greater acceptance in the software development industry.

While Card and Glass' model is for the system level, the system values of the metrics in the model are aggregates (averages) of module-level data. Therefore, it is feasible to correlate these metrics to defect level at the module level. The meanings of the metrics at the module level are as follows:

- $D_i$: data complexity of module $i$, as defined earlier
- $S_i$: structural complexity of module $i$, i.e., a measure of the module's interaction with other modules
- $C_i = S_i + D_i$: the module's contribution to overall system complexity.

In Troster's study (1992) discussed earlier, data at the module level for Card and Glass' metrics are also available. It would be interesting to compare these metrics with McCabe's cyclomatic complexity with regard to their correlation with defect rate. Not unexpectedly, the rank-order correlation coefficients for these metrics are very similar to that for McCabe's (0.27). Specifically, the coefficients are 0.28 for $D_i$, 0.19 for $S_i$, and 0.27 for $C_i$. More research in this area will certainly yield more insights into the interrelationships of various design and module metrics and their predictive power in terms of software quality.

## 10.6  An Example of Module Design Metrics in Practice

In this section we describe an analysis of several module design metrics as they relate to defect level, and how such metrics can be used to develop a software quality improvement plan. Special attention is given to the significance of cyclomatic complexity. Data from all program modules of a key component in the AS/400 software system served as the basis of the analysis. The component provides facilities for message control between users, programs, and the operating system. It was written in PL/MI (a PL/1-like language) and has about 70 KLOC. Because the component functions are complex and involve numerous interfaces, the component has consistently experienced high reported error rates from the field. The purpose of the analysis was to produce objective evidences so that data-based plans can be formulated for quality and maintainability improvement.

The metrics in the analysis include:

- McCabe's cyclomatic complexity index (CPX).
- Fan-in: the number of modules that call a given module (FAN-IN).
- Fan-out: the number of modules that are called by a given module. In AS/400 this metric refers to the number of MACRO calls in the module (MAC).

☐ Number of INCLUDES in the module. In AS/400 INCLUDES are used for calls such as subroutines and declarations. The difference between MACRO and INCLUDE is that for INCLUDE there are no parameters passing. For this reason INCLUDES are not counted as fan-out. However, INCLUDES do involve interface, especially for the common INCLUDES.

☐ Number of design changes and enhancements since the initial release of AS/400 (DCR).

☐ Previous defect history. This metric refers to the number of formal test defects and field defects in the same modules in System/38, the predecessor midrange computer system of AS/400. This component reused most of the modules in System/38. This metric is denoted as PTR38 in the analysis.

☐ Defect level in the current system (AS/400). This is the total number of formal test defects and field defects for the latest release when the analysis was done. This metric is denoted as DEFS in the analysis.

Our purpose was to explain the variations in defect level among program modules by means of the differences observed in the metrics described earlier. Therefore DEFS is the dependent variable and the other metrics are the independent variables. The means and standard deviations of all variables in the analysis are shown in Table 10.2. The large mean values of MACRO calls (MAC) and FAN-IN illustrate the complexity of the component. Indeed, as the component provides facilities for message control in the entire operating system, numerous modules in the system have MACRO-call links with many modules of the component. The large standard deviation for FAN-IN also indicates that the chance for significant relationships between fan-in and other variables is slim.

| Variable | Mean | Standard Deviation | n |
|----------|------|--------------------|---|
| CPX | 23.5 | 23.2 | 72 |
| FAN-IN | 143.5 | 491.6 | 74 |
| MAC | 61.8 | 27.4 | 74 |
| INCLUDES | 15.4 | 9.5 | 74 |
| DCR | 2.7 | 3.1 | 75 |
| PTR38 | 8.7 | 9.8 | 63 |
| DEFS | 6.5 | 8.9 | 75 |

TABLE 10.2

Means, Standard Deviations, and Number of Modules

| Variable | Pearson Correlation | n | Significance (p Value) |
|----------|---------------------|---|------------------------|
| CPX | .65 | 72 | .0001 |
| FAN-IN | .02 | 74 | not significant |
| MAC | .68 | 74 | .0001 |
| INCLUDES | .65 | 74 | .0001 |
| DCR | .78 | 75 | .0001 |
| PTR38 | .87 | 75 | .0001 |

TABLE 10.3
Correlation Coefficients Between Defect Level and Other Metrics

Table 10.3 shows the Pearson correlation coefficients between defect level and other metrics. The high correlations for many factors were beyond expectation. The significant correlations for complexity indexes and MACRO calls support the theory that associates complexity with defect level. McCabe's complexity index measures the complexity within the module. Fan-out, or MACRO calls in this case, is an indicator of the complexity between modules.

As expected, the correlation between FAN-IN and DEFS was not significant. Because the standard deviation of FAN-IN is large, this finding is tentative. More focused analysis is needed. Theoretically speaking, modules with a large fan-in are relatively simple and are usually located at lower layers in the system structure. Therefore, fan-in should not positively correlate with defect level. The correlation should either be negative or insignificant, as the present case showed.

The high correlation for module changes and enhancement simply illustrates the fact that the more changes, the more chances for injecting defects. Moreover, small changes are especially error-prone. Because most of the modules in this component were designed and developed for the System/38, changes for AS/400 were generally small.

The correlation between previous defect history and current defect level was the strongest (0.87). This finding confirms the view of the developers that many modules in the component are chronic problem components, and systematic plans and actions are needed for any significant quality improvement.

The calculation of Pearson's correlation coefficient is based on the least-squares method. Because the least-squares method is extremely sensitive to outliers, examination of scatterplots to confirm the correlation is mandatory. Relying on the correlation coefficients alone sometimes may be erroneous. The scatter diagram of defect level with McCabe's complexity index is shown in Figure 5.9 in Chapter 5 when we discussed the seven basic quality tools. The diagram appears radiant in shape: low-complexity modules at the low defect level; however, for high-complexity modules, while more are at the high defect level, there are others with low defect levels as well. Perhaps the most impressive finding from the diagram is the blank area in the upper left-hand part, confirming the correlation between low complexity and low defect level. As can be seen, there are many modules with a complexity index far beyond McCabe's recommended level of 10—probably due to the high complexity of system programs in general, and the component functions specifically.

Figure 10.3 shows the scatter diagrams for defect level with MAC, INCLUDE, DCR, and PTR38. The diagrams confirm the correlations. Because the relationships appear to be linear, the linear regression lines and confidence intervals are also plotted.

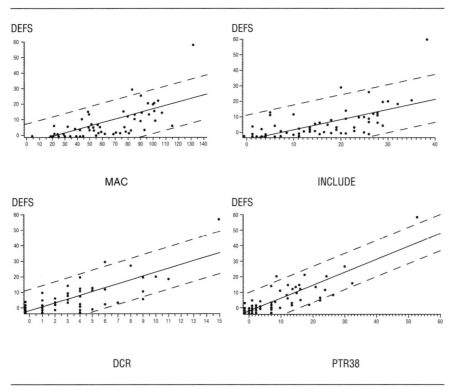

FIGURE 10.3
Scatter Diagram—DEFS with MAC, INCLUDE, DCR, and PTR38

The extreme data point at the upper right-hand corner in the diagrams represents the best known module in the component, which formats a display of messages in a queue and sends it either to the screen or printer. With more than 5000 lines of source code, it is a highly complex module with a history of many problems.

The next step in our analysis was to look at the combined effect of these metrics on defect level simultaneously. To achieve this task we used the multiple regression approach. In a multiple regression model, the effect of each independent variable is adjusted for the effects of other variables. In other words, the regression coefficient and the significance level of an independent variable represent the net effect of that variable on the dependent variable—in this case the defect level. We found that in the combined model, MAC and INCLUDE become insignificant. When we excluded them from the model, we obtained the following:

$$DEFS = -1.796 + 0.597 \times PTR38 + 0.628 \times DCR + 0.051 \times CPX$$

With an $R^2$ of 0.83, the model is highly signifcant. Each of the three independent variables is also significant at the 0.05 level. In other words, the model explains 83% of the variations in defect level observed among the program modules.

To further verify the findings, we must also control for the effect of program size—lines of code. Since LOC is correlated with DEFS and other variables, its effect must be partialled out in order to conclude that there are genuine influences of PTR38, DCR, and CPX on DEFS. To accomplish the task, we did two things: (1) We normalized the defect level by LOC and used defects per KLOC (DEFR) as the dependent variable and (2) we included LOC as one of the independent variables (control variable) in the multiple regression model. We found that with this control, PTR38, DCR, and CPX were still significant at the 0.1 level. In other words, these factors truly represent something for which the length of the modules cannot account. However, the $R^2$ of the model was only 0.20. We contended that this again is due to the wide fluctuation of the dependent variable, the defect rate. The regression coefficients, their standard errors, $t$ values, and the significance levels are shown in Table 10.4.

This analysis indicates that other than module length, the three most important factors affecting the defect rates of the modules are the number of changes and enhancements, previous defect history, and complexity level. From the intervention standpoint, since developers have no control over release enhancements, the latter two factors become the best clues for quality improvement actions. The relationships among previous defect history, complexity, and current defect level are illustrated in Figure 10.4. The best return on investment, then, is to concentrate efforts on modules with high defect history (chronic problem modules) and high complexity.

| Variable | Regression Coefficients | Standard Error | t Value | Significance (p Value) |
|----------|------------------------|----------------|---------|------------------------|
| Intercept | 4.631 | 2.813 | 1.65 | .10 |
| CPX | .115 | .066 | 1.73 | .09 |
| DCR | 1.108 | .561 | 1.98 | .05 |
| PTR38 | .359 | .220 | 1.63 | .10 |
| LOC | −.014 | .005 | 2.99 | .004 |
| R² | .20 | | | |

TABLE 10.4
Results of Multiple Regression Model of Defect Rate (DEFR)

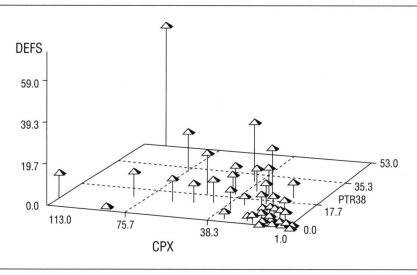

FIGURE 10.4
Scatter Diagrams of DEF, PTR38, and CPX

Based on the findings from this analysis and other observations, the component team established a quality improvement plan with staging implementation. The following list includes just some of the actions related to this analysis:

☐ Scrutinize the several modules with moderate complexity and yet high defect level. Examine module design and code implementation and take proper actions.

□   Identify high complexity and chronic problem modules, do intramodule restructuring and clean up (for instance, better separation between mainline and subroutines, better comments, better documentation in the prologue, removal of dead code, better structure of source statements, etc.). The first-stage target is to reduce the complexity of these modules to 35 or lower.

□   Closely related to above, another target is to reduce the number of compilation warning messages to zero for all modules.

□   New module design will include complexity as a key factor, with the maximum not to exceed 35.

□   Improve test effectiveness, especially for complex modules. Use test coverage measurement tools to ensure that such modules are adequately covered.

□   Improve component documentation and education.

The preceding analysis was conducted in 1990. Since then the component team has been making consistent improvements according to their quality plan. Field data from new releases indicated significant improvement in the component's quality.

## 10.7 Summary

In this chapter we described several major metrics and models with regard to software module and design. Our discussion was from the viewpoint of the metrics' correlation with defect level. Regardless of whether it is lines of code, the software science metrics, cyclomatic complexity, other syntactic constructs, or structure metrics, these metrics seem to be operational definitions of the complexity of the software design and module implementation. In retrospect, the key to achieving good quality is to reduce the complexity of software design and implementation, given a problem domain for which the software is to provide a solution.

The criteria for evaluation of complexity metrics and models, therefore, rest on their explanatory power and applicability. *Explanatory power* refers to the model's ability to explain the interrelationships among complexity, quality, and other programming and design parameters. Applicability refers to the degree to which the models and metrics can be applied by software engineers to improve their work in design, code, and test. This is related to whether the model or metric can provide clues from which actions can be taken. As a secondary criteria to explanatory power, congruence between the underlying logic of the model and the reasoning patterns of software engineers also plays a significant role. As a case in point, McCabe's complexity metrics may appeal more to programming development professionals than Halstead's token-based software science. During design, code, and test, software engineers' line of reasoning is determined more in terms of decision points, branches, and paths, rather than in terms of the number of operators and operands.

Like software reliability models, perhaps even more so, the validity of complexity metrics and models often depends on the product, the development team, and the development environment. Therefore, one should always be very careful when generalizing findings from specific studies. In this regard, the concept and approach of local software quality metrics seem quite appealing. Specific improvement actions, therefore should be based on pertinent empirical relationships.

## References

1.  Basili, V. R., and B. T. Perricone, "Software Errors and Complexity: An Empirical Investigation," *Communications of the ACM,* January 1984, pp. 42–52.
2.  Belady, L. A., and C. J. Evangelisti, "System Partitioning and Its Measure," *Journal of Systems and Software,* 2, 1981, pp. 23–39.
3.  Binder, L., and J. Poore, "Field Experiments with Local Software Quality Metrics," *Software—Practice and Experience,* Vol. 20, No. 7, July 1990, pp. 631–647.
4.  Card, D. N., and Robert L. Glass, *Measuring Software Design Quality,* Englewood Cliffs, N.J.: Prentice-Hall, 1990.
5.  Craddock, L. L., "Analyzing Cost-Of-Quality, Complexity, and Defect Metrics for Software Inspections," Technical Report TR07.844, IBM Rochester, Minn., April 1987.
6.  Halstead, M. H., *Elements of Software Science*, New York: Elsevier North Holland, 1977.
7.  Henry, S. M., and D. Kafura, "Software Structure Metrics Based on Information Flow," *IEEE Transactions on Software Engineering,* Vol. SE-7, 1981, pp. 510–518.
8.  Henry, S. M., and C. Selig, "Predicting Source-Code Complexity at the Design Stage," *IEEE Software,* March 1990, pp. 36–44.
9.  Lo, B., "Syntactical Construct Based APAR Projection," IBM Santa Teresa Laboratory Technical Report, California, 1992.
10. McCabe, T. J., "A Complexity Measure," *IEEE Transactions on Software Engineering,* Vol. 2, No. 4, December 1976, pp. 308–320.
11. McClure, C. L., "A Model for Program Complexity Analysis," *Proceedings IEEE Third International Conference on Software Engineering,* May 1978, pp. 149–157.
12. Myers, G. J., *Composite Structured Design,* Wokingham, U.K.: Van Nostrand Reinhold, 1978.
13. Shen, V., T. Yu, S. Thebaut, and L. Paulsen, "Identifying Error-Prone Software—an Empirical Study," *IEEE Transactions on Software Engineering,* Vol. SE-11, No.4, April 1985, pp. 317–324.
14. Troster, J., "Assessing Design-Quality Metrics on Legacy Software," Software Engineering Process Group, IBM Canada Ltd. Laboratory, North York, Ontario, September 1992.
15. Withrow, C., "Error Density and Size in Ada Software," *IEEE Software,* January 1990, pp. 26–30.
16. Yau, S. S., and J. S. Collofello, "Some Stability Measures for Software Maintenance," *IEEE Transactions on Software Engineering,* Vol SE-6, 1980, pp. 545–552.
17. Yourdon, E., and L. L. Constantine, *Structured Design,* Englewood Cliffs, N.J.: Prentice-Hall, 1979.

# 11

Measuring and Analyzing Customer Satisfaction

Customer satisfaction is the ultimate validation of quality. Product quality and customer satisfaction together form the total meaning of quality. Indeed, what differentiates total quality management (TQM) from the sole focus on product quality in traditional quality engineering is that TQM is aimed at long-term business success by linking quality with customer satisfaction. In this modern-day quality era, enhancing customer satisfaction is the bottom line of business success. With ever-increasing market competition, customer focus is the only way to retain the existing customer base and to expand market share. Studies show that it is five times more costly to recruit a new customer than it is to keep an old customer, and that dissatisfied customers tell 7 to 20 people about their experiences, while satisfied customers tell only 3 to 5.

As a result of TQM, more and more companies are conducting surveys to measure their customers' satisfaction. In this chapter we discuss customer satisfaction surveys and the analysis of survey data. As an example, we describe an analysis of the relationship between overall customer satisfaction and satisfaction with specific attributes for a software product. In the last section we discuss the question of how good is good enough.

## 11.1 Customer Satisfaction Surveys

There are various ways to obtain customer feedback with regard to their satisfaction levels with the product(s) and the company. For example, telephone follow-up regarding a customer's satisfaction at a regular time after the purchase is a frequent practice by many companies. Other sources include customer complaint data, direct customer visits, customer advisory councils, user conferences, and the like. To obtain representative and comprehensive data, however, the time-honored approach is conducting customer satisfaction surveys that are representative of the entire customer base.

### 11.1.1 Methods of Survey Data Collection

There are three common methods to gather survey data: personal face-to-face interviews, telephone interviews, and mail questionnaires (self-administered). The personal interview method requires the interviewer to ask questions based on a prestructured questionnaire and to record the answers. The primary advantage of this method is the high degree of validity of the data. Specifically, the interviewer can note specific reactions and eliminate misunderstandings about the questions being asked. The major limitations are costs and factors concerning the interviewer. If not adequately trained, the interviewer may deviate from the required protocol, thus introducing biases into the data. If the interviewer cannot maintain neutrality, any statement, movement, or even facial expression by the interviewer could affect the response. Errors in recording the responses could also lead to erroneous results.

Telephone interviews are less expensive than face-to-face interviews. Different from personal interviews, telephone interviews can also be monitored by the research team to ensure that the specified interview procedure is being followed. The computer-aided approach can further reduce costs and increase efficiency. Telephone interviews should be kept short and impersonal to maintain the interest of the respondent. The limitations of this method are the lack of direct observation, the lack of using exhibits for explanation, and the limited group of potential respondents—those who can be reached by telephone.

The mailed questionnaire method does not require interviewers and is therefore less expensive. However, this savings in cost is usually at the expense of lower response rates. Low response rates can introduce biases to the data because if the respondents are different from the nonrespondents, the sample will not be representative of the population. Nonresponse can be a problem in any method of surveys, but the mailed questionnaire method usually has the lowest rate of response. For this method, extreme caution should be used when analyzing data and generalizing the results. Moreover, the questionnaire must be carefully constructed, validated, and pretested before final use. Questionnaire development requires professional knowledge and experience and should be dealt with accordingly. Texts on survey research methods provide useful guidelines and observations (for example, Babbie, 1986).

Figure 11.1 shows the advantages and disadvantages of the three survey methods with regard to a number of attributes.

| Type of survey | Cost | Sampling | Response Rate | Speed | Flexibility | Observations | Length of Interview | Exhibits | Validity |
|---|---|---|---|---|---|---|---|---|---|
| In person | – – | + – | + – | + – | + + | + + | + | + | + + |
| Phone | + | + | + + | + | + | – | – | – | + |
| Mail | + + | – | – – | – | – | – | + | + – | – |

| | | |
|---|---|---|
| – | = | Disadvantage (– – = Worst) |
| + | = | Advantage (+ + = Best) |
| + – | = | Could be either an Advantage or a Disadvantage |

FIGURE 11.1
Advantages and Disadvantages of Three Survey Methods

## 11.1.2 Sampling Methods

When the customer base is large, it is too costly to survey all customers. Estimating the satisfaction level of the entire customer population through a representative sample is more efficient. To obtain representative samples, scientific probability sampling methods must be used. There are four basic types of probability sampling: simple random sampling, systematic sampling, stratified sampling, and cluster sampling.

If a sample of size $n$ is drawn from a population in such a way that every possible sample of size $n$ has the same chance of being selected, the sampling procedure is called simple random sampling. The sample thus obtained is called a simple random sample (Mendenhall *et al.,* 1971). Simple random sampling is often mistaken as convenient sampling or accidental sampling for which the investigator just "randomly" and conveniently selects individuals he or she happen to come across. The latter is not a probability sample. To take a simple random sample, each individual in the population must be listed once and only once. Then some mechanical procedure (such as using a random number table, or using a random number generating computer program) is used to draw the sample. To avoid repeated drawing of the same individual, it is usually more convenient to sample without replacement. Notice that on each successive draw the probability of an individual being selected increases slightly because there are fewer and fewer individuals left unselected from the population. If, on any given draw, the probabilities are equal of all remaining individuals being selected, then we have a simple random sample.

Systematic sampling is often used interchangeably with simple random sampling. Instead of using a table of random numbers, in systematic sampling one simply goes down a list taking every $k$'th individual, starting with a randomly selected case among the first $k$ individuals. ($k$ is the ratio between the size of the population and the size of the sample to be drawn. In other words, $1/k$ is the sampling fraction.) For example, if we wanted to draw a sample of 500 customers from a population of 20,000, then $k$ is 40. Starting with a random number between 1 and 40 (say, 23), then we would draw every fortieth on the list (63, 103, 143, . . . .).

Systematic sampling is simpler than random sampling if a list is extremely long or a large sample is to be drawn. However, there are two types of situations in which systematic sampling may introduce biases: (1) The entries on the list may have been ordered so that a trend occurs and (2) the list may possess some cyclical characteristic that coincides with the $k$ value. For example, if the individuals have been listed according to rank and salary and the purpose of the survey is to estimate the average salary, then two systematic samples with different random starts will produce systematic differences in the sample means. As another example for (2), suppose in a housing development every twelfth dwelling unit is a corner unit. If the sampling fraction happens to be $1/12$ ($k = 12$), then one could obtain a sample either with all corner units or no corner units depending on the random start. This sample could be biased. Therefore, the ordering of a list should be examined before applying systematic sampling. Fortunately, neither type of problem occurs frequently in practice, and once discovered, they can be dealt with accordingly.

In a stratified sample we first classify individuals into nonoverlapping groups, called *strata,* and then select simple random samples from each stratum. The strata are usually formed based on important variables pertaining to the parameter of interest. For example, customers with complex network systems may have a set of satisfaction criteria for software products that is very different from those who have stand-alone systems and simple applications. Therefore, a stratified sample should include customer type as one of the stratification variables.

Stratified sampling, when properly designed, is more efficient than simple random sampling and systematic sampling. Stratified samples can be designed to yield greater accuracy for the same cost, or for the same accuracy with less cost. By means of stratification we ensure that individuals in each stratum are well represented in the sample. In the simplest design, one can take a simple random sample within each stratum. The sampling fractions within each stratum may be equal (proportional stratified sampling) or different (disproportional stratified sampling). If the goal is to compare different subpopulations that differ in size, it may be desirable to use disproportional stratified sampling. To yield the maximum efficiency for a sample design, the following guidelines for sample size allocation can be used: Make the sampling fraction for each stratum directly proportional to the standard deviation within the stratum and inversely proportional to the square root of the cost of each case within the stratum.

In stratified sampling we sample within each stratum. Sometimes it is advantageous to divide the population into a large number of groups, called *clusters,* and to sample among the clusters. A cluster sample is a simple random sample in which each sampling unit is a cluster of elements. Usually geographical units such as cities, districts, schools, or work plants are used as units for cluster sampling. Cluster sampling is generally less efficient than simple random sampling, but it is much more cost effective. The purpose is to select clusters as heterogeneous as possible but which are small enough to cut down on expenses such as travel costs involved in personal interviews. For example, if a company has many branch offices throughout the country and an in-depth face-to-face interview with a sample of its customers is desired, then a cluster sample using branch offices as clusters (of customers) may be the best sampling approach.

For any survey, the sampling design is of utmost importance in obtaining unbiased, representative data. If the design is poor, then despite its size, chances are the sample will yield biased results. There are plenty of real-life examples in the literature with regard to the successes and failures of sampling. The *Literary Digest* story is perhaps the most well known. The *Literary Digest,* a popular magazine in the 1930s, had established a reputation for successfully predicting winners of presidential elections on the basis of "straw polls." In 1936 the *Digest's* history of successes came to a halt when it predicted a 3-to-2 victory for the Republican nominee, Governor Alf Landon, over the incumbent Franklin Roosevelt. As it turned out, Roosevelt won by great landslides, carrying 62% of the popular votes and 46 of the 48 states. The magazine suspended publication shortly after the election.

For the prediction, the *Digest* chose a sample of ten million persons originally selected from telephone listings and from the list of its own subscribers. Despite the huge sample, the prediction was in error because the sample was not representative of the voting population. In the 1930s more Republicans than Democrats had telephones. Furthermore, the response rate was very low, at about 20% to 25%. Therefore, the responses that were obtained from the poll and used for the prediction were not representative of those who voted (Bryson, 1976).

### 11.1.3 Sample Size

How large a sample is sufficient? The answer to this question depends on the confidence level we want and the margin of error we can tolerate. The higher the level of confidence we want from the sample estimate, and the smaller the error margin, the larger the sample we need, and vice versa. For each probability sampling method, specific formulas are available for calculating sample size, some of which (such as that for cluster sampling) are quite complicated. The following formula is for the sample size required to estimate a population proportion (for example, percent satisfied) based on simple random sampling:

$$n = \frac{N_x Z^2 \times p(1-p)}{NB^2 + \left[ Z^2 \times p(1-p) \right]}$$

where

$N$ = population size

$Z$ = Z statistic from normal distribution:

    for 80% confidence level, $Z = 1.28$

    for 85% confidence level, $Z = 1.45$

    for 90% confidence level, $Z = 1.65$

    for 95% confidence level, $Z = 1.96$

$p$ = estimated satisfaction level

$B$ = margin of error.

A common misconception with regard to sample size is that the size of a sample must be a certain percentage of the population in order to be representative, whereas in fact the power of a sample depends on its absolute size. Regardless of the size of its population, the larger the sample the smaller its standard deviation will become and therefore the estimate will be more stable. When the sample size is up to a few thousands, it gives satisfactory results for many purposes, even if the population is extremely large. For example, sample sizes of national fertility surveys (representing all women in childbearing ages for the entire nation) in many countries are in the range of 3000 to 5000.

Figure 11.2 illustrates the sample sizes for 10,000 customers for various levels of confidence with both 5% and 3% margins of error. Note that the required sample size decreases as customer satisfaction level increases. This is because the larger the $p$ value, the smaller its variance, $p(1 - p) = pq$. When an estimate for the satisfaction level is not available, using a value of 50% ($p = 0.5$) will yield the largest sample size that is needed because $pq$ is largest when $p = q$.

| Expected Satisfaction | 80% Confidence | | 85% Confidence | | 90% Confidence | | 95% Confidence | |
|---|---|---|---|---|---|---|---|---|
| | +/− 5% | +/− 3% | +/− 5% | +/− 3% | +/− 5% | +/− 3% | +/− 5% | +/− 3% |
| 80% | 104 | 283 | 133 | 360 | 171 | 462 | 240 | 639 |
| 85% | 83 | 227 | 106 | 289 | 137 | 371 | 192 | 516 |
| 90% | 59 | 161 | 75 | 206 | 97 | 265 | 136 | 370 |
| 95% | 31 | 86 | 40 | 110 | 51 | 142 | 72 | 199 |

FIGURE 11.2
Examples of Sample Size (for 10,000 customers) in Relation to Confidence
Level and Error Margin

## 11.2  Analyzing Satisfaction Data

The five-point satisfaction scale (very satisfied, satisfied, neutral, dissatisfied, and very dissatisfied) is often used in customer satisfaction surveys. The data are usually summarized in terms of percent satisfied. In presentation, run charts or bar charts to show the trend of percent satisfied are often used. We recommend that confidence intervals be formed for the data points so that the margins of error of the sample estimates can be observed immediately (Figure 11.3).

Traditionally, the 95% confidence level is used for forming confidence intervals and the 5% probability ($p$ value) is used for significance testing. This $p$ value means that if the true difference is not significant, the chance we wrongly conclude that the difference is significant is 5%. Therefore, if a difference is statistically significant at the 5% level, it is indeed very significant. When analyzing customer satisfaction it is not necessary to stick to the traditional significance level. If the purpose is to be more sensitive in detecting changes in customers' satisfaction levels, or to trigger actions when a significant difference is observed, then the 5% level is not sensitive enough. Based on our experience, a $p$ value as high as 20%, or a confidence level of 80%, is still reasonable: sensitive enough to detect substantial difference, yet not giving false alarms when the difference is trivial.

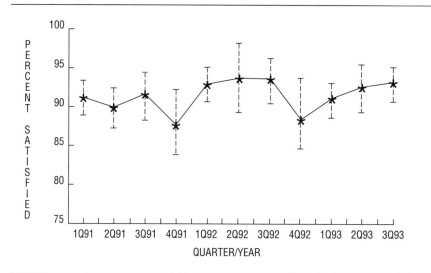

FIGURE 11.3

Quarterly Trend of Percent Satisfied with a Hypothetical Product

While percent satisfied is perhaps the most used metric, some companies, such as IBM, choose to monitor the inverse, the percent nonsatisfied. Nonsatisfied includes the neutral, dissatisfied, and very dissatisfied in the five-point scale. The rationale to use percent nonsatisfied is to enable focus on areas that need improvement. This is especially the case when the value of percent satisfied is quite high. Figure 12.3 in Chapter 12 shows an example of IBM Rochester's percent nonsatisfied in terms of CUPRIMDA categories (capability, usability, performance, reliability, installability, maintainability, documentation/information, and availability) and overall satisfaction.

## 11.2.1 Specific Attributes and Overall Satisfaction

The major advantage of monitoring customer satisfaction with specific attributes of the software, in addition to overall satisfaction, is that such data provide specific information for improvement. The profile of customer satisfaction with those attributes (for example, CUPRIMDA) indicates the areas of strength and weakness of the software product. One easy mistake in customer satisfaction analysis, however, is to equate the areas of weakness with the priority of improvement, and hence investment. For instance, if a product has low satisfaction with documentation (D) and high satisfaction with reliability (R), that does not mean that there is no need to continually improve the product's reliability and that the first priority of the development team is to improve documentation. Reliability may be the very reason the customers decide to buy this product and that customers may expect even further improvement. On the other hand, customers may not like the product's documentation but it may still be tolerable given other considerations. To answer the question on priority of improvement, therefore, the subject must be looked at within the broader context of overall customer satisfaction with the product. Specifically, the correlations of the satisfaction levels of specific attributes with overall satisfaction need to be examined. After all, it is the overall satisfaction level that the software developer aims to maximize; it is the overall satisfaction level that affects the customer's purchase decision.

Here we describe an example of analyzing the relationship between satisfaction level with specific attributes and overall satisfaction for a hypothetical product. For this product, data are available on the UPRIMD parameters and on availability (A). The purpose of the analysis is to determine the priority for improvement by assessing the extent to which each of the UPRIMD-A parameters affects overall customer satisfaction. The sample size for this analysis is 3658. Satisfaction is measured by the five-point scale ranging from very dissatisfied (1) to very satisfied (5).

To achieve the objectives, we attempted two statistical approaches: least-squares multiple regression and logistic regression. In both approaches overall customer satisfaction is the dependent variable, and satisfaction levels with UPRIMD-A are the independent variables. The purpose is to assess the correlations between each of the specific attributes and overall satisfaction simultaneously. For the ordinary regression approach, we use the original five-point scale. The scale is an ordinal variable and data obtained from it represent a truncated continuous distribution. Sensitivity research in the literature, however, indicated that if sample size is large (such as our case), violation of the interval scale and the assumption of Gaussian distribution results in very small bias. In other words, the use of ordinary regression is quite robust for the ordinal scale with large samples.

For the logistic regression approach, we classified the five-point scale into a dichotomous variable: very satisfied and satisfied (4 and 5) versus nonsatisfied (1, 2, and 3). Categories 4 and 5 were recoded as 1 and categories 1, 2, and 3 were recoded as 0. The dependent variable, therefore, is the odds ratio of satisfied and very satisfied versus nonsatisfied. The odds ratio is a measurement of association that has been widely used for categorical data analysis. In our application it approximates how much more likely customers will be positive in overall satisfaction if they were satisfied with specific UPRIMD-A parameters versus if they were not. For instance, let customers who were satisfied with the performance of the system form a group and those not satisfied with the performance form another group. Then an odds ratio of 2 indicates that the overall satisfaction occurs twice as often among the first group of customers (satisfied with the performance of the system) than the second group. The logistic model in our analysis, therefore, is as follows:

$$\log\left(\frac{sat + v.\ sat}{v.\ dis + dis + neut}\right) = \beta_0 + \beta_1 x_1 + \ldots + \beta_k x_k + e$$

The correlation matrix, means, and standard deviations are shown in Table 11.1. Two rows of means are shown: the five-point scale and the 0–1 scale. Means for the latter reflect the percent satisfaction level (for example, overall satisfaction is 85.5% and satisfaction with reliability is 93.8%). Among the parameters, availability and reliability have the highest satisfaction levels, whereas documentation and installability have the lowest.

| | Overall | U | P | R | I | M | D | A |
|---|---|---|---|---|---|---|---|---|
| Overall | | | | | | | | |
| U—usability | .61 | | | | | | | |
| P—performance | .43 | .46 | | | | | | |
| R—reliability | .63 | .56 | .42 | | | | | |
| I—installability | .51 | .57 | .39 | .47 | | | | |
| M—maintainability | .40 | .39 | .31 | .40 | .38 | | | |
| D—documentation | .45 | .51 | .34 | .44 | .45 | .35 | | |
| A—availability | .39 | .39 | .52 | .46 | .32 | .28 | .31 | |
| Mean | 4.20 | 4.18 | 4.35 | 4.41 | 3.98 | 4.15 | 3.97 | 4.57 |
| Standard deviation | .75 | .78 | .75 | .66 | .90 | .82 | .89 | .64 |
| % SAT | 85.5 | 84.1 | 91.1 | 93.8 | 75.3 | 82.9 | 73.3 | 94.5 |

TABLE 11.1
Correlation Matrix, Means, and Standard Deviations

As expected, there is moderate correlation among the UPRIMD-A parameters. Usability with reliability, installability, and documentation, and performance with availability are the more notable ones. In relation to overall satisfaction, reliability, usability, and installability have the highest correlations.

Results of the multiple regression analysis are summarized in Table 11.2. As indicated by the $p$ values, all parameters are significant at the 0.0001 level except the availability parameter. The total variation of overall customer satisfaction explained by the seven parameters is 52.6%. In terms of relative importance, reliability, usability, and installability are the highest, as indicated by the $t$ value. This finding is consistent with what we observed from the simple correlation coefficients in Table 11.1. Reliability being the most significant variable implies that although customers are quite satisfied with the software's reliability (93.8%), reliability is still the most determining factor for achieving overall customer satisfaction. In other words, further reliability improvement is still demanded. For usability and installability, the current low and moderate levels of satisfaction, together with the significance finding, really pinpoint the need for drastic improvement.

More interesting observations can be made on documentation and availability. Although being the lowest satisfied parameter, intriguingly, documentation's influence on overall satisfaction is not too strong. This may be because customers have become more tolerant with documentation problems. Indeed, data from software systems within and outside IBM often indicate that documentation/information usually receive the lowest ratings among specific dimensions of a software product. This does not mean that one doesn't have to improve documentation; it means that documentation is not as sensitive as other variables when measuring its effects on the overall satisfaction of the software. Nonetheless, it still is a significant variable and should be improved.

Availability is the least significant factor. On the other hand, it has the highest satisfaction level (94.5%, average 4.57 in the five-point scale).

| Variable | Regression Coefficient (Beta) | t value | Significance Level (p Value) |
|---|---|---|---|
| R—reliability | .391 | 21.4 | .0001 |
| U—usability | .247 | 15.2 | .0001 |
| I—installability | .091 | 7.0 | .0001 |
| P—performance | .070 | 4.6 | .0001 |
| M—maintainability | .067 | 5.4 | .0001 |
| D—documentation | .056 | 4.5 | .0001 |
| A—availability | .022 | 1.2 | .22 (not significant) |

TABLE 11.2

Results of Multiple Regression Analysis

Results of the logistic regression model are shown in Table 11.3. The most striking observation is that the significance of availability in affecting customer satisfaction is in vivid contrast to findings from the ordinary regression analysis, as just discussed. Now availability ranks third, after reliability and usability, in affecting overall satisfaction. The difference observed from the two models lies in the difference in the scaling of the dependent and independent variables in the two approaches. Combining the two findings, we interpret the data as follows:

☐   Availability is not very important in influencing the average shift in overall customer satisfaction from one level to the next (from dissatisfied to neutral, from neural to satisfied, etc.).

☐   However, availability is very important in affecting whether customers are satisfied versus nonsatisfied.

☐   Therefore, availability is a sensitive factor in customer satisfaction and should be improved further despite its current level of high satisfaction.

Because the dependent variable of the logistic regression model (satisfied versus nonsatisfied) is more appropriate for our purpose, we use the results of the logistic model for the rest of our example.

| Variable | Regression Coefficient (Beta) | Chi Square | Significance Level (p Value) | Odds Ratio |
|---|---|---|---|---|
| R—reliability | 1.216 | 138.6 | <.0001 | 11.4 |
| U—usability | .701 | 88.4 | <.0001 | 4.1 |
| A—availability | .481 | 16.6 | <.0001 | 2.6 |
| I—installability | .410 | 33.2 | <.0001 | 2.3 |
| M—maintainability | .376 | 26.2 | <.0001 | 2.1 |
| P—performance | .321 | 14.3 | .0002 | 1.9 |
| D—documentation | .164 | 5.3 | .02 | 1.4 |

TABLE 11.3
Results of Logistic Regression Analysis

The odds ratios indicate the relative importance of the UPRIMD-A variables in the logistics model. That all ratios are greater than 1 means that each of the UPRIMD-A variables has a positive impact on overall satisfaction, the dependent variables. Among them, reliability has the largest odds ratio, 11.4. So the likelihood of overall satisfaction is much higher for customers who are satisfied with reliability than those who aren't. On the other hand, documentation has the lowest odds ratio, 1.4. This indicates that the impact of documentation on overall satisfaction is not very strong, but there is still a positive effect.

Table 11.4 presents the probabilities for customers being satisfied depending on whether or not they are satisfied with the UPRIMD-A parameters. These conditional probabilities are derived from the earlier logistic regression model. When customers are satisfied with all seven parameters, chances are they are 96.32% satisfied with the overall software product. From row 2 to row 8, we show the probabilities that customers will be satisfied with the software when they are not satisfied with one of the seven UPRIMD-A parameters, one at a time. The drop in probabilities in row 2 through row 8 compared with row 1 indicates how important that particular parameter affects whether customers are satisfied or not. Reliability (row 6), usability (row 8), and availability (row 2), in that order, again, are the most sensitive parameters. Data in rows 9 to 16 shows the reverse view of rows 1 to 8: the probabilities that customers will be satisfied with the software when they are satisfied with one of the seven parameters, one at a time. This exercise, in fact, is a reconfirmation of the odds ratios shown in Table 11.3.

By now we have a good understanding of how important each UPRIMD-A variable is in terms of affecting overall customer satisfaction in the example. Now let us come back to the initial question of how to determine the priority of improvement among the specific quality attributes. We propose the following method:

1. Determine the order of significance of each quality attribute on overall satisfaction by statistical modeling (such as the regression model and the logistic model in the example).

2. Plot the coefficient of each attribute from the model (Y-axis) against its satisfaction level (X-axis).

3. Use the plot to determine priority by:

   □    Going from top to bottom, and

   □    Going from left to right, if the coefficients of importance have the same values.

| Row | P(Y=1/X) | U | P | R | I | M | D | A | Frequency |
|-----|----------|---|---|---|---|---|---|---|-----------|
| 1 | .9632 | 1 | 1 | 1 | 1 | 1 | 1 | 1 | 1632 |
| 2 | .9187 | 1 | 1 | 1 | 1 | 1 | 1 | 0 | 14 |
| 3 | .9552 | 1 | 1 | 1 | 1 | 1 | 0 | 1 | 267 |
| 4 | .9331 | 1 | 1 | 1 | 1 | 0 | 1 | 1 | 155 |
| 5 | .9287 | 1 | 1 | 1 | 0 | 1 | 1 | 1 | 212 |
| 6 | .7223 | 1 | 1 | 0 | 1 | 1 | 1 | 1 | 12 |
| 7 | .9397 | 1 | 0 | 1 | 1 | 1 | 1 | 1 | 42 |
| 8 | .8792 | 0 | 1 | 1 | 1 | 1 | 1 | 1 | 47 |
| 9 | .0189 | 0 | 0 | 0 | 0 | 0 | 0 | 0 | 20 |
| 10 | .0480 | 0 | 0 | 0 | 0 | 0 | 0 | 1 | 8 |
| 11 | .0260 | 0 | 0 | 0 | 0 | 0 | 1 | 0 | 2 |
| 12 | .0392 | 0 | 0 | 0 | 0 | 1 | 0 | 0 | 9 |
| 13 | .0132 | 0 | 0 | 0 | 1 | 0 | 0 | 0 | 1 |
| 14 | .1796 | 0 | 0 | 1 | 0 | 0 | 0 | 0 | 12 |
| 15 | .0353 | 0 | 1 | 0 | 0 | 0 | 0 | 0 | 4 |
| 16 | — | 1 | 1 | 0 | 0 | 0 | 0 | 0 | 0 |

Y=1: satisfied, Y=0: nonsatisfied; X: the UPRIMDA vector

TABLE 11.4
Conditional Probabilities

To illustrate this method based on our example, Figure 11.4 plots the estimated logistic regression coefficients against the satisfaction level of the variable. The $Y$-axis represents the beta values and the $X$-axis represents the satisfaction level. From the plot, the order of priority for improvement is very clear: reliability, usability, availability, installability, maintainability, performance, and documentation. As this example illustrates, it is useful to use multiple methods (including scales) to analyze customer satisfaction data—so as to understand better the underlying relationships hidden beneath the data. This is exemplified by our seemingly contradictory findings on availability from ordinary regression and logistic regression models.

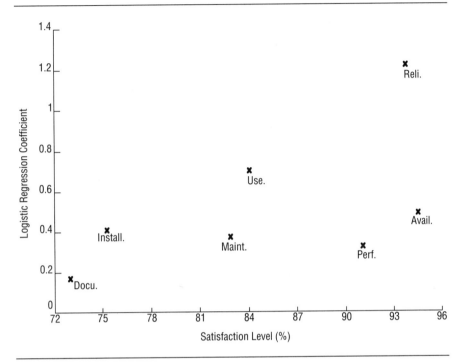

FIGURE 11.4
Logistic Regression Coefficients Versus Satisfaction Level

Our example focused on the relationships between specific quality attributes and overall customer satisfaction. There are many other meaningful questions that our example did not address. For example, what are the interrelationships among the specific quality attributes (e.g., CUPRIMDA) in a cause-and-effect manner? What are the other variables, other than specific quality attributes, that also affect overall customer satisfaction? For instance, in our regression analysis, the $R^2$ is 52.8%. What are the factors that may explain the rest of the variations in overall satisfaction? Given the current level of overall customer satisfaction, what does it take to improve one percentage point (in terms of CUPRIMD-A and other factors)?

To seek possible answers to questions such as these, apparently a multitude of techniques is needed for analysis. Regardless of the analysis to be performed, it is always beneficial to take into consideration issues in measurement theory such as those discussed in Chapter 3, whenever possible.

## 11.3 Satisfaction with Company

Thus far our discussion on customer satisfaction has been product oriented—satisfaction with the overall software and with specific attributes. A broader scope of the subject deals with customers' overall satisfaction with the company. This broad definition of customer satisfaction includes a spectrum of variables in addition to the quality of the products. For instance, in their study of the customers' view model with regard to IBM Rochester, Hoisington and associates (1993) found that customers' overall satisfaction and loyalty is attributed to a set of common attributes of the company (as perceived by the customers) and satisfaction levels with specific dimensions of the entire company. The common attributes include ease of doing business with, partnership, responsiveness, knowledge of customer's business, and the company being customer driven. The key dimensions of satisfaction about the company include technical solutions, support and service, marketing, administration, delivery, and company image. It is under the dimension of technical solutions that product quality attributes come into play. In the following, we list several attributes under each dimension:

- ☐ *Technical solutions:* quality/reliability, availability, ease of use, pricing, installation, new technology, etc.
- ☐ *Support and service:* flexible, accessible, product knowledge, etc.
- ☐ *Marketing:* solution, central point of contact, information, etc.
- ☐ *Administration:* purchasing procedure, billing procedure, warranty expiration notification, etc.
- ☐ *Delivery:* on time, accurate, postdelivery process, etc.
- ☐ *Company image:* technology leader, financial stability, executives image, etc.

It is remarkable that in Hoisington's customer view model, company image is one of the dimensions of customer satisfaction. Whether this finding holds true in other cases remains to be seen. However, this finding illustrates the importance of both a company's actual performance and how it is perceived with regard to customer satisfaction.

It is apparent that customer satisfaction at both the company level and the product level needs to be analyzed and managed. Knowledge about the former enables a company to take a comprehensive approach in total quality management; knowledge about the latter provides specific clues for product improvements.

Yet another type of analysis centers on why customers choose a company's products over other companies', and vice versa. This kind of analysis requires information that is not available from regular customer satisfaction surveys, be they product level or company level. It requires data about customers' decision making for purchases and requires the responses from those who are not the company's current customers as well as those who are. This type of analysis, albeit difficult to conduct, is worthwhile to pursue because it deals directly with the issue of gaining new customers to expand the customer base.

## 11.4 How Good Is Good Enough?

How much customer satisfaction is good enough? Of course, the long-term goal should be 100%—total customer satisfaction. However, there are specific business questions that need better answers. Should my company invest \$2,000,000 to improve satisfaction from 85% to 90%? Given that my company's customer satisfaction is at 95%, should I invest another million dollars to improve it further or should I do this later?

The key for answering questions such as these lies in the relationship between customer satisfaction and market share. The basic assumption is that satisfied customers continue to purchase products from the same company and dissatisfied customers will buy from others. Therefore, as long as market competition exists, customer satisfaction is key to customer loyalty. Even if a company has no direct competitors, customers may purchase substitute products if they are dissatisfied with that company's products. Even in monopoly markets customer dissatisfaction encourages the development and emergence of competition. Studies and actual cases in business have lent strong support to this assumption.

With the above assumption, Babich (1992) studied the "how good is good enough" question based on a simplified model of customer satisfaction and market share that contains only three companies: A, B, and C. Therefore, when customers are dissatisfied with company A, they choose company B or C, and so forth. Babich further assumed that the distribution of dissatisfied customers among the alternative suppliers is in proportion to the suppliers' current market share. Babich then determined the algorithm for the market shares of the three companies at time $t + 1$ as follows:

$$A_{t+1} = A_t(1-x) + B_t y \left[ A_t/(A_t + C_t) \right] + C_t z \left[ A_t/(A_t + B_t) \right]$$
$$+ G \left[ A_t/(A_t + B_t + C_t) \right]$$

$$B_{t+1} = B_t(1-y) + A_t x \left[ B_t/(B_t + C_t) \right] + C_t z \left[ (B_t/A_t + B_t) \right]$$
$$+ G \left[ B_t/(A_t + B_t + C_t) \right]$$

$$C_{t+1} = C_t(1-z) + A_t x \left[ C_t/(B_t + C_t) \right] + B_t y \left[ C_t/(A_t + C_t) \right]$$
$$+ G \left[ C_t/(A_t + B_t + C_t) \right]$$

where:

$A$ = number of A customers

$B$ = number of B customers

$C$ = number of C customers

$G$ = number of new customers to market

$x$ = dissatisfaction level with A products

$y$ = dissatisfaction level with B products

$z$ = dissatisfaction level with C products

$t$ = time.

Based on this model, Babich computed the market shares of the three companies assuming satisfaction levels of 95%, 91%, and 90% for A, B, and C, respectively, over a number of time periods. The calculations also assume equal initial market share. As shown in Figure 11.5, after 12 time periods the 95% satisfaction product (company A) would basically own the market. However, had the satisfaction levels of companies B and C been 98% and 99%, respectively, and company A's satisfaction level remained at 95%, company A's product would have less than 10% market share in 24 time periods, as shown in Figure 11.6.

From Babich's simple model and examples, the answer to the "how good is good enough" is obvious: you have to be better than your competitors. Therefore, it is important to measure not only one's customer satisfaction level, but also the satisfaction level of one's competitors. Indeed, many companies have been doing exactly that. As an example, Figure 12.4 in Chapter 12 shows the comparison (% nonsatisfied) between AS/400's software system versus one of its key competitors over time, based on AS/400's survey data.

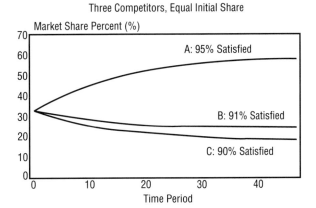

**FIGURE 11.5**

## Satisfaction Levels and Market Share—I

(*Source:* Babich, P., "Customer Satisfaction: How Good Is Good Enough?" *Quality Progress,* December 1992, pp. 65–67, Fig. 3. Copyright © 1992 American Society For Quality Control. Reprinted with permission from ASQC *Quality Progress.*)

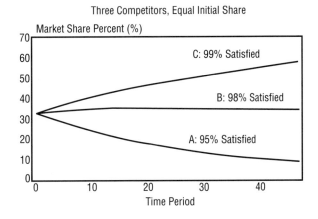

**FIGURE 11.6**

## Satisfaction Levels and Market Share—II

(*Source:* Babich, P., "Customer Satisfaction: How Good Is Good Enough?" *Quality Progress,* December 1992, pp. 65–67, Fig. 4. Copyright © 1992 American Society For Quality Control. Reprinted with permission from ASQC *Quality Progress.*)

Finally, we emphasize that measuring and analyzing customer satisfaction is but one element of customer satisfaction management. A good customer satisfaction management process must form a closed loop between measurement, analysis, and actions. While it is not the intent of this chapter to cover the customer satisfaction management process, we recommend that such a process should at least cover the following elements:

☐ Measure and monitor the overall customer satisfaction over time, one's own as well as key competitors'.

☐ Perform analyses on specific satisfaction dimensions, quality attributes of the products and their strengths, weaknesses, prioritization, and other relevant issues.

☐ Perform root cause analysis to identify inhibitors for each dimension and attribute.

☐ Set satisfaction targets (overall and specific) by taking competitors' satisfaction levels into consideration.

☐ Formulate and implement action plans based on the above.

## 11.5  Summary

Various methods are available to gauge customer satisfaction; the most common one is to conduct representative sampling surveys. The three major methods of survey data collection are face-to-face interview, telephone interview, and mailed questionnaire. Each method has its advantages and disadvantages. To obtain representative samples, scientific probability sampling methods must be used. There are four basic types of probability sampling: simple random sampling, systematic sampling, stratified sampling, and cluster sampling.

Given a probability sample, the larger the sample size, the smaller the sampling error. A common misconception with regard to sample size is that it must be a certain percentage of the population in order to be representative, whereas in fact the power of a sample depends on its absolute size. However, the sample must be a scientific (probability) sample. If the sample is drawn unscientifically, then even a huge size does not guarantee its representativeness. There are many real-life examples of huge and unrepresentative samples, which are results of unscientific design.

When analyzing and presenting customer satifaction survey data, the confidence interval and margin of error must be included. Furthermore, good analysis is paramount in transforming data into useful information and knowledge. In satisfaction surveys, satisfaction with specific quality attributes of a product are often queried, in addition to overall satisfaction. However, it does not mean that attributes with the lowest levels of satisfaction should be accorded the highest priority for improvement and, hence, investment. To answer the priority question, the subject must be looked at within the broader context of customers' overall satisfaction with the product; the correlations of the satisfaction levels of specific attributes with overall satisfaction need to be examined; and the improvement actions should aim to maximize overall satisfaction.

Beyond satisfaction with a product, customers' satisfaction with the company should also be analyzed. A customer view model at the company level often entails improvement actions in areas in addition to product improvement, such as marketing, order process, delivery, support, and so forth. As a simple market-share model illustrated in this chapter, one must be better than one's competitors in overall customer satisfaction in order to retain customer loyalty and to expand market share.

## References

1. Babbie, E., *The Practice of Social Research,* Belmont, Calif.: Wadsworth Publishing, 1986.
2. Babich, P., "Customer Satisfaction: How Good Is Good Enough?" *Quality Progress,* December 1992, pp. 65–67.
3. Bryson, M. C., "The Literary Digest Poll: Making of a Statistical Myth," *The American Statistician,* Vol. 30, No. 4, November 1976, pp. 184–185.
4. Hoisington, S., T. H. Huang, T. Suther, and T. Cousins, "Customer View of Ideal Business Machine Enterprise (Part I—Methodology and Results)," Technical Report TR 07.2010, IBM Rochester, Minn., January 1993.
5. Hosmer, D. W., and L. Stanley, *Applied Logistic Regression,* New York: John Wiley & Sons, 1989.
6. Mendenhall, W., L. Ott, and R. L. Scheaffer, *Elementary Survey Sampling,* Belmont, Calif.: Duxbury Press, 1971.

# 12

## AS/400 Software Quality Management*

IBM Rochester develops and manufactures the Application System/400 (AS/400) computer system. Generally available to customers since August 1988, the initial release of the AS/400 had 7.1 million lines of source code in its software system—the base operating system and licensed program products. Since then, many new functions and enhancements have been added with at least one new release each year. The customer base has been expanding, with more than 250,000 licenses at year-end 1993. The typical release usually has about two million lines of new and changed source code. With such a large development effort and so many customers, continuous quality improvement is a necessity. Indeed, quality focus has always been one of the top priorities at IBM Rochester. The site's quality focus can best be reflected by its winning of the Malcolm Baldrige National Quality Award in 1990, and its obtaining ISO 9000 registration for the entire site at the end of 1992.

*This chapter is based on "AS/400 Software Quality Management," by S. H. Kan, S. D. Dull, D. N. Amundson, R. J. Lindner, and R. J. Hedger in *IBM Systems Journal,* Vol. 33, No.1, February 1994. Copyright © 1994 International Business Machines Corporation. Permission to reprint obtained from *IBM Systems Journal.*

In early 1990, IBM began deploying the corporate strategy of Market Driven Quality (MDQ) to its divisions and business units. Capitalizing on the new MDQ momentum and the ongoing effort, the software development laboratory at IBM Rochester quickly undertook several important activities: benchmarking studies of quality leaders such as Motorola and IBM Houston (which develops the NASA onboard shuttle flight software system and has achieved defect-free quality); assessment of the AS/400 development process; analysis of in-process and field-defect data to guide improvement efforts; and development of a long-term quality improvement strategy. A quality action road map was soon established and deployment of key action items followed immediately. These included the laboratory-wide implementation of the defect prevention process (DPP) (Jones, 1985; Mays *et al.,* 1990), a strong focus on the design review/code inspection (DR/CI) process (referred to as the "back to the basics" focus in the laboratory), component test improvements, departmental 5-UP measurements, quality recognition based on peer nomination, and others. Strong management commitment, the entire team's passion for quality, and the excitement with the MDQ vision formed the best climate for improvement actions.

Since the initial MDQ roll-out, Rochester's AS/400 software quality management system has evolved significantly; it now encompasses all aspects of software quality. This chapter describes the key elements of the system: people, product quality management [both in-process and post-general availability (GA)], continuous process improvement, and customer satisfaction management. The AS/400 quality road map is presented, which describes the goals and key action items that drive these elements, including examples of the results achieved as described through empirical data. Where appropriate, the climate for quality improvement (such as management commitment and mind-set change of the entire team) is also discussed.

It should be noted that discussions in the following sections are about the AS/400 software quality management system. There are no "silver bullets." Many quality improvement techniques and recommended solutions exist in the literature. Placing these techniques into practice systematically and persistently makes the difference. It is important to continue to look for new technology for quality breakthroughs; it is equally important to focus on implementation and to bridge the gap between state of the art and state of practice.

Furthermore, we confine our discussions to the two key ingredients of quality: reducing product defects and improving customer satisfaction. The lack of functional defects, or reliability, is the most basic measure of quality. Customer satisfaction, on the other hand, represents the final evaluation of the product and service by the customer, based on all variables. Other quality attributes such as performance, installability, usability, and so forth are discussed only in the context of customer satisfaction. Improving those quality attributes is important. In IBM Rochester software development, specialized groups address each of those key attributes. However, detailed discussion of them are beyond the scope of this chapter.

## 12.1 AS/400 Software Quality Management System (SQMS)

After customers receive and use a product they chose, they grade the product based on their personal usage experience. If they experience many problems or frustrations in using the product, their opinion of the product will be negative. If the product is essentially defect free or solves a key problem for their business, their opinion of the product may be very positive. A quality management system must focus on reducing the number of defects a customer experiences with a product and, if a customer does experience a problem, the quality management system must ensure that the customer receives a quality fix in an acceptable amount of time. In other words, the end result of a quality management system is to reduce defects and increase customer satisfaction. These results are the key objectives of the various elements of the AS/400 Software Quality Management System (SQMS) of Figure 12.1. There are five elements of the AS/400 SQMS: (1) people, (2) in-process product quality management, (3) continuous process improvement, (4) post-GA product quality management, and (5) customer satisfaction management.

As shown in Figure 12.1, before development begins, competition, marketing, and customer requirements are analyzed, prioritized, and selected for implementation based on resources. These analyses and activities provide direction for the system and form the release definition for development. A release plan is developed that defines the detailed contents and schedules of a release. The AS/400 SQMS also requires a quality plan. This plan documents the specific quality actions from the quality road map that will be leveraged in this release. The quality road map describes the quality technologies that can be deployed across many releases of AS/400 that will help achieve the quality goals. During the development of the release, the people factor, the in-process quality management element, the continuous process improvement element (which encompasses tools and technology used in the development process), and the overall release management are the significant pieces affecting the deliverables. When the release development is complete and the product is delivered to customers, the post-GA product quality management element and the customer satisfaction management element are in full operation. Feedback from customers is then incorporated into the customer requirements analysis, which influences the definition for future releases.

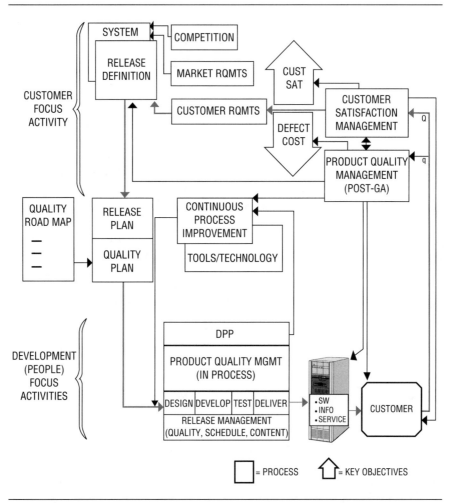

FIGURE 12.1
AS/400 Software Quality Management System

The most important element of the quality management system is people. People must be highly motivated and talented to execute and improve the development processes to deliver a high-quality product to customers release after release, with each release quality goal more challenging than the previous one.

In-process product quality management is another important element of the AS/400 SQMS. The objective of this element is to measure the results of the various process steps used in developing a product. These in-process measurements help to determine if the product is on target for achieving product quality goals. Action plans are created to improve the quality of functions that are not meeting the quality plan goals. The release management process uses the in-process quality measurements at checkpoints during the release to assess the ongoing overall quality of the release. Content and schedule are also critical parts of this assessment.

Another very important element of the AS/400 SQMS is continuous process improvement. This element provides a foundation for improving the processes used in the development cycle. Process improvement is triggered by defects reported by customers using the product; by DPP, which is a mechanism for preventing recurrence of defects that are found while developing the product; and by use of tools and technology that enable process automation, increase defect discovery, or reduce defect injection. Process owners continually look for ways to improve their processes and communicate improvements to their users.

The post-GA product quality management element addresses the problems that AS/400 customers may experience with software products, both defect oriented (requiring a fix) and nondefect oriented (user errors, usability problems, etc.). The key objectives of this element are to fix customer problems quickly, with quality, and to learn from the errors that were made. The number of problems customers report, defects found in the product, defective fixes that affected customers, and the response time to problems are measured. Some problems reported by customers may become new requirements that in turn are fed into the software planning process. Others may result in suggested improvements to the software development processes.

The objective of the customer satisfaction management element is to improve customer satisfaction via a closed-loop process. To understand overall customer satisfaction and customer satisfaction in different parameters of the product, large-scale surveys are conducted. Analysis of survey data identifies areas of the product that are deficient. This results in defining a set of new product requirements that can lead to improving the product and, it is hoped, customer satisfaction. Customer satisfaction management also addresses critical problems that customers are experiencing, problems that need immediate and high priority attention by developers, marketing, and service teams. A team monitors critical situations and reacts to resolve problems quickly before they seriously affect the customer's business. Such quick responsive action can turn a dissatisfied customer into a satisfied one.

In the following sections, each of these elements is described in more detail. Real examples of results achieved from the AS/400 SQMS are included. For a better flow of information, were align the order of discussions as follows:

- Customer satisfaction
- Product quality: in-process and post-GA
- Continuous process improvement
- People.

### 12.1.1 Customer Satisfaction Management

The ultimate goal of IBM's MDQ is to satisfy customers totally with the products and services provided. The AS/400's goal in customer satisfaction is to be the undisputed leader worldwide. To work toward this goal, a customer satisfaction management process is in place (Figure 12.2) and, in addition to overall satisfaction, specific categories called CUPRIMDA are monitored and measured for improvement. As mentioned in previous chapters, CUPRIMDA is an acronym for:

- ☐ Capability (function)
- ☐ Usability (ease of use)
- ☐ Performance (response time and throughput)
- ☐ Reliability (defect free)
- ☐ Installability (ease of upgrade)
- ☐ Maintainability (ease of maintenance)
- ☐ Documentation (information)
- ☐ Availability (nonoutage time).

Each of these categories has been assigned to an owner and is measured at the system and product level by continuous surveys. As Figure 12.2 indicates, each CUPRIMDA owner is responsible for gathering and analyzing customer satisfaction information from various sources (such as surveys, problems reported, critical situations, competitive analysis, and customer calls), identifying inhibitors for improvement, and recommending solutions to improve customer satisfaction. When the recommended solutions call for specific items to be added or changed in the development plan, formal plan change requests (PCRs) are created. These solutions (PCRs) are reviewed by a core team of category owners and chaired by a development director. The director is also a member of the system plan team and provides the necessary focus in the plan change process. The core team becomes the champion of customer satisfaction line items for inclusion in the software planning process. These line items are presented to the system plan team for consideration for inclusion in the official plan. The plan team evaluates the line items against other customer wants and needs and determines the resources available to develop them.

In addition to initiating line items that address improvement in their parameters, the CUPRIMDA owners are responsible for (1) coordinating and driving other actions to improve their parameters and (2) monitoring and projecting customer satisfaction levels for their parameters.

On rare occasions a customer may run into a critical AS/400 problem. The causes of these problems vary and are often unique situations. When they occur, the critical situation management process goes to work. The primary focus of the team assigned to use this process is to resolve the critical situation as quickly as possible, and to turn a dissatisfied customer into a satisfied customer. This process enables people from development, manufacturing, marketing, and service to address the critical problems immediately. On-site assistance may be required to understand the problem or provide the fix. Causal analysis is performed on these problems to prevent future recurrences.

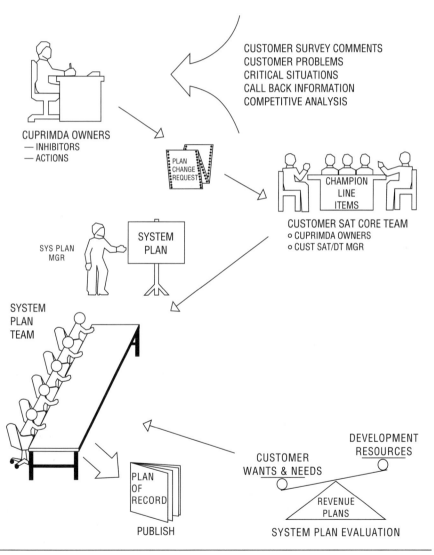

FIGURE 12.2
Customer Satisfaction Management Process

Figure 12.3 shows an example of customer satisfaction in each of the CUPRIMDA categories based on the IBM Marketing and Services (M&S) surveys. It compares customer nonsatisfaction in each of the CUPRIMDA categories and for the overall operating system for the baseline (year-end 1989) and two recent releases. Customer nonsatisfaction is the percent of customers who are either neutral, dissatisfied, or very dissatisfied. Analyzing customer satisfaction in terms of percent nonsatisfied enables us to focus on areas that need improvement. The M&S surveys are conducted in the United States by an independent consulting company. They are blind surveys; the interviewee does not know which company the consulting firm represents. Customer responses are obtained through telephone interviews based on structured questionnaires.

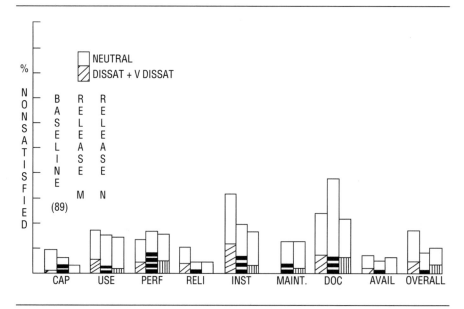

FIGURE 12.3
AS/400 M&S Customer Satisfaction Survey Results

In Figure 12.3 the first bar of each group represents the percent of nonsatisfied of the parameter at baseline; the second and third bar represent the percent of nonsatisfied for two recent releases. For the maintainability parameter there are only two bars because data were not available for the baseline. For each bar the upper empty segment represents the percent of neutral responses, and the lower shaded segment represents the percent of dissatisfied and very dissatisfied in a five-point Likert scale. The total length of the bar thus represents the percent of nonsatisfied customers.

Compared to the baseline, capability, reliability, installability, and overall satisfaction have significantly improved in recent releases. For capability and reliability, the nonsatisfied level is quite low; in fact, there were 0% of dissatisfied customers for the latest release in the survey. For installability, the percent of dissatisfied and very dissatisfied has dropped to a very low level; however, additional improvement is needed as the percent of neutral customers was still relatively high. For usability, documentation, and availability, some improvement was observed. For performance, no clearly perceived improvement was observed; this parameter is clearly a continuing challenge to our improvement effort. (It should be noted that the data are with respect to customers' satisfaction with software, based on surveys. We have been continually focusing on performance improvement of the software system. Furthermore, compared to the original hardware models in 1988, AS/400s in 1993 are 2 to 10 times more powerful. Performance of the high-end AS/400 models has increased an average of 60% to 70% per year.)

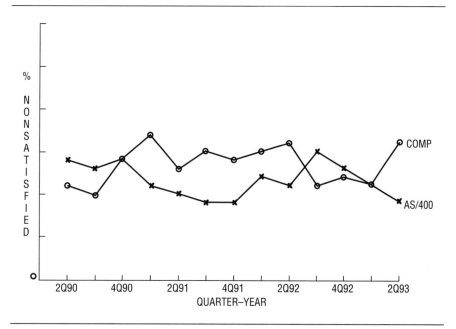

FIGURE 12.4

Trend of Overall Customer Satisfaction with Operating System: AS/400 and Competitor

In Figure 12.4 the quarterly trend of percent of nonsatisfied with the overall operating system quality is shown for AS/400 and a major U.S. competitor. The data are also from the IBM M&S surveys. Data are shown starting from the second quarter of 1990; earlier data on the competitor is not available. For AS/400, the data are based on the latest release in the field.

The M&S data show that AS/400 lagged behind the competitor in overall satisfaction with the operating system before 1991. Since then, AS/400 has gained substantially and had a lower percent of nonsatisfied than the competitor. However, AS/400 lost this advantage in the second half of 1992, only to be back on the improvement trend again in 1993.

The data in Figure 12.4 show the volatile nature of customer satisfaction, which needs constant focus. Our analysis also indicated that overall customer satisfaction is affected not only by product quality, but also by factors such as marketing, distribution, support, and how the company is perceived by the customers. Recently, the AS/400 division director of development commissioned a special task force on customer satisfaction, which is now evaluating all possible factors affecting satisfaction from the customers' view, and studying the mechanisms for improvement.

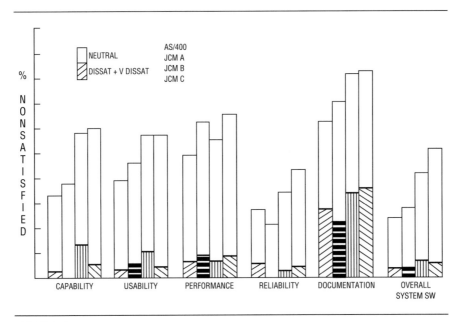

FIGURE 12.5

Customer Satisfaction: AS/400 and Three Japanese Computer Manufacturers

Figure 12.5 compares the customer satisfaction data for the AS/400 software system with the products of three Japanese computer manufacturers (JCMs). The data are based on a survey conducted by IBM Japan in 1992. In the figure, the first bar in each group represents the percent of nonsatisfied AS/400 customers. The other three bars represent data for three JCM products: A, B, and C, respectively. AS/400 had the best customer satisfaction overall and for specific categories except reliability, where it ranked second. It should be noted that the scale is the same for Figures 12.5 and 12.3. The difference between the data in the two figures is intriguing. However, we cannot validly compare data across the two figures because the sources of data are from two entirely different surveys.

## 12.1.2 Product Quality Management

To reduce defects and improve reliability in all aspects, the dynamics of software reliability must be understood. Figure 12.6 shows a schematic representation of the software reliability dynamics. When a software product is developed and becomes available to the marketplace, there is a certain level of latent defects (defects that have not manifested). Customers use the product, detect the defects, and report them. As defects are discovered, reported, and fixed, the latent defect rate in the system decreases. Over time, the system becomes more and more stable and its reliability grows. This process is known as *aging* or *reliability growth*. Fix quality and old code improvement are pertinent factors for a smooth aging process. If fix quality is not perfect (for instance, incorrect or with unintended consequences that may or may not be found immediately), then new errors are injected into the system. Perhaps even more significant is that defective fixes are detrimental to customer satisfaction. From the customer's perspective, encountering defects while using the product is bad enough. If a fix turns out to be defective, frustration will only multiply.

Theoretically, with aging, the software system's reliability can only get better and the curve will be a monotonically decreasing function. This pattern of software reliability is different from the hardware "bathtub" reliability pattern in which the reliability deteriorates at the end of the product life when hardware components begin to wear out (hence, the defect rate curves up again at the tail). If fix quality is good, through normal aging a software product could reach six sigma quality (Harry and Lawson, 1992) within a few years. In reality, after the first release of a software product, enhancements and new functions are made, and new releases of the product become available at regular intervals. The latent defect rate of the new and changed source instructions (CSI) is usually higher than that of the base system, which has been undergoing aging. Therefore, when a new release is available, the overall system latent defect rate will increase and the reliability worsens slightly. This phenomenon is represented by the spikes in Figure 12.6. The more CSI a new release contains, the higher the spike will become. If the base system has been aging for many years and CSI quality has not improved, the gap between the two (base code quality and CSI quality) will continue to widen. As a result, the overall latent-defect-rate function may curve up again at the tail, resembling the hardware "bathtub curve."

Therefore, continuous improvement in CSI quality is necessary to minimize the impact of new releases on system quality. CSI quality is the genuine indicator of the quality of the development process. It must be tracked separately using in-process measurements and dealt with specifically in quality road maps and plans. The next section on in-process product quality management describes how we manage CSI quality indicators.

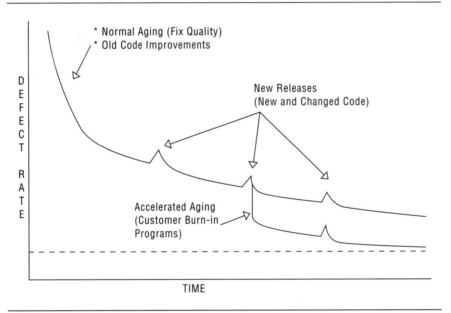

FIGURE 12.6
Software Reliability Dynamics

Another way to improve reliability (reduce defects) relies on the concept of accelerated aging (similar to accelerated testing of hardware). Many customer burn-in programs are based on this concept. In such programs, high-defect-finding customers are invited to participate in special programs to accelerate the defect discovery process. Customer burn-in programs are conducted when programming development is complete and before the general availability of the product. Customers are encouraged to move their production applications over to the new release so that defect discovery is effective. At the same time, the development organization provides special technical support to these customers so that potential risks to their businesses are minimized. The defects found are fixed as quickly as possible with excellent quality. Therefore, when the majority of customers receive the new release after the burn-in program(s), they will benefit from better quality. The AS/400's customer burn-in program is called the Customer Quality Partnership (CQP) program.

By understanding the software reliability dynamics, we can address all possible aspects for better reliability from the customers' perspectives.

### In-Process Product Quality Management

The in-process product quality management element focuses on improving code quality, particularly CSI quality. Two key directions must be taken to improve CSI quality: (1) reduce the number of errors injected during the development process and (2) remove defects as early as possible. These directions are illustrated by the defect removal curves shown in Figure 9.2 in Chapter 9. Again, the purpose is to shift the peak of the curves in two directions simultaneously: to the left as much as possible and at the same time push the curve downward. A key intermediate goal is to minimize the defect rate during formal machine testing, therefore leading to low field-defect rates. In formulating the AS/400 quality road map, improvement actions for both directions were addressed. For example, the pre-I0 inspection process was developed to specifically reduce error injection. Mini-builds, which provide the developer with a preintegration test environment, is a good example of an early-defect-removal-type action item that was implemented.

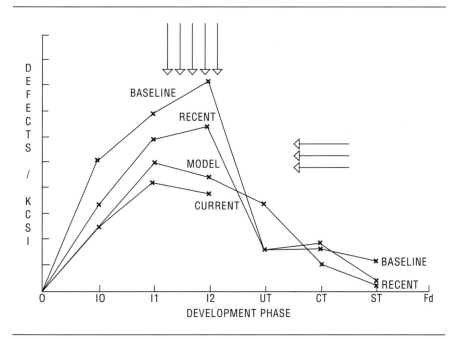

FIGURE 12.7
AS/400 Defect Removal Patterns

We have made significant progress in AS/400 quality since year-end 1989. Because of the systematic implementation of improvement actions within the context of the quality road map, improvements in development effectiveness have been made. For instance, overall error injection during the development process was reduced by more than one-fourth. The front-end phases (before system integration and build) were executed better. Due to the front-end improvement, a 30% reduction in the overall formal machine testing defect rate, and a reduction in the system test defect rate by more than 60% have been achieved. Our overall strategy of pushing for earlier defect removal and reducing error injection is being realized. Figure 12.7 shows a concise summary of the shifting of the defect removal patterns for the AS/400 development. The patterns compared are the 1989 baseline measurement, the most recent release shipped, the projected model for the current release (under development), and the current release results through the I2 (code) inspection phase. Compared to the baseline pattern, substantial reduction in error injection has occurred at both the front-end inspection phases (I0, I1, I2) and the back-end formal testing phases (CT, ST). Also, the peak of defect removal has been shifting from the I2 phase toward the I1 phase. The defect removal pattern of the current release (under development) seems to be quite close to the model curve.

Not surprisingly, the field defect rates of the AS/400 software system have decreased significantly over the past several years. As Figure 12.8 shows, the CSI defect rate improved by about 40% and the defect rate for the entire system (SSI: total shipped source instructions) improved even more. In the figure the Y-axis is expressed in terms of defects per million lines of code (MLOC), either CSI or SSI; the X-axis shows the year and quarter in which new AS/400 releases became available to the general market. The defect rates are based on actual defect arrivals after general availability of the releases and have been normalized to a four-year life-of-product (LOP). Therefore, valid release-to-release comparisons can be made. The SSI defect rates are much lower than the CSI defect rates because SSI defect rates are a function of several variables:

   □   The size of CSI for each release
   □   Reduction in CSI defect rates
   □   Defect reduction due to aging
   □   Defect reduction through customer burn-in programs.

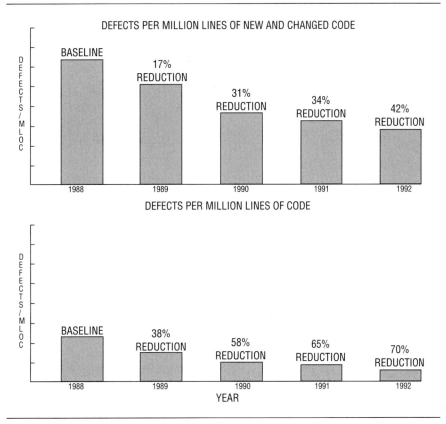

FIGURE 12.8
Reductions in AS/400 Field Defect Rate

Note that not only have the defect rates been reduced; the absolute number of product defects has also been decreasing. In summary, through the focus applied to improving CSI quality and accelerated aging, the level of product defects customers experience has reduced substantially release to release.

## Post-GA Product Quality Management

The post-GA product quality management element tracks the quality of the product after it has been shipped. This is done to ensure that AS/400 customers are receiving timely answers and fixes to their product problems.

The problems customers encounter when using the software product can be classified into three categories. The first are the functional defects in the product. At IBM, when a customer problem appears to be a defect in the product, an APAR (authorized program analysis report) is written. In the previous section and in Figure 12.9, we have described the reduction in the product defect rates (and defects) for the AS/400 software system for the past several years. Because the defect rate is low, the overwhelming majority of AS/400 customers have never opened an APAR. The second category of customer problems, and by far the most common, occurs when the product does not do what was expected, but the solution does not require a change to the product. These are called non-defect-oriented problems. When these problems occur, IBM provides information to the customers to resolve them. The third category of problems is a defective fix to a customer problem. Defective fixes have a significant negative impact on customer satisfaction. That is why the goal is always zero defects.

Each of these categories of problems is measured weekly and reviewed monthly in order to understand progress toward achieving specific goals for each release and to be able to take immediate and appropriate action if any of these measurements gets out of control.

Figure 12.9 shows results of tracking non-defect-oriented problems over a three-year period. Presented is the trend for problems per user month (PUM): the average number of problems a customer encountered monthly. The PUM rate peaked in early 1990, and soon after started to decline through September 1990. It then fluctuated at a more or less consistent level. From October 1991 to February 1992 another drop was observed but was less significant than the first one.

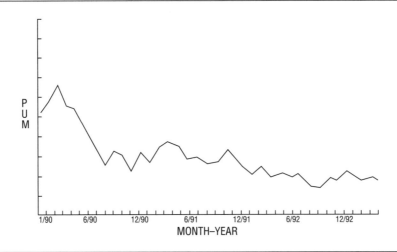

FIGURE 12.9
AS/400 Non-Defect-Oriented Problems Per User Month

Although significant improvement in the PUM rate was observed compared to the baseline (early 1990), the bigger challenge is to curb or even reduce the absolute number of problems. We have begun to address this. In cases where many customers call service for the same non-defect-oriented problem, an analysis is done by the development and service team to determine if a change can be made to the software product or documentation that would eliminate repetitive service calls. It is too early to see the results of this effort, but our goal is to reduce the PUM rate further and to curb the growth of the raw number of non-defect-oriented problems while continuing to expand the customer base.

Significant improvement in fix quality has been observed. It is summarized in Figure 12.10, which shows the year-to-year number of defective fixes. In 1992, the percent of correct fixes exceeded 99.9%; the absolute number of defective fixes is close to zero (in single digit). Of the 32 AS/400 licensed program products, 30 had no defective fixes for a year or more. The goal is to achieve zero defective fixes for the system.

Key factors that contributed to the improvement of fix quality include the rigorous practice of DPP, use of the formal inspection process on fixes, and a system that was developed internally and used to enhance the fix process. For instance, fix stage kickoff sessions are conducted weekly so developers who have an APAR to fix are kept up to date with the fix process and the various ways to prevent defects. When a defective fix is discovered, we take a proactive approach to determine which customers ordered the fix so they may be alerted in advance. Our experience shows that this customer call-back process with regard to defective fixes has enhanced customer satisfaction.

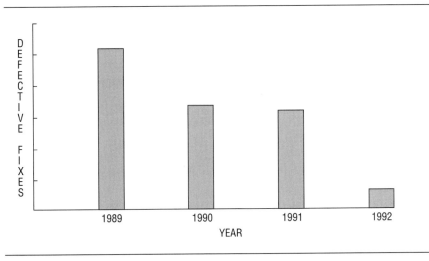

FIGURE 12.10
AS/400 Fix Quality Improvement—Number of Defective Fixes by Year

### 12.1.3 Continuous Process Improvement

The continuous process improvement element of the AS/400 SQMS provides the basic foundation for improving any software development process. The foundation consists of process ownership, definition, documentation, measurements (including baseline measurements), yearly goals, maturity assessments, and corrective actions for improvement. Having all development processes laid across this foundation enables effective and efficient process improvement. The Development Quality and Process Technology team keeps the process foundation strong through ongoing process owner education, establishing documentation consistency, performing yearly maturity assessments, establishing measurement and tracking guidelines, enabling cross-process synergy, and enabling compliance to standards such as ISO 9000.

Process optimization through data and analysis, strong process discipline, process benchmarking, and the introduction of object-oriented technology are the major process improvement activities that have been deployed.

The AS/400 software development process (modified waterfall process) was analyzed based on objective data and resulted in recommendations for improvement. For instance, we found significantly higher defect rates associated with interfaces and small changes. Therefore, the high-level design and review subprocess (I0) and the design change request (DCR) subprocess were modified so that interface issues are resolved early. We recommended that development managers use top-notch developers to fix defects reported from the field (small changes are highly error-prone activities). Based on defect origin data, the highest error injection was found in the code development phase. (This is not surprising given that the transition from low-level design to actual code involves an explosion of details, which means numerous chances for injecting defects.) Thus, a renewed focus on front-end inspection was initiated.

For significant quality improvement in a large-scale development environment, and for complex system software with numerous interdependencies such as the AS/400, strong process discipline is required. A Back to the Basics Program was deployed to emphasize strong process discipline. The benefits of process discipline have been demonstrated by Japanese computer companies. The formula for success in advancements in development productivity and quality by some Japanese computer manufacturers is a combination of continuous refinement of the classical development methodology, wide-scale use of quality control techniques, and development and use of CASE (computer-aided software engineering) tools.

Benchmarking other companies in the industry and other IBM facilities was also used to assess and implement various approaches for process improvement. For instance, a benchmark exchange took place in 1991 between IBM Rochester and Hewlett-Packard Commercial Systems (the HP 3000 computer system). By examining the "IBM Rochester way" and the "HP way" in areas such as product development process, release cycle, process and quality management, and human resources, both sites were able to institute improvements. Another example of wide-scale implementation is the defect prevention process from IBM Networking Systems (Research Triangle Park, North Carolina) (Mays *et al.,* 1990). DPP adds intelligence to the process and makes it more iterative. After a successful pilot in 1989, DPP was implemented throughout the entire Rochester software development laboratory. Other approaches evaluated included the Cleanroom methodology (Mills *et al.,* 1987), the experience factory (Basili *et al.,* 1992), the small team approach, the object-oriented design/object-oriented programming (OOD/OOP) process and technology, and various modeling and metrics approaches.

Continuous process improvement also requires equipping people with the right tools and technology that lead to quality improvements. Long-term investment for technological transfer (such as powerful workstations and the support for the OOD/OOP process) was necessary. On the other hand, the learning curve for new processes and technology is long; continuous incremental tool improvements were needed for the immediate needs when optimizing the current process. DPP and the network of technical process owners were the key identifiers of requirements for tool improvement. Through causal analysis and the assessment by action teams and technical process owners, the costs and benefits of any tool improvement were well understood and prioritized.

To date, powerful workstations have been rolled out according to plan, several large-scale OOD/OOP projects are in progress, and numerous tool-related DPP items have been implemented to improve the current process. Significant progress was made in developing an environment and a library system for distributed development.

Our continuous process improvement can be summarized as follows: continually optimize the current process; strongly enforce process discipline for better execution and results, while selectively using the small-team approach for flexibility and innovations; use benchmarking to apply both IBM and non-IBM knowledge and experience for process improvement; and continue to move toward the OOD/OOP process with related technology.

### 12.1.4 People

People are the most important element of the AS/400 SQMS. The human side of quality and productivity, although less tangible, is more important than process and technology. Given a certain process and technology, it is people who make the difference. "Conscientious programmer" is our key assumption in terms of the people's aspect of quality improvement. According to Maslow (1970), it is human nature to strive for self-actualization when basic needs are fulfilled.

This assumption has significant implications. It means that to formulate specific plans for quality and process improvement, the programmer's perspective must be taken into account, especially in terms of feasibility. In fact, many actions in the quality road map originated from the development teams (see the subsection about the quality road map in the next section). The assumption also means that process improvement does not always mean adding more requirements, checklists, and process steps. The optimization effort must continuously look for ways to simplify the process. A good example is the simplification made to the inspection defect-gathering process. Two old inspection defect databases were merged into a single new database that was tightly integrated with the current project management process. At the same time, inspection defect reports were improved.

We must ask what motivates individuals and teams to perform the necessary tasks that will result in excellent product quality. Although the answers may vary, a well-accepted one is that people are motivated by incentives, awards, public recognition, peer respect, and so forth. In fact, incentives together with public recognition is a key principle in quality management. Public recognition takes many forms and does not always involve monetary awards. Incentives programs could be difficult to formulate and implement. However, it would be remiss if quality road maps and plans fail to include this positive and powerful approach. A good program should be based on measurable product quality outcome and targeted to the teams and groups that directly influence product quality.

Several quality incentive programs, in addition to the regular IBM award programs, have been implemented at IBM Rochester. The AS/400 Division MDQ Award is a team award designed to promote MDQ initiatives and foster teamwork. It runs three cycles per year and its scoring guidelines include assessments on approach, deployment, and results. It includes quality contributions in all areas in the AS/400 Division such as planning, engineering, programming, production, market support, site support, and so forth.

In software development there is a monthly quality award in all functional areas. The award, started in 1990, is based on peer nomination. It is well received and widely used by team members to recognize their peers for quality contributions in terms of process, product, and support of the AS/400 software development. This is an individual award. Compared to the MDQ Award, this award is less formal and is given out monthly in each third-line area in the software community.

The third award, recently announced in a large development area, focuses on development quality. It is specifically targeted for innovative successes that enable the product to achieve excellent quality. It focuses on good development characteristics such as good design, less rework, meeting key dates, low testing defects, and minimal field defects. A key feature of this award is that improvements must be measurable. There are two tiers of the award: The in-process award relies on indicators such as driver stability, low testing defects, and client satisfaction (the other teams that use the candidate's code); the long-term award relies on the actual field-defect rate after GA and customer feedback. In addition to the objective criteria, a peer review board also considers factors such as code complexity, usage, previous history of code quality, and relative improvement. The award program is funded from the savings derived from having fewer maintenance costs due to reductions in the product defect rates. Submissions can be self-nominated or nominated by management and can be awarded to teams or individuals.

## 12.2 AS/400 SQMS Structure, Deployment, and Measurement

A quality management system cannot exist without some structure that enables its implementation. At IBM Rochester we devised a key structural element called a quality road map that defines the goals the system is to achieve for each release of AS/400, and the key actions that must be deployed to achieve those results. Details of what actions are deployed are documented in a quality plan for each release. Metrics, measurements, and analysis are used to track implementation progress and to guide improvement effort. The following sections describe the AS/400 software quality road map, give examples of key actions that were deployed, describe how a detailed quality plan for each release was developed, discuss the deployment of key quality practices in the software development community, and describe the tracking, measurement, and analysis in the AS/400 SQMS.

### 12.2.1  Quality Road Map

A quality road map describes the various quality technologies and actions that will be used over a period of time to leverage improvements to overall software product quality. In the road map the quality goals are specified by each year and each release of AS/400, along with the actions to achieve the goals. Detailed descriptions of these actions are documented in the quality plan for each release. A simplified version of the AS/400 software quality road map is shown in Figure 12.11. Symbols such as QI-91a and QI-91b represent the specific system quality goals for CSI and SSI for each release. The road map has been revised several times since the initial MDQ roll-out in early 1990. It is updated continuously based on accumulated experiences and knowledge, making it a living document. The action items in the road map cover all elements of the AS/400 SQMS. Its purpose is to achieve defect elimination and customer satisfaction goals. For each product release, the action list is cumulative. For instance, actions implemented for the 1992 release include those listed under both the first and second columns. For the 1993 and 1994 releases, the items are subject to change as the releases are under development. We continuously assess the effectiveness and feasibility of each action.

| YEAR | 1991 RELEASE | 1992 RELEASE | 1993 RELEASE | 1994 RELEASE |
|------|--------------|--------------|--------------|--------------|
| GOALS | | | | |
| MSSI | QI-91a | QI-92a | QI-93a | QI-94a |
| MCSI | QI-91b | QI-92b | QI-93b | QI-94b |

- Development line item cutoff date
- Improved DR/CI effectiveness
    Increased coverage
    Better reviews
- Phase-based defect removal model
- Mini-builds
- Integration/build defect feedback loop
- Double byte characters set testing focus
- Improved CT—network of component team leaders
- Experimental pre-ST code freeze
- Enforced ST entry criteria
- 5* component actions
- Prototyping projects— user-centered design (UCD)
- CQP (customer burn-in)
- CUPRIMDA actions
- DPP lab-wide roll-out
- Third-line areas monthly quality awards—peer nominations
- Departmental 5-UP

- Release kickoff sessions
- Improved front-end change control process
- Simplified DR/CI and UT defect data collection
- Front-end (DR/CI) in-process measurements
- ST—RAISE testing
- Pre-ST code freeze (development complete)
- Compiler improvements
- DPP lab-wide implementation
- Non-defect-oriented customer problems closed-loop process
- Special quality line items in development plan

FIGURE 12.11 (Page 1 of 2)

## AS/400 Software Quality Road Map

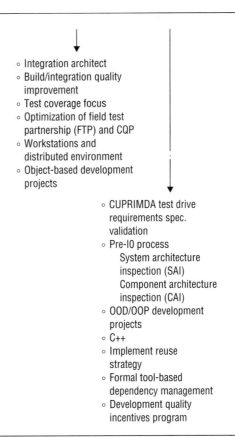

FIGURE 12.11 (Page 2 of 2)
AS/400 Software Quality Road Map

Note that some actions on the quality road map were originated by development teams. An example is the use of mini-builds by the database development team. A mini-build is a process that creates an isolated test environment for testing a new function. This test environment gives developers an opportunity to remove defects prior to integrating the function with the remaining parts of the system being developed. This is a significant improvement because integration and build are on the critical path of the development process and driver problems can cause schedule delays and significant quality and productivity loss (especially drivers for external development locations). From this positive experience, many areas are now taking advantage of this approach. The build and integration team took this approach one step further and established the build/integration defect feedback (to development teams) closed-loop process so as to reduce the chance of similar problems recurring in the future.

Another instance is the adoption of test coverage measurement and the development of a new test coverage measurement tool by a developer. These examples attest to the importance of the people aspect of software development and that a transformation to a quality-oriented culture is taking place.

It is worth noting that the position of release integration architect was established recently as a result of a benchmarking exchange with the HP 3000 system and a continuous focus on integration quality. The integration architect oversees the interdependent nature of the release line items and serves as the gatekeeper for integration and build quality. He/she oversees detailed code integration plans and schedules, defines, and manages code integration procedures, and ensures that cross-product and cross-component dependencies are met.

### 12.2.2  Examples of Key Quality Road Map Actions

Described next in more detail are some examples of quality actions that were deployed.

**Defect Prevention Process**

The merits of DPP were first recognized at an IBM Software Engineering Interdivisional Liaison (ITL) conference. A pilot program was started shortly afterward in mid-1989. With positive experience from the pilot and developers' enthusiasm, DPP was positioned as a strategic action in the MDQ roll-out in early 1990. Robert Mays of IBM Research Triangle Park, North Carolina, co-founder of DPP, was invited to Rochester to present two special seminars, to which the responses were overwhelming. One session was videotaped and later shown to the entire programming community. A mind-set change to a prevention-oriented focus was under way. With strong management commitment, a roll-out team was formed that developed and rolled out DPP seminars and formulated a long-term strategy of self-sufficiency of DPP education. Rochester developers were trained to deliver the formal education. An action team structure and a network of technical process owners were established. An action tracking tool was also developed. To date, most programmers and managers have been formally trained in the DPP process. Figure 12.12 shows the number of DPP actions that have been implemented and closed through the first quarter of 1993. The graph indicates that more than 3400 suggested actions were closed, of which more than 2000 have been implemented since the creation of the DPP program. Many of the proposed actions are extensive in the amount of effort required to implement them; some cannot be implemented because of resource limitations.

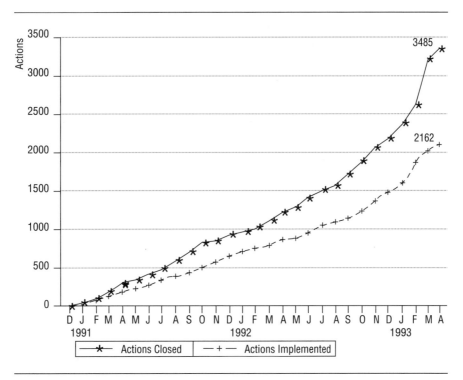

FIGURE 12.12
DPP Actions Implemented

The scope of the DPP actions that were implemented varies. Many were small items such as adding entries to the common error lists and stage kickoff meetings. Other items such as the postcompiler module checker and the release kickoff sessions were fairly significant. Regardless of the scope, all items are pertinent to the improvement of the development process and quality. The following example is perhaps better at providing the flavor of the DPP actions. From statistical analysis at the system level as well from the development team's causal analysis sessions, defects related to interface problems needed to be dealt with. Interface defects constitute a large percentage of total defects during all phases of development and from the field (APARs). Interface problems, to a large extent, are human communications problems that are preventable. One action proposed and implemented was to add a new command in the AS/400 development support environment that would allow developers to subscribe to the modules on which their code depends. If the modules change, the tool automatically notifies the subscribers. Therefore, developers are better able to manage dependencies and reduce interface defects.

There are several key characteristics of Rochester's DPP deployment: strong buy-in from both management and nonmanagement, developers as DPP instructors (after training), and the integration of DPP and process improvement (action teams and the network of technical process owners).

### "Back to the Basics" Design Review/Code Inspection Focus

The "Back to the Basics" focus refers to executing the design review/code inspection (DR/CI) process much better. Benchmarking analysis of the IBM Houston Space Shuttle onboard software system project indicated that rigorous implementation of the process can make an order of magnitude difference in development quality. Furthermore, causal analysis of APAR data indicated that often the bugs could have been caught early in the development cycle. Analysis of defect origin data indicated that the code development phase had the highest defect injection. Hence, a renewed focus on the front-end reviews and inspections was initiated, and a series of actions related to DR/CI then undertaken. This strong DR/CI focus led to significantly higher inspection coverage and better execution. The result was that the front-end execution became much better and fewer defects escaped to the testing phases, as described in earlier sections.

It is worth noting that software reviews and inspections are distinctly different from manufacturing inspections, which are at the back end of the production process and are known to be an ineffective method for quality assurance. Quality improvement teachings often call for the abandonment of manufacturing inspections in favor of acceptance sampling (with the front-end focus on design quality). Software reviews and inspections, on the contrary, are the vital techniques at the front end of the software development process.

Furthermore, software design reviews and code inspections are more efficient in defect removal, as Fagan's study (1976) showed. In our analysis, the ratio of the cost of finding and fixing a defect during design, test, and field is 1 to 13 to 92. This ratio, interestingly, is very similar to the ratio reported by IBM Santa Teresa, California, some years ago, 1 to 20 to 82 (Remus, 1983).

### Customer Quality Partnership (CQP) Program

The CQP program was designed to accelerate the normal field aging process to achieve further defect reduction before GA. It was based on the concept of accelerated aging in quality engineering and the results of the analysis of the AS/400 customers in terms of their defect discovery patterns. For AS/400, the dominant majority of APARs are reported by a small percentage of customers. These customers and those who will exercise the new release functions are good candidates for customer burn-in programs. The CQP program works as follows:

- ☐ Motivate a group of high APAR-writing customers and customers who use specific new-release functions to move their production over to the new release as soon as possible. Defect discovery is thus accelerated. The program starts at the end of the development cycle after code freeze (when code quality has reached a satisfactory level) but before GA.

- ☐ Provide a streamlined process and additional technical support to facilitate the installation of the new release and for problem solving. The bottom line is to minimize customers' business risk and to enhance their satisfaction.

- ☐ Fix the defects as quickly as possible with unsurpassed quality focus.

- ☐ When a sufficient number of defects are detected and fixed, integrate the fixes into the system library so the defects are eliminated before GA.

The AS/400 CQP program was conceived and proposed at the end of 1990. With strong management support and intensive planning and preparation, the program moved into implementation in early 1991, a few months after the conception phase. Now it is implemented for each new AS/400 release. Defects found by the program are subject to DPP causal analysis and findings are used to improve the development process. For each implementation, postmortem analysis is done to improve the next implementation. At the end of each implementation, customers are surveyed. Their responses have been positive.

### 5* Component Quality Analysis

This is an analysis that was done to identify error-prone components in the system. A component in the AS/400 software system is a group of program modules that perform specific functions, for example, workstation manager, print function, spooling, storage management, message handling, and so forth. The analysis has been done for each release of the AS/400 software system since 1989. A composite index is formed based on CSI defect rate, SSI defect rate, and raw number of APARs (customers do not care about the normalized rate). The composite index gives a more balanced view of component quality than any of the individual indicators. Components are ranked based on the composite index from 0* to 9* (9* being the most error-prone). Components with 5* or more are submitted to special improvement actions. During the past several years the 5* component analysis has become a key driving force for code quality improvement.

Components have taken various approaches for improvement: involve customers in early requirements and design phases, place rigorous focus on front-end design and reviews, conduct causal analysis on defects, invite external experts for early testing during development, test coverage measurement, selective module break-up for error-prone modules, special customer testing via the Field Test Partnership program, recommend their high-APAR customers to join the CQP program, and so forth.

### 12.2.3  Quality Plan

At the beginning of each release cycle, a system quality plan is established in which the committed quality goals are defined and improvement actions to achieve the goals are described. To make the quality plan effective, a bottom-up commitment approach is used. The Development Quality and Process Technology team first develops a proposal. After a series of brainstorming sessions with groups of developers, the proposal is revised. The proposal is then reviewed with upper management in the software laboratory. The agreed-to proposal then becomes the basis of the bottom-up commitment process to be conducted in each development area from the component level and up. The committed quality goals and actions from all areas, together with system-level actions, form the system quality plan. The final written document, after review and approval by management, is then made available to the entire software development community.

Note that the system quality plan represents the overall system approach to quality improvement. Quality improvement is everyone's responsibility. It is made clear that each component, department, area, and product manager owns its quality activities including planning, implementation, and outcome. Indeed, each department and area in the software development community has established its quality improvement plan.

For each department, the committed quality goals and actions are described in the department's Quality Control Book (QCB). This on-line QCB, together with other on-line repositories in which the process documents and system quality plans reside, are available to all members at IBM Rochester via the IBM Rochester's Quality Management System (RQMS) tool. This tool basically provides a single user interface to important quality management system information, which is also essential for meeting ISO 9000 certification requirements.

Moreover, to make efforts in quality improvement a part of the overall development effort, quality investment is also included in the development plan process. Several plan line items have been used to address the resources needed for the deployment of several major quality practices. Good examples of quality line items include the funding of the formal action teams of DPP, 5* component improvement, and the work and resource needed to improve the products to reduce the problems customers encounter, even though such problems may not be defect related (non-defect-oriented problems).

## 12.2.4 Deployment

Thus far, quality road maps and quality plans have been presented. This section discusses the approach to implementing key quality practices in the software development community. Note that for quality improvement to happen, bottom-up commitment is the most important factor. Indeed, the improvement of AS/400's software quality, as discussed in earlier sections, is due to the efforts by everyone on the software team. Many improvement actions were also self-initiated by development teams. In the following discussion on deployment of pervasive quality practices, the importance of individual commitment should not be forgotten.

Management commitment is equally important. According to Townsend and Gebhardt (1990), upper management participation is a prerequisite to practicing total quality management (TQM). Without management participation, the organization practices quality by proclamation instead of TQM. In Rochester, active management participation is one of the key factors that makes the quality management system work and the deployment of actions successful. Each month the AS/400 Division general manager reviews the overall quality of the AS/400. Separately, the AS/400 Division director of development reviews the progress and status of development quality. For software development there is also a monthly quality meeting in which the directors and third-line managers review status and make operational decisions.

Perhaps the strong top-down management commitment to quality in Rochester can best be illustrated by the establishment of the Rochester Development Quality Council by the AS/400 Division director of development. Its focus is on the use of the MDQ techniques and practices in development programs. Several times a year high-leverage development programs are reviewed by Rochester senior management, technical professionals, and development managers. The review meetings provide a communications link between the various program teams and facilitate the exchange of good quality practices across development. The scope of influence of this program covers the entire ABS development laboratory, not just the software community.

Bottom-up and top-down commitment together ensures success. In deploying key quality practices to the entire software community, this two-way approach is used as much as possible. For instance, the successful laboratory-wide implementation of DPP clearly is a result of strong commitment and effort from both management and all members of the programming community and the mind-set change of all. On some occasions, either the bottom-up or the top-down approach has been observed to play a more significant role than the other. For instance, the mini-build approach is clearly a developer's own initiative. The CQP program represents a well-planned approach with strong management support and resource commitment.

**Deployment Model**

Deploying quality practices differs between large organizations and small groups. In small groups new practices can be experimented on at anytime. Large organizations, however, cannot afford broad experiments. A regular deployment pattern has been observed from Rochester's experience with deploying DPP, DR/CI focus, CQP, and other quality practices. From this experience the following deployment model was developed:

1. Given a new practice or innovative process, and after study and evaluation, the first step is to develop an informal proposal for small-scale implementation and to obtain management's initial approval. This can be done by anyone.

2. The most important step is to get developers committed and start a small-scale pilot project. If the pilot is voluntary and does not require management funding, its chance for success is good. It is vital to have the developers' commitment because without it the chance for future success is minimal.

3. Upon completion of the pilot(s), conduct analysis in terms of empirical data as well as causal analysis sessions.
   - [ ] If the results are overwhelmingly positive, proceed to next step.
   - [ ] If the results are moderate, or the buy-in is not enthusiastic, refine the process or practice and its implementation procedures and loop back to step 2.
   - [ ] If the results are neutral or negative and the pilot members' buy-in is lukewarm, then pursue another approach.

4. Prepare a formal proposal. Present it to management and request formal management commitment, especially if resources are required.

5. Upon formal management approval, prepare a detailed roll-out plan for the entire organization and start the implementation. Aggressive schedules with highly intensive effort have the best chance of success. A comfortable roll-out schedule may run the risk of losing momentum.

## 12.2.5 Supplier Quality Requirements

Because the development of AS/400 involves many other IBM locations and suppliers, the quality of products developed by other sites and non-IBM suppliers is reviewed. Their product quality must not adversely affect the AS/400 system quality. For each release, specific goals are set. All suppliers are required to meet these goals. In terms of outcome, their product quality must be as good or better than the quality of Rochester-developed products. In this respect, the Rochester team has the challenge to demonstrate its ability to achieve the aggressive quality goals.

Supplier quality requirements are documented in the product management plan (PMP) for each supplier or external-site product. The PMP is part of the contractual agreement between IBM Rochester and its suppliers.

For supplier products, quality plans are required by the release commit checkpoint. Each product is also required to have its own quality assessment and certification. To be consistent with Rochester development, in-process measurements are required. Suppliers that use the IBM Rochester development process must provide similar indicators that IBM Rochester development uses. For those that have their own development process, whatever data that are indicative of in-process quality must be provided to Rochester. This requirement reduces the risk of project failure.

IBM Rochester provides the AS/400 system quality plan to all suppliers and IBM sites that develop AS/400-licensed products, and provides input to their product quality plans when needed. To the extent possible, Rochester also provides consultation to other IBM sites and suppliers on quality improvement actions, metrics, defect models, and quality projections.

The product quality goal of defect rate, expressed in terms of numbers of defects per thousand source lines of instructions, is a life-of-product requirement. Therefore, before a supplier product is accepted by Rochester, the quality level must meet certain defect rate criteria, which indicate that the life-of-product quality goal is likely to be met. Defect rate criteria are established for an acceptance test (just prior to system test) that are based on the system defect removal model. This methodology is consistent with literature and actual AS/400 experience. By the acceptance test time, product development is complete. The defect rate detected during this period is a good indicator of the projected field quality.

Myers (1979) has a counterintuitive principle in software testing which basically states that the more defects found during formal testing, the more will be found later. For AS/400, actual data confirmed the positive relationship between formal machine test defect rate and field defect rate. The reason for this relationship is that at the late stage of formal testing, error injection in the product is already formed. Higher testing defects are an indicator of high error injection in the product. An analogy can be drawn between the total defect rate since formal test (formal test defects and field defects) and an iceberg—the tip of the iceberg is the formal test defects and the submerged part the field defects. Therefore, high defect rate during acceptance test means more defects will escape to the field unless extraordinary actions (extra testing, customer burn-in, and so forth) are implemented.

### 12.2.6 Tracking, Measurement, and Analysis

Tracking, measurement and analysis make up an important element of the structure of the AS/400 SQMS (Kan *et al.,* 1991). We believe that software development must move in the direction of a quantitative approach to become a true engineering discipline and to be more efficient and effective. Such an approach is especially important for complex, large development projects with numerous interdependencies such as the AS/400 software system. It is important to note that the data collected, and the metrics used and analyzed, need not be overwhelming; it is more important that the information from these activities be focused, accurate, and useful. Such information enables data-based decision making for project and quality management.

Quality management measurements and tracking are an integral part of IBM Rochester's business checkpoint process when developing a new product or enhancing an existing product. The four major business checkpoints that our products must achieve prior to shipping to customers are commitment, announce readiness, announcement, and general availability. Each checkpoint requires a specific quality activity to be completed. For example, a quality plan is required for the release commit checkpoint. An interim quality assessment is required at the mid-release announcement checkpoint. At the general availability checkpoint, we conduct the final quality assessment and projection. By merging quality management with the business checkpoint process, quality becomes a key factor in business decision making.

In addition to the in-process metrics that are used for quality management during the development process, post-GA metrics and customer satisfaction survey results are examined to assess product quality in the field. In-process and post-GA measurements, and customer satisfaction survey results are reviewed monthly by executives.

## In-Process Measurements

In-process quality measurements enable one to implement real-time quality management. To achieve this task we use a defect tracking system for the entire development cycle. It is integrated with the change control process of the AS/400 software development process. Metrics, such as the phase-based defect removal pattern, phase effectiveness (Kan, 1990; Kan *et al.,* 1991), inspection effort and coverage, percent of interface defects, integration/build defect arrivals, number of unit test defects found before and after code integration, testing defect arrivals and defect rates by phase, severity distribution of defects, late performance changes, and so forth are used and interpreted in the context of an overall defect removal model. These metrics, combined with the standard project status metrics (for example, the cumulative curves of actual versus plan for various phase activities such as the completion of design reviews and the execution of text cases), provide a sound basis for informed decision making with regard to project and quality management.

We have been using in-process metrics at the system and product levels for AS/400 since the development of its first release. For each release we continue to refine our metrics and improve our analysis. The major vehicle being used is a set of standard reports under a common report interface. We have discussed examples of these metrics and reports in Chapter 9.

## Post-GA Measurements

Post-GA measurements are used to examine the quality of software products that have been shipped to customers against product quality goals. Analysis of the post-GA measurements results in actions to improve the overall software development process so that the next software release will be better than the previous release. As discussed earlier, the 5* component analysis is a key driving force for the improvement of component quality for the past several years. Another form of analysis performed regularly is the root cause analysis of APARs.

The key post-GA measurements tracked monthly are product defects (APARs) and defect rates by release, number of defective fixes, total number of problems reported by customers, and average problem fix time. Other indicators that are tracked include number of APARs by severity, number of valid versus invalid APARs, number of APARs that are delinquent in providing a fix, and the number of non-defect-oriented problems. Each metric serves specific purposes. The number of defects and problems, and defect or problem rates for that matter, indicate the quality of the product that is being used by customers. Average problem fix time, number of delinquent APARs, and number of defective fixes measure the efficiency and quality of the fix process. The ratio of valid versus invalid APARs reflects the effectiveness and efficiency of problem determination and the skill level of the service team.

## Customer Satisfaction Measurements

The following data are used to gauge AS/400's customer satisfaction and provide input to the product improvement plans:

- ☐ IBM M&S survey data and questions, as discussed earlier.
- ☐ AS/400 customer feedback survey data, questions, and comments sorted by CUPRIMDA category.
- ☐ Customer-critical situation data sorted by category.
- ☐ Customer partnership call-back comments sorted by category (this is a 90-day-after-install customer contact call).
- ☐ Customer problems sorted by category.

This information is presented regularly to software development executives. Like the in-process and post-GA metrics, analysis is an inseparable part of the tracking and reporting system. Our experience indicated that good analysis is paramount in transforming data into useful information and knowledge.

## 12.3 Summary

We have described the various elements of the AS/400 SQMS: customer satisfaction management, product quality management (in-process and post general availability), continuous process improvement, and people. The structure of the quality management system—quality road maps, quality plans, deployment, supplier quality requirements, tracking, measurement, and analysis—was explained. Examination of empirical data indicates we have achieved substantial quality improvement.

It is absolutely essential to establish goals and to use those goals to drive continuous improvement. Establishment of a quality plan ensures that goals are documented and are used to drive change and innovation in the development of each new release.

Continuous improvement of process and tools requires an ongoing focus and a closed feedback loop so changes are made as a result of past mistakes. It is important that focus is placed both on defect prevention and on defect detection. The advantage of prevention and early defect removal is very clear.

Once a quality plan has been established by the development team, it becomes very important that quality be measured as the release is being developed. In-process quality management is the key to being able to recognize quality problems early, in time to take actions before the product is made available to customers.

After a product is made generally available, it remains essential that measurements and analyses continue so problem areas are identified early. A closed-loop system should be used to feed back those problems in order to prevent them in the future.

All of the above requires a dedicated team—a team that is committed to making improvements happen and delighting all of our customers. A dedicated team makes the quality management system function.

With a systematic approach, we continue to refine the AS/400 software quality management system based on feedback and learning through measurement and analysis. With the total participation of the entire team, and based on process, technology, and measurements and analyses, we continually strive for further improvement in AS/400's product quality and customer satisfaction.

## References

1.  Basili, V. R., G. Caldiera, F. McCarry, R. Pajersky, G. Page, and S. Waligora, "The Software Engineering Laboratory: An Operational Software Experience Factory," *International Conference on Software Engineering,* IEEE Computer Society, May 1992, pp. 370–381.
2.  Fagan, M. E., "Design and Code Inspections to Reduce Errors in Program Development," *IBM Systems Journal,* Vol. 15, No. 3, 1976, pp. 182–211.
3.  Harry, M. J., and J. R. Lawson, *Six Sigma Producibility Analysis and Process Characterization,* Reading, Mass.: Addison-Wesley, 1992.
4.  Jones, C. L., "A Process-Integrated Approach to Defect Prevention," *IBM Systems Journal,* Vol. 24, 1985, pp. 150–167.

5. Kan, S. H., "Determining the Phase Effectiveness of the AS/400 Software Development Process," presented at the First International Conference on Applications on Software Measurement, sponsored by American Society for Quality Control and Software Quality Engineering, Inc., San Diego, November, 1990.

6. Kan, S. H., R. J. Lindner, and R. J. Hedger, "In-Process Metrics of the AS/400 Software Development Process," presented at the 38th Annual ASQC Minnesota Quality Workshops and Conference, Minneapolis, Minn., March 5–6, 1991.

7. Maslow, A. H., *Motivation and Personality,* 2nd ed., New York: Harper and Row, 1970.

8. Mays, R. G., C. L. Jones, G. J. Holloway, and D. P. Studinski, "Experiences with Defect Prevention," *IBM Systems Journal,* Vol. 29, 1990, pp. 4–32.

9. Mills, H. D., M. Dyer, and R. C. Linger, "Cleanroom Software Engineering," *IEEE Software,* September 1987, pp. 19–25.

10. Myers, G. J., *The Art of Software Testing,* New York: John Wiley & Sons, 1979.

11. Remus, H., "Integrated Software Validation in the View of Inspections Review," *Proceedings of the Symposium on Software Validation,* Darmstadt, Germany, Amsterdam: North Holland, 1983, pp. 57–64.

12. Townsend, P. L., and J. E. Gebhardt, *Commit to Quality,* New York: Wiley Press, 1990.

# 13

## Concluding Remarks

The past 12 chapters covered a spectrum of topics on the theme of metrics and models in software quality engineering. Beginning with the definition of software quality and the need to measure and drive improvement via metrics and models, we surveyed the major existing software development process models; examined the fundamentals in measurement theory; discussed major software quality metrics that cover the entire software life cycle; and looked into the application of techniques from traditional quality engineering, such as the seven basic quality tools, in software development. Then we examined the concept of defect removal effectiveness, which is central to software development, and its measurements; presented the three categories of models in software quality engineering: reliability models, quality management models, and complexity metrics and models; discussed the measurement and analysis of customer satisfaction; and described the software quality management system for the AS/400 computer system. Throughout the discussions, many examples were presented. Our purpose has been to establish and illustrate a framework for the application of software quality metrics and models.

In this final chapter we discuss several observations with regard to software measurements in general and software quality metrics and models in particular, and offer a perspective on the future role of measurement in software engineering.

## 13.1  Data Quality Control

Few would argue against that software measurement is critical and necessary to provide a scientific basis for software engineering. What is measured is improved. For software development to be a true engineering discipline, measurement must be an integral part of the state of practice. For measurements, metrics, and models to be useful, the data quality must be good. On the contrary software data are often error-prone (as discussed in Chapter 4). Despite its importance, data quality has not received much attention from either the quality or the software engineering communities. In our view, the data quality issue is a big obstacle for software measurement to gain wide-scale acceptance in practice. It is even more important than the techniques of metrics and models *per se;* it is the most basic element on which the techniques of metrics and models can build in software engineering—garbage in, garbage out. Without adequate accuracy and reliability in the raw data, the value added from metrics, models, and analysis will diminish. The software industry will see little benefit in adopting the quantitative-measurement approach. Therefore, strong focus should be placed on the quality of the data in the data collection and analysis process. The data collection or project tracking process must encompass validation as an integral element. Any analysis and modeling work should assess the validity and reliability of the data and its potential impact on the findings (as discussed in Chapter 3).

Note that the data quality problem goes far beyond software development; it appears to permeate the entire information system and data processing industry. The accuracy of data in many databases is surprisingly low; error rates of roughly 10% are not uncommon (Huh *et al.,* 1992). In addition to accuracy, completeness, consistency, and currency appear to be the most pertinent issues in data quality. Furthermore, the magnitude of the problem often multiplies when databases are combined and when organizations update or replace old applications. It usually results in unhappy customers, useless reports, and financial loss. In a survey conducted by *Information Week* in 1992, 70% of the information system (IS) managers responding said their business processes had been interrupted at least once by bad data (*Information Week,* 1992). The most common causes were inaccurate entry, 32%; incomplete entry, 24%; error in data collection, 21%; and system design error, 15%.

Information technology has permeated every facet of the institutions of modern society, so the impact of poor data quality is enormous. Software engineering (or for that matter, software quality engineering) has the responsibility to take on this issue for both software development and information technology. Fortunately, efforts are under way by some quality practitioners. For instance, at the *International Software Quality Exchange* (Juran Institute, 1992), which was held in San Francisco in 1992, the panel on prospective methods for improving data quality discussed their experiences with some data quality improvement methods. Current approaches include:

- ☐ Engineering (or reengineering) the data collection process and entry processes for data quality
- ☐ Human factors in data collection and manipulation for data quality
- ☐ Joint information system and process design for data quality
- ☐ Data editing, error localization, and imputation techniques
- ☐ Sampling and inspection methods
- ☐ Data tracking—follow a random sample of records through the process to trace the root sources of error in the data collection and reporting process.

We recommend that methods like these be considered for software engineering data collection and analysis.

## 13.2  Getting Started with a Software Metrics Program

Once a development organization begins collecting software data, there is a tendency for overcollection and underanalysis. The amount of data collected and the number of metrics need not be overwhelming. It is more important that the information extracted from the data is accurate and useful, as discussed earlier. Indeed, a large volume of data may lead to low data quality and casual analysis, instead of serious study; it may also incur a sizable cost on the project and a burden on the development team. Note that to transform raw data into pieces of information, and to turn information into knowledge, analysis is the key. Analysis and its result, understanding and knowledge, are what drive improvement, which is the payback of the measurement approach. Therefore, it is essential for a measurement program to be analysis driven instead of data driven.

By analysis driven we mean the data to be collected and the metrics used should be determined by the models we use for development (such as models for development process, quality management, and reliability assessment) and the analysis we intend to perform. Associated with the analysis-driven approach, a key to operating a successful metrics program is knowing what to expect from each metric. In this regard, measurement paradigms such as Basili's Goal/Question/Metrics (GQM) approach proves to be useful (Basili, 1989). (In Chapters 1 and 4 we briefly discussed the GQM approach and gave examples of implementation.)

Metrics and measurements must progress and mature with the development process of the organization. If the development process is still in the initial stage of the maturity spectrum, a heavy focus on metrics may be counterproductive. For example, if there is not a formal integration control process, tracking integration defects will not be meaningful; if there is no formal inspection or verification, collecting defect data at the front end provides no help. In general, the starting metrics ought to be closely related to the final product deliverable.

As an example, suppose we are to begin a simple metrics program with only three metrics. We would highly recommend these metrics be the size of the product, the number of defects found in the field (or other reliability measures), and the number of defects found during the final phase of testing. Assuming that the data collection process put in place ensures high accuracy and reliability, then here are a few examples of what can be done from these pieces of data:

☐ Calculate the product defect rate (per specified time frame) (A).

☐ Calculate the test defect rate (B).

☐ Determine a desirable goal for A, and monitor the performance of the products developed by the organization. One can even use the control chart technique to monitor if any product is conspicuously above or below the norm.

☐ Monitor B for the products in the same way as A.

☐ Assess the correlation between A and B when at least several data points become available.

☐ If a correlation is found between A and B, then form the metric of testing effectiveness (final phase), (B/A) × 100%. Or one can derive a simple regression model predicting A from B (a simple static reliability model).

☐ Use the B/A metric to set the test defect removal target for new projects, given a predetermined goal for the product defect rate.

☐ Monitor and use a control chart for the B/A metrics for all products to determine the process capability of the test defect removal of the organization's development process.

This simple example illustrates that good use of simple data can be quite beneficial. Of course, in real-life situations we would not stop at the B/A metrics. To improve the B/A value, a host of questions and metrics will naturally arise: Is the test coverage improving? How can we improve the test suite to maximize test defect removal effectiveness? Is a test-focused defect removal strategy good for us? What are the alternative methods that make us more cost effective in removing defects? Our point is that for metrics programs to be successful it is important to make good use of small amounts of data, then build on the proven metrics in order to maximize the benefits of quantitative software quality engineering. As more metrics are used and more data collected, they should progress in reverse direction of the development process—from the end product to the back end of the process, then to in-process data. Metrics and data are usually more clear-cut at the back end and more difficult to define and collect in the front end.

As illustrated on numerous occasions in previous chapters and in the preceding example, investment in a metrics program is required for continuous improvement and for long-term success. When the development organization is small, data collection and analysis can be done by managers and project leaders. In large organizations, full-time metrics professionals are warranted for a successful program. We recommend that organizations with more than 100 members should have at least one full-time metrics person. The metrics personnel design the metrics that support the organization's quality goals, design and implement the data collection and validation system, oversee the data collection process, ensure data quality, analyze data, provide feedback to the development team, and engineer improvements in the development process.

Developers play a key role in providing data. Our experience indicated that it is essential that developers understand how the data are to be used. They need to know the relationship between the data they collect and the issues to be solved. Such an understanding enhances cooperation and, hence, the accuracy and completeness of the data. Of course, the best situations are where the metrics can be used by the developers themselves. Unless the data are collected automatically without human intervention, the development team's willingness and cooperation is the most important factor in determining data quality.

When the process is mature enough, the best approach is to incorporate software data collection with the project management and the configuration management process, preferably supported by automated tools. In contrast, analysis should never be fully automated. It is helpful to use tools for analysis. However, the analyst ought to retain intellectual control of the process, the sources of the data, the techniques involved, the meaning of each piece of the data within the context of the product, development process, and environment, and the outcome. This is the part of software quality engineering that the human mind cannot relegate. We have seen examples of ridiculous outcomes when the analysts lost control over the automated analysis process.

## 13.3 Software Quality Engineering Modeling

Software quality engineering, in particular software quality models, is a relatively new field for research and application. Of the three types of models we covered in this book, reliability models are more advanced than the other two. Quality management models are perhaps still in their infancy stage. It is safe to say that in spite of a good deal of progress in the past decade, none of the three types of models has reached the mature stage. The need for improvement will surely intensify in the future as software plays an increasingly critical role in modern society and quality has been brought to the center of the development process. Large-scale software projects need to be developed in a much more effective way with much better quality.

Note that the three types of models are developed and studied by different groups of professionals. Software reliability models are developed by reliability experts who were trained in mathematics, statistics, and operations research; complexity models and metrics are studied by computer scientists. The differing originations explain why the former tends to take a black-box approach (monitoring and describing the behavior of the software from an external viewpoint), and the latter tends to take a white-box approach (looking into the internal relationships revolving around the central issue of complexity). Quality management models emerged from the practical needs of large-scale development projects and draw on principles and knowledge in the field of quality engineering (traditionally being practiced in manufacturing and production operations). For software quality engineering to become mature, an interdiscipline effort to combine and merge the various approaches is needed. A systematic body of knowledge in software quality engineering should encompass seamless links among the internal structure of design and implementation, the external behavior of the software system, and the logistics and management of the development project.

From the standpoint of the software industry, perhaps the most urgent challenge is to bridge the gap between state of the art and state of practice. On the one hand, better training in software engineering in general and metrics and models in particular needs to be incorporated into the curriculum for computer science. Some universities and colleges are taking the lead in this regard; however, much more needs to be done and at a faster pace. Developers need not become experts in measurement theory, failure analysis, or other techniques. However, they need to understand the quality principles, the impact of various development practices on the software's quality and reliability, and the findings accumulated over the years in terms of effective software engineering. Now that software is playing a more and more significant role in all institutions of our society, such training is very important. Indeed, the implications of poor software quality to the functioning of society has even caught the mass media's attention recently; it was suggested that software engineers for safety-critical systems be certified.

On the other hand, this gap poses a challenge for academicians and researchers in metrics and modeling. Many models, especially the reliability models, are expressed in sophisticated mathematical notations and formulas that are difficult to understand. To facilitate practices by the software industry, models, concepts, and algorithms for implementation need to be communicated to the software community (managers, software engineers, designers, testers, quality professionals) in their language. The model assumptions need to be clarified; the robustness of the model needs to be investigated and presented when some assumptions are not met; and much more applied research using industry data needs to be done.

With regard to state of the art in reliability models, it appears that the fault count models give more satisfactory results than the time between failures models. In addition, the fault count models are usually used for large-scale commercial projects where the estimation precision required is not as stringent. In contrast, for safety-critical systems, precise and accurate predictions of the time of the next software failure is needed. Thus, the time between failures software reliability models are largely unsuccessful. Furthermore, the validity of reliability models depends on the size of the software. The models are suitable for large-size software; small-size software may make some models nonsensical. For small projects we recommend using simple methods such as the test effectiveness example (simple ratio method) discussed in the previous section, or a simple regression model.

A common feature of the existing software reliability models is the probability assumption. Recently, researchers started to challenge this assumption in software reliability. For the probability assumption to hold, three conditions must be satisfied: (1) The event is defined precisely, (2) a large size of samples is available, and (3) sample data must be repetitive in the probability sense. Cai and associates (1991) challenged the probability assumption. They observed that software reliability behavior is fuzzy in nature and cannot be precisely defined: Reliability is workload dependent; test case execution and applications of various testing strategies are time variant; software complexity is defined in a number of ways; human intervention in the testing/debugging process is extremely complex; failure data are sometimes hard to specify; and so forth. Furthermore, software is unique; a software debugging process is never replicated. Therefore, Cai and associates contended that the probability assumption is not met and that is why software reliability models are largely unsuccessful. They strongly advised that fuzzy software reliability models, based on fuzzy set methodologies, be developed and used. Hopefully this new line of reasoning will shed light on the research of software reliability models.

Another technology that could be very valuable in quality modeling and projection is the reemerging neural network computing technology. Based loosely on biological neural networks, a neural network computer system consists of many simple processors and many adaptive connections between the processors. Through inputs and outputs, the network learns mapping of inputs to outputs by performing mathematical functions and adjusting weight values. Once trained, the network can produce good outputs given new inputs. Different from expert systems, which are expertise based (i.e., from a set of inference rules), neural networks are data based. Neural network systems can be thought of as pattern recognition machines, which are especially useful where fuzzy logic is important. In the past several years, applications of neural networks have begun in areas such as diagnosis, forecasting, inventory control, risk analysis, process control, scheduling, and so forth. Several neural network program products are also available in the market. Examples include the Neural Network Utility/400 for the AS/400 platform and the Neural Network Utility/2 for the PS/2 platform.

For software quality and reliability, neural networks could be used to link various in-process indicators to the field performance of the final product. As such, neural networks can be regarded as machines for automatic empirical modeling. However, as mentioned, to use this approach, large samples with good quality data must be available. Therefore, it seems until measurements become ingrained in practice, the software industry may not be able to take good advantage of this technology. When in use, quality engineers or process experts must also retain intellectual control of the models produced by the networks, discern spurious relationships from the genuine ones, interpret the results, and, based on the results, plan for improvements.

In the meantime, for a software development organization to choose its models, the criteria for model evaluation discussed in Chapters 8 to 10 can serve as a guideline. Moreover, our experience indicated that it is of utmost importance to establish the empirical validity of the models based on historical data relative to the organization and its development process. Once the empirical validity of the models is established, the chance for satisfactory results is significantly enhanced. At times, calibration of the model or the projection may be needed. Furthermore, it is good practice to use more than one model. For reliability assessment, cross-model reliability can be examined. In fact, recent research in reliability growth models indicated that combining the results of individual models may give more accurate predictions (Lyu and Nikora, 1992). For quality management, the multiple-model approach can increase the likelihood of achieving the criteria of timeliness of indication, scope of coverage, and capability.

## 13.4 Statistical Process Control in Software Development

For manufacturing production the use of control charts is synonymous to statistical process control (SPC). In Chapter 5 we discussed the differences between software development and manufacturing processes. The use of control charts in software development, while helpful, is far from achieving SPC because the parameters being control-charted are usually some in-process measures instead of the final product quality. We also cannot control-chart the final product quality because when the data are available the software development is complete. It is not possible to effect changes at that time. (In manufacturing production the unit of analysis is parts. When the process is out of the control, the samples or the parts involved are excluded from the final deliverables.)

It is now clear we need an overall defect model (or models) that relates the phase-based parameters to the end-product quality goal, as well as phase-specific models and the application of the control chart technique. A good model ought to have theoretical backings and at the same time should be relevant to actual experience. The parameters of the model ought to be able to relate in-process characteristics to end-product quality. Control charts and other quality control tools enhance the chance the model parameter values can be achieved. For example, if the model sets a certain in-process-escape-rate target (e.g., Figure 9.16 in Chapter 9) for the product, control charts can be used to identify the components or the inspections that are out of the control limits. Without a good overall model, the use of control charts may become a piecemeal approach. In contrast, without rigorous in-process monitoring such as the application of control charts, the model may become empty. When a project meets the in-process targets according to the model(s) and at the end achieves the end-product quality goal, then we can say it is under statistical process control, in the relaxed sense of the term.

The above is confined to the narrow meaning of quality control. In a broader sense other parameters such as schedule, resource, and cost should be included. In other words, a software project can be said to be under process control when all the major parameters are achieved according to plan. Considering that projects with schedule delays, cost overrun, and low quality still constitute the majority, it will take a long time for the software industry to achieve such a state of practice—when software development becomes a mature discipline of software engineering.

## 13.5 Measurement and the Future

Measurement is becoming more important in software development. In this modern-day quality era, customers demand complex software solutions of high quality. To ensure effective development, software development organizations must gain control over the entire development process. Measurement is the key to achieving such a state of control and to make software development a true engineering discipline. Without good use of measurement the tasks of planning and controlling software development and maintenance will remain stagnant in a craft-type mode, whereby learning and experience transfer do not occur effectively and systematically.

Furthermore, various software engineering techniques have emerged in the past decade: CASE tools, formal methods, software fault tolerance, object technology, and the like. To improve productivity and quality, software developers are faced with an enormous choice of methods, tools, and standards. However, as Fenton (1993) contended, there is very little quantitative data and objective evaluation of various methods in software engineering. There is an urgent need for proper measurements to quantify the benefits and costs of these competing technologies. Such evaluations will help the software engineering discipline grow and mature. Progress will be made at adopting those innovations that work well, and discarding or improving those that do not.

In contrast, in other areas such as software reliability the challenge is not the lack of measurements. There are hundreds of proposed metrics and models. Empirical validation is the key for natural selection and for these measurements to improve and mature.

A "state of practice" challenge that needs to be overcome is the inappropriate use of measurements. In software development organizations where a metrics program exists, cases of misuse of measurement and data, even outright abuse, are not uncommon. As a result, the intended benefits of measurements are not realized. To make their metrics program successful, development organizations should place strong focus on the data tracking system, the data quality, and the education and experience of the personnel involved. The quality of measurement practice plays a pivotal role in determining whether software measurement will become ingrained in the state of practice in software engineering.

## References

1. Basili, V. R., "Software Development: A Paradigm for the Future," *Proceedings 13th International Computer Software and Applications Conference (COMPSAC),* Keynote Address, Orlando, Fla., September 1989.
2. Cai, K. Y., C. Y. Wen, and M. L. Zhang, "A Critical Review on Software Reliability Modeling," *Reliability Engineering and System Safety,* Vol. 32, 1991, pp. 357–371.
3. Fenton, N., "How Effective Are Software Engineering Methods?" *Journal of Systems Software,* Vol. 22, 1993, pp. 141–146.
4. Huh, Y. U., R. W. Pautke, and T. C. Redman, "Data Quality Control," *ISQE 92 Conference Proceedings,* Wilton, Conn.: Juran Institute, 1992, pp. 7A-1–7A-27.
5. *Information Week,* August 31, 1992, p. 48, "Devil in Your Data" by Linda Wilson.
6. "Session 7A Data Quality," *ISQE 92 Conference Proceedings,* p. 7A-29. Wilton, Conn., Juran Institute, 1992.
7. Lyu, M. R., and A. Nikora, "Applying Reliability Models More Effectively," *IEEE Software,* July 1992, pp. 43–52.

# Index

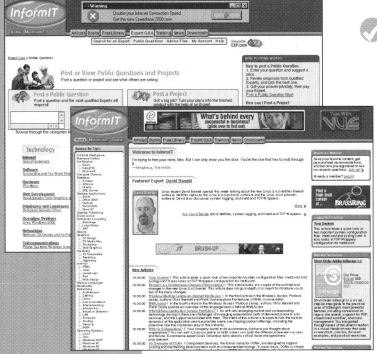

# Register
## Your Book
### at www.aw.com/cseng/register

You may be eligible to receive:
- Advance notice of forthcoming editions of the book
- Related book recommendations
- Chapter excerpts and supplements of forthcoming titles
- Information about special contests and promotions throughout the year
- Notices and reminders about author appearances, tradeshows, and online chats with special guests

## Contact us

If you are interested in writing a book or reviewing manuscripts prior to publication, please write to us at:

Editorial Department
Addison-Wesley Professional
75 Arlington Street, Suite 300
Boston, MA 02116 USA
Email: AWPro@aw.com

**Addison-Wesley**

Visit us on the Web: http://www.aw.com/cseng